JOURNAL FOR THE STUDY OF THE NEW TESTAMENT
SUPPLEMENT SERIES
98

JSOT Press
Sheffield

Filling up the Measure

Polemical Hyperbole in
1 Thessalonians 2.14-16

Carol J. Schlueter

Journal for the Study of the New Testament
Supplement Series 98

To my parents, in memoriam:
Martha Scott Schlueter 1914–1976
Pembroke Schlueter 1911–1993

Copyright © 1994 Sheffield Academic Press

Published by JSOT Press
JSOT Press is an imprint of
Sheffield Academic Press Ltd
343 Fulwood Road
Sheffield S10 3BP
England

Typeset by Sheffield Academic Press
and
Printed on acid-free paper in Great Britain
by Bookcraft
Midsomer Norton, Somerset

British Library Cataloguing in Publication Data

A catalogue record for this book is available
from the British Library

ISBN 1-85075-479-9

CONTENTS

ACKNOWLEDGMENTS

It gives me great pleasure to acknowledge those who were part of the process of the writing of this work, either in its form as a PhD dissertation or in its transformation to a monograph. First, I owe to my thesis supervisor, Dr E.P. Sanders, sincere thanks for his support of my research, for his comments and questions which helped to sharpen my thinking on the topic, and for his encouragement which helped to keep the process in motion. To Dr Stephen Westerholm I am grateful for his careful reading and appraisal of my work which helped to clarify my thoughts and writing. To Dr George Paul I give sincere appreciation for being a valuable resource for my investigation of rhetoric in the Graeco-Roman era.

There are others who have encouraged my academic work. I would like to thank Dean Barry McPherson and the Graduate Studies Office of Wilfrid Laurier University for their support of my research by awarding me a Book Preparations Grant. This award made it possible for me to hire a graduate student to assist with the preparation of the manuscript. I am grateful to Brad Prentice and Annemarie Klassen without whose careful assistance in preparing the text, indices, checking the references, and reading the proofs, it would not have been possible to produce this monograph at this time. Many colleagues, members of my family and friends have been supportive. I wish to single out for special recognition, Oscar Cole Arnal, Lucille Marr and Dorothy Sly. To them, I offer my sincere thanks and friendship.

Finally, I wish to thank my editor, Steve Barganski, for his careful work, helpful suggestions, and good cheer throughout the production of the book.

ABBREVIATIONS

AB	Anchor Bible
ATR	*Anglican Theological Review*
AusBR	*Australian Biblical Review*
BARev	*Biblical Archaeology Review*
Bib	*Biblica*
BNTC	Black's New Testament Commentaries
CII	*Corpus inscriptionum iudaicarum*
ETL	*Ephemerides theologicae lovanienses*
HKNT	Handkommentar zum Neuen Testament
HNT	Handbuch zum Neuen Testament
HTKNT	Herders theologischer Kommentar zum Neuen Testament
HTR	*Harvard Theological Review*
IBS	*Irish Biblical Studies*
ICC	International Critical Commentary
IEJ	*Israel Exploration Journal*
Int	*Interpretation*
JAC	*Jahrbuch für Antike und Christentum*
JBL	*Journal of Biblical Literature*
JEH	*Journal of Ecclesiastical History*
JJS	*Journal of Jewish Studies*
JQR	*Jewish Quarterly Review*
JRE	*Journal of Religious Ethics*
JSNT	*Journal for the Study of the New Testament*
JSNTSup	*Journal for the Study of the New Testament*, Supplement Series
JTS	*Journal of Theological Studies*
MeyerK	H.A.W. Meyer (ed.), Kritisch-exegetischer Kommentar über das Neue Testament
MNTC	Moffatt NT Commentary
NCB	New Century Bible
NovT	*Novum Testamentum*
NTS	*New Testament Studies*
SBT	*Studies in Biblical Theology*
ST	*Studia Theologica*
TAPA	*Transactions of the American Philological Association*
TZ	*Theologische Zeitschrift*

UBSGNT	United Bible Societies' *Greek New Testament*
ZNW	*Zeitschrift für die neutestamentliche Wissenschaft*
ZTK	*Zeitschrift für Theologie und Kirche*

The abrasive statements in 1 Thess. 2.14-16 have long posed a problem for understanding Paul's relationship to the Jewish people. In this passage Paul castigates the Jews and finishes by saying that God's judgment upon them is extended without limit, whereas in Romans 9–11 he finds a positive place for them in God's plan of salvation. This contradiction has puzzled many scholars and therefore made 1 Thess. 2.14-16 an intriguing passage to investigate as a dissertation topic. That work has been transformed here into a monograph.

Traditional solutions to the problem are reviewed, including theories of the inauthenticity of 1 Thess. 2.14-16 and attempts at harmonizing it with the passage in Romans. Such approaches are shown to be inadequate and a fresh examination of the content of the statements about the Jews is initiated.

Through historical investigation a link is revealed between most of the statements in 1 Thess. 2.14-16: they appear to be exaggerations. As a result, the Greek and Roman rhetors are used as an entry point into the nature and function of extreme language. How statements in 1 Thess. 2.14-16 are exaggerated, and how they function in the chapter and the letter are investigated.

The resultant hypothesis is that Paul, a skilled debater, used polemical hyperbole to polarize issues and to move his readers to his side while casting his opponents (in this case, the Jews) completely on the wrong side. The hypothesis is tested in other letters where Paul addresses opponents. Evidence from Galatians, the Corinthian correspondence and Romans supports the hypothesis. It is argued that Paul frequently amplified his main points through the use of hyperbole, exhibiting various levels of polemical intensity against his opponents. A comparison of these letters reveals that his polemic against other Christians is at least as strong as—if not stronger than—that against the Jews. Recognition of his responses to competition from other

Christians brings more balance to the historical picture of his polemical hyperbole against the Jews in 1 Thess. 2.14-16. By the time he wrote Romans 9–11, Paul's rhetoric against the Jews was more subdued. He was explaining God's plan and not battling Jewish opposition. Finally, Paul's statements about the Jews in 1 Thessalonians indicate a lively and continuing relationship between compatriots and not a separation of religions.

Chapter 1

THE PROBLEM PASSAGE AND ITS PAST SOLUTIONS

For scholars of the New Testament 1 Thess. 2.14-16[1] has long been a puzzle, even an irritation. Verses 14-16 list severe charges against the Jews and seem unlike Paul's discussion of the Jewish people in Romans. These charges include their persecuting the Judaean churches, killing the Lord Jesus and the prophets, driving out Paul, displeasing God, opposing all humanity, and hindering the preaching to the Gentiles. The accusations culminate in the statement 'But God's wrath has come upon them at last!' (v. 16c). Since 1 Thess. 2.14-16 is the focus of this study, I shall cite the passage in its transliterated form and in translation:

> *humeis gar mimētai egenēthēte adelphoi, tōn ekklēsiōn tou theou tōn ousōn en tē Ioudaia en Christō Iēsou, hoti ta auta epathete kai humeis hupo tōn idiōn symphyletōn kathōs kai autoi hupo tōn Ioudaiōn, tōn kai ton kyrion apokteinantōn Iēsoun kai tous prophētas kai hēmas ekdiōxantōn kai theō mē areskontōn kai pasin anthrōpois enantiōn, kōlyontōn hēmas tois ethnesin lalēsai hina sōthōsin, eis to anaplērōsai autōn tas hamartias pantote. ephthasen de ep' autous hē orgē eis telos.*[2]

For you, brethren, became imitators of the churches of God in Christ Jesus which are in Judea; for you suffered the same things from your own [compatriots] as they did from the Jews, who killed both the Lord Jesus and the prophets, and drove us out, and displease God and oppose all [people] by hindering us from speaking to the Gentiles that they may be saved—so as always to fill up the measure of their sins. But the wrath has come upon them at last![3]

1. In order to limit the number of repetitions of the phrase '1 Thess. 2.14-16' in this study, the phrase 'the problem passage' is often substituted for it and refers *only* to this passage.
2. All quotations from the New Testament in Greek are from *UBSGNT*.
3. English translations of the Greek text are taken from the RSV, except where

This passage in its abundance of negative comments about the Jewish people may be contrasted with statements in Romans 9 and 11 in which Paul expresses sorrow over the unbelief of the Jews but recognizes their positive role in salvation history. His praise of their privileged position in obtaining gifts from God culminates in a blessing which seems to indicate approval. In Rom. 9.1-5, he says,

> I am speaking the truth in Christ, I am not lying; my conscience bears me witness in the Holy Spirit, that I have great sorrow and unceasing anguish in my heart. For I could wish that I myself were accursed and cut off from Christ for the sake of my brethren, my kinsmen by race. They are Israelites, and to them belong the sonship, the glory, the covenants, the giving of the law, the worship, and the promises; to them belong the patriarchs, and of their race, according to the flesh, is the Christ. God who is over all shall be blessed for ever. Amen.

Similarly, Paul affirms the positive place that Jewish people hold in God's plan in Rom. 11.1-2:

> I ask, then, has God rejected his people? By no means! I myself am an Israelite, a descendant of Abraham, a member of the tribe of Benjamin. God has not rejected his people whom he foreknew...

Also in 11.11:

> So I ask, have they stumbled so as to fall? By no means! But through their trespass salvation has come to the Gentiles, so as to make Israel jealous.

His positive attitude towards the Jews is also expressed in Rom. 11.30-32:

> Just as you were once disobedient to God but now have received mercy because of their disobedience, so they [the Jews] have now been disobedient in order that by the mercy shown to you they also may receive mercy. For God has consigned all people to disobedience, that he may have mercy upon all.

To be sure, Paul's positive comments here about the Jewish people must be set alongside his negative comments in Romans. He seems to agree with Neh. 9.26 that Israel is 'a disobedient people', that most of the nation failed to attain or receive what the elect did because they were hardened (Rom. 11.7). Then, quoting Isa. 29.10, he writes that

otherwise indicated. Words enclosed in brackets are my alterations of the RSV translation.

God has given the Jews 'a spirit of stupor, eyes that should not see and ears that should not hear' (11.8). A denunciation from Psalm 69 follows: 'Let their table become a snare and a trap, a pitfall and a retribution for them; let their eyes be darkened so that they cannot see, and bend their backs for ever' (11.9-10). These criticisms of the Jewish people notwithstanding, the overall tenor of the assertions is positive and appreciative. Paul's negative statements about the Jewish people in 1 Thess. 2.14-15 and his absolute judgment about their destiny in v. 16c stand in contrast to his ultimately positive views in Romans 9–11.

As we shall see, the history of interpretation of the problem passage shows that scholars have long doubted whether Paul could have written 1 Thess. 2.14-16 because of the discrepancy between it and the passages in Romans. Doubts have persisted and scholars have even proposed that the passage be excised from the letter.[1] Yet, the problem passage is firmly embedded within the chapter, with no manuscripts showing it to be missing. Although this evidence suggests that it is authentic, scholars are still puzzled. To what historical situation could Paul's strong statements refer? The passage, its problems and attempted solutions still merit serious consideration—and call out for a fresh approach.

For more than a century scholars have questioned the authenticity of 1 Thess. 2.14-16 on historical, stylistic and theological grounds. Some nineteenth and early twentieth century scholars rejected the entire letter; others rejected only 1 Thess. 2.13-16, or some part of it. We begin a survey of such 'solutions' by turning to F.C. Baur.

Nineteenth and Early Twentieth Century Solutions

Rejection of the Letter
Many factors led F.C. Baur to conclude that the entire letter could not have been written by Paul,[2] but among them, our passage stood out as a major factor. On historical grounds Baur noted that Paul's comparison of 'the troubles raised by Jews and Gentiles conjointly and the

---

1. See N.A. Beck, *Mature Christianity: The Recognition and Repudiation of the Anti-Jewish Polemic in the New Testament* (London and Toronto: Associated University Press, 1985), p. 46.

2. For a full discussion, see T. Zahn, *Introduction to the New Testament* (Edinburgh: T. & T. Clark, 1927), pp. 69-73.

persecution of Christians in Judea was far-fetched'[1] for the 40s and 50s of the common era. He insisted that their suffering probably refers to a time after 70 CE. Further, he pointed out that Paul did not usually hold up the Judaeo-Christians as a model for the Gentile Christians. In addition, Baur could determine in Paul's time no event of significant magnitude to serve as the referent of the 'wrath' in v. 16. Above all, he noted, Paul's theological attitude towards the Jewish people, as expressed in Romans, was different from that of the problem passage. Baur put his assessment this way:

> Is this polemic against the Jews [vv.14-16] at all natural to him; a polemic so external and so vague that the enmity of the Jews to the Gospel is characterized solely in the terms of that well-known charge with which the Gentiles assailed them, the *odium generis humani*?[2]

The theological disparity between Paul's views of the Jewish people in 1 Thessalonians and Romans led Baur to conclude that the problem passage had a 'thoroughly un-Pauline stamp'.[3] The implication is that Paul's authentic view of the Jewish people resides in Romans. Baur proposed that the entire letter of 1 Thessalonians was spurious. Had his proposal gained the approval of scholars it would have solved the dilemma of how to understand 1 Thess. 2.14-16, but the rejection of the letter itself was short-lived. One generation later scholars had generally accepted the epistle as an authentic writing by Paul. Their arguments are summarized below.

Acceptance of the Letter
The main arguments for the letter's authenticity include the following points:[4]

---

1. F.C. Baur, *Paul the Apostle of Jesus Christ: His Life and Work, his Epistles, and his Doctrine* (ed. E. Zeller; trans. A. Menzies; London: Williams, 2nd edn, 1875–76), II, p. 87. The first to raise doubts was C. Schrader (*Der Apostel Paulus* [Leipzig, 1836], V) but it was Baur who developed vigorous arguments against the letter's authenticity.

2. Baur, *Paul the Apostle of Jesus Christ*, p. 87.

3. Baur, *Paul the Apostle of Jesus Christ*, p. 87.

4. For a more detailed discussion, see G. Milligan, *St Paul's Epistles to the Thessalonians* (London: Macmillan, 1908), pp. lxxii-vi; J.E. Frame, *A Critical and Exegetical Commentary on the First Epistle of St Paul to the Thessalonians* (ICC, 38; Edinburgh: T. & T. Clark, 1912), pp. 37-38. See D.A. Jülicher, *Einleitung in das Neue Testament* (Tübingen: Mohr, 1906), p. 37.

1.   The content of 1 Thessalonians is sufficiently specific to be considered an occasional letter designed to provide support for a church which Paul founded.

2.   The letter reveals characteristic Pauline ideas of the indwelling Christ or Spirit and the hope of imminent future salvation.

3.   There is sufficient disagreement between 1 Thessalonians and Acts to preclude dependence. Consider, for example, how Acts presents Paul as preaching first in the synagogue and then to the Gentiles, whereas 1 Thessalonians indicates that Paul conducted no activity among Jews prior to his preaching to the Gentiles. Moreover, the account in Acts 17 indicates that the Jews in Thessalonica were jealous, whereas Paul's view in 1 Thess. 2.14-16 is that it was the *symphyletōn* who were troubling the Thessalonians.

4.   A later writer would not have written about Paul's expectation of the parousia during his lifetime (4.15-17).

Rejection of the Passage

Although many of the late nineteenth and early twentieth century scholars accepted 1 Thessalonians as an authentic letter of Paul, they still found our passage problematic and rejected all or part of it as inauthentic. Sometimes, like Baur, they asked whether Paul actually could have uttered what is said in vv. 14-16. They also were vexed by the problem of trying to decipher the historical situation to which v. 16c referred. To what event do the words *orgē* (wrath), *ephthasen* (from the root *phthanō*, 'to precede', 'to arrive') and *eis telos* refer? Let us examine the language of the text.

1. The verb *ephthasen*, in the aorist tense, can be translated in several different ways. The simplest translation of the verb is 'has come upon', referring to a fixed point in time. In this sense *ephthasen* refers to a particular event that 'has happened'[1] and the difficulty is to determine what event has happened in the past which Paul called God's wrath.

It is also appropriate for the translation 'has come upon' to indicate an action in the past, the results of which stand operative in the

---

1.   J.H. Moulton, *The Grammar of New Testament Greek*. I. *Prolegomena* (Edinburgh: T. & T. Clark, 2nd edn, 1906), p. 135.

present.[1] Sometimes this employment of the aorist is understood as dramatic.[2] This use is found in Homer and in the dramatic poets where a sudden change occurs or in passionate speech.[3] It is also found in the Gospels. For example, in Mt. 12.28 the verb *ephthasen* is used for dramatic effect ('But if it is by the finger of God that I cast out demons, then the kingdom of God has come upon you'). Thus, in the case of 1 Thess. 2.16c it may be a recent event to which the *orgē* referred, the effects of which were dramatic and are still being felt. The aorist is also sometimes translated as an English pluperfect, which raises the question of the sequence of events.

There is also a proleptic use of the aorist, involving 'a vivid transference to the future'.[4] However, the proleptic use is infrequent in the New Testament. Robertson cites *emeristhē* and *ephthasen* in Mt. 12.26, 28 ('if Satan cast out Satan, he is divided...'; for 12.28, see above) as examples. The point is that the matter has already been decided, but will be effective in the future. If *ephthasen* is to be understood proleptically, the meaning is that God's wrath has been decided and will become effective upon the Jews in the future.

In any interpretation the decision about how to translate the verb affects the determination of what it was that came upon the Jews, as we shall see below.

2. The phrase *eis telos* can be translated temporally ('finally' or 'at last'[5]) or intensively ('to the uttermost',[6] 'completely, forever'[7]). The LXX uses *eis telos* both temporally (cf. the parallel *eis ton aiōna* in Pss. 9.19; 76.8-9; 102.9) and intensively (Josh. 3.16; 2 Chron. 12.12). Scholars who looked for events in the recent past that could be the referent of *orgē* also tended to a temporal meaning ('finally' or 'at last') for *eis telos*.

Faced with the difficulties of how to translate 1 Thess. 2.16, Albert Ritschl[8] took the aorist *ephthasen* in its simplest meaning ('has come

---

1. Moulton, *The Grammar of New Testament Greek*, p. 843.
2. Moulton, *The Grammar of New Testament Greek*, pp. 841-42.
3. Moulton, *The Grammar of New Testament Greek*, pp. 841-42.
4. Moulton, *The Grammar of New Testament Greek*, p. 846.
5. RSV, JB.
6. KJV.
7. See the note on 1 Thess. 2.16 in the RSV.
8. A. Ritschl, *Rechtfertigung und Versöhnung* (Bonn: Adolph Marcus, 2nd edn, 1882), II, pp. 142-44. Spitta and Moffatt thought that v. 16c was an

upon') as referring to an event which had occurred in the recent past. He could locate no event from the time of Paul to which this 'wrath' could refer. Instead he thought that the 'wrath' could more logically refer to a catastrophic event like the destruction of the Jerusalem temple, an event of great consequence for Jews. He proposed that v. 16 was from the hand of a later author, thereby rejecting it as an inauthentic insertion which reflected the Jewish–Christian conflicts of the period post 70 CE. Paul Wilhelm Schmiedel[1] agreed, but suggested that the interpolation included vv. 15-16 because the severe accusations against the Jews are unlike anything found in Paul's other letters. On literary and historical grounds Heinrich Holtzmann[2] argued that the interpolation included vv. 14-16 because Paul's holding up of the Judaean churches as an example for one of his Gentile churches is peculiar to this letter. Further, the period when the Judaean churches experienced significant suffering does not seem to coincide with Paul's lifetime, but rather the period after 70 CE.

To sum up, in the nineteenth century the arguments against 1 Thess. 2.14-16 as originating from Paul's hand were based on theological, historical and literary grounds. The main points were: (1) the early suffering of the Judaean churches is questionable, as is Paul's use of these churches as examples; (2) the accusations against the Jews seem to be unlike anything Paul says about them elsewhere; and (3) in the case of v. 16 the wrath which has come upon the Jews seems to be anachronistic for the period in which Paul was writing.

Defence of the Passage

Some scholars who defended the passage as authentic pointed to the possibility of *orgē* and *ephthasen* referring to an event of the past such as the loss of Jewish independence, the famine in 46 CE (Acts 11.28),

---

interpolation. See J. Moffatt, *Introduction to the Literature of the New Testament* (Edinburgh: T. & T. Clark, 3rd edn, 1927), p. 73, and *The First and Second Epistles of Paul the Apostle to the Thessalonians* (The Expositor's Greek Testament, 4; London: Hodder & Stoughton, 1910), p. 29. For F. Spitta, see 'Der zweite Brief an die Thessalonicher', in his *Zur Geschichte und Literatur des Urchristentums* (Göttingen: Vandenhoeck & Ruprecht, 1893), pp. 109-54.

1.   P.W. Schmiedel, *Die Briefe an die Thessalonicher und an die Korinther* (HKNT, 2; Freiburg: Mohr, 1891), p. 17.

2.   See H. Holtzmann, *Praktische Erklärung des I. Thessalonicherbriefes* (Tübingen: Mohr, 1911), pp. 74-79. See further Moffatt, *Introduction*, p. 73, and *First and Second Thessalonians*, p. 29.

the banishment from Rome in 49 CE (Acts 18.2),[1] a series of persecutions such as that which befell Theudas (Acts 5.36), or the persecutions under Tiberius Alexander (Josephus, *Ant.* 20.102, 105-115, 118-122).

Ernst von Dobschütz was not able to settle upon an event of the past. He asserted that if Paul was indeed referring to such an event, then his statement in v. 16c was an exaggeration.[2] I shall return to this point later. Here it is important to note that Dobschütz sought instead an event to which the 'wrath' could refer by reading *ephthasen* as proleptic.[3] As discussed above, the proleptic sense of the aorist projects the meaning forward to an event which has *already been decided and is about to occur.*[4] In this case the wrath is a divine decision which would culminate in the day of judgment.[5] As James Everett Frame put it, 'The denunciation is unqalified; no hope for their future is expressed'.[6] Some scholars thought that what had been decided in the past was the destruction of the Jerusalem temple (Jesus' prediction)[7] or the rejection of Jews by God because of the crucifixion. This rejection would continue and culminate in the final judgment.[8] R.J. Knowling proposed that the 'wrath' referred to the 'hardening and unbelief of the Jews'.[9] He understood Paul as saying that God had so decided, completely and utterly. Knowling put it this way: 'The Jews, in their rejection of the Messiah, had cut themselves

---

1. See P.W. Schmidt, *Der erste Thessalonicherbrief neu erklärt* (Berlin: G. Reimer, 1885), pp. 86-90. See also E. von Dobschütz, *Die Thessalonicher-Briefe* (MeyerK, 10/7; Göttingen: Vandenhoeck & Ruprecht, 1909), pp. 116-17.

2. Dobschütz, *Die Thessalonicher-Briefe*, p. 117.

3. Dobschütz, *Die Thessalonicher-Briefe*, pp. 115-16.

4. G.G. Findlay, *The Epistles to the Thessalonians* (Cambridge: Cambridge University Press, 1904), p. 77.

5. Dobschütz, *Die Thessalonicher-Briefe*, p. 117; Frame, *Thessalonians*, p. 114, and the earlier work by G. Lünemann, *Critical and Exegetical Handbook to the Epistles of St Paul to the Thessalonians* (trans. P.J. Gloag; Edinburgh: T. & T. Clark, 1880).

6. Frame, *Thessalonians*, p. 111.

7. A. Plummer, *A Commentary on Paul's First Letter to the Thessalonians*, (London: Robert Scott, 1918), pp. 34-35.

8. E.J. Bicknell, *First and Second Epistles to the Thessalonians* (London: Methuen, 1932), p. 27; Plummer, *Thessalonians*, pp. 34-35.

9. R.J. Knowling, *The Testimony of St Paul to Christ* (New York: Charles Scribner's Sons, 1905), p. 21.

off from salvation, and were appointed unto wrath, the wrath which would come upon them, which was coming upon them, without a remedy'.[1] By treating the aorist proleptically, scholars were able to maintain that the passage was authentic, and that the 'wrath' referred to a divine decision in the past which was to be carried out in the future.

The view of George Milligan is only slightly different. He thought that what triggered the statement in v. 16c was something which was happening at the time of the writing. He argued that, although Paul's attack against the Jews is startling when compared with his views in Romans, it reflects the 'strenuous opposition which at the time they were offering to him in his work (note the participles *areskontōn*, *kōluontōn*)'.[2] The mere mention of 'the Jews' was

> sufficient to recall to the Apostle what he himself had suffered at the hands of his fellow-countrymen, and accordingly he 'goes off' at the word into a fierce attack upon them.[3]

Like other scholars of his time, Milligan believed that v. 16 referred to a divine decision which was initiated by the rejection of Jesus as messiah:

> The language is too vague to be understood of any such literal and outward event and... clearly refers to the 'judgment' passed upon the Jewish people in the rejection of the Messiah.[4]

Frame's argument advanced Milligan's conclusion about a divine decision. Without agreeing with Frame's general conclusion about the meaning of the passage, I think that his claims for a temporal meaning of *eis telos* here are correct. Frame contends that a temporal meaning ('at last') is best because of the parallelism of the clauses in 1 Thess. 2.16[5]:

| (2.16b) | *anaplērōsai* | *autōn* | *tas hamartias* | *pantote* |
| (2.16c) | *ephthasen* | *ep' autous* | *hē orgē* | *eis telos* |

---

1. Knowling, *The Testimony of St Paul to Christ*, p. 21.
2. Milligan, *Thessalonians*, p. lxxiv. See also W. Neil, *The Epistles of Paul to the Thessalonians* (London: Hodder & Stoughton, 1950), p. 50.
3. Neil, *Thessalonians*, p. 29. See too Bicknell, *Thessalonians*, p. 127; Plummer, *Thessalonians*, p. 31.
4. Milligan, *Thessalonians*, p. lxxiv.
5. Frame, *Thessalonians*, p. 114.

Since *pantote* in the first clause requires a temporal sense, it is likely that *eis telos* in the second clause requires the same.

Although Frame settled on a temporal meaning for *eis telos*, curiously enough he did not look to an event in the past to explain v. 16c. He concluded instead that the 'wrath' referred to 'the well-known principle of the wrath of God which is revealed (Rom. 1.18) at the ends of the ages (1 Cor. 10.11) in which Paul lives, and which is shortly to be expressed in the day of wrath (Rom. 2.5)'.[1] Using the theological principle of God's revealed 'wrath' at the end of the age, he was able to connect the 'wrath' and the general sins of the Gentiles against the creator in Rom. 1.18 with the 'wrath' and the sins of the Jews in 1 Thess. 2.14-16.

The method underlying Frame's approach becomes clear when he argues that the sins of the Jews (1 Thess. 2.14-16) are under the control of God for positive purposes. He used Paul's views in Romans 11 (especially vv. 25-31) as the basis for his interpretive principle without paying attention to the particular context of either letter. Thus he stated, 'The obstinacy of the Jews is viewed as an element in the divine plan'.[2] Surely this view is derived from Romans 11, although he did not say so. In Chapter 4 the tendency to use Romans to interpret the problem passage will be discussed.

Frame also employed the *Testament of Levi*, which contains a statement paralleling that in 1 Thess. 2.14-16, to support his argument. In *T. Levi* 6.11 we read, *ephthasen de autous hē orgē tou theou eis telos* ('But the wrath of God came upon them to the uttermost').[3] Frame acknowledged the textual variants of this verse and noted that the sentence may well be a Christian interpolation from our 1 Thessalonians passage or derive from some other source. The Armenian recension omits *T. Levi* 6.11 altogether, indicating that this verse may be a later addition.

If the verse is borrowed from Paul's letter, it attests to its authentic presence in 1 Thessalonians—or in the form of it known to the writer or editor of the *Testament of Levi*. If the verse comes from another source, it could point to a standard Jewish formula for declaring

---

1.   Frame, *Thessalonians*, p. 113.
2.   Frame, *Thessalonians*, p. 113.
3.   *The Apocrypha and Pseudepigrapha of the Old Testament* (ed. and trans. R.H. Charles; Oxford: Clarendon Press, repr. 1979 [1913]), II.

God's judgment which was used both by the *Testament of Levi* and by Paul.[1]

The internal evidence of *T. Levi* 6.8 ('But I saw that the sentence of God was for evil against Shechem...') seems to anticipate the judgment in v. 11 (see above). Thus the verse seems to be authentic to the *Testament of Levi*. Similarly, 1 Thess. 2.16c seems to be anticipated by 'so as always to fill up the measure of their sins'. It seems to me that either both authors likely knew of the sentence 'But the wrath...' from some other source or that the author of the *Testament of Levi* borrowed it from Paul's letter.

Unfortunately, the *Testament of Levi* cannot illuminate the meaning of 1 Thess. 2.14-16 and to what event v. 16 referred. Today, as in the early twentieth century, the relationship of *T. Levi* 6.11 to 1 Thess. 2.16 is still unsettled and cannot resolve the meaning of the words in our passage.

Defenders of the passage have also addressed the historical question about the sufferings of the Judaean churches. Milligan noted that there was no actual record of the persecution of the Judaean churches in Acts—except for a short period in the Jerusalem church (Acts 8.1)—but contended that it would 'doubtless consist in excommunication and social outlawry, as well as in actual legal persecution'.[2] Frame suggested that the Jews in Thessalonica, in opposing Christianity, had insinuated that it was a false religion. In his view, this is why Paul argues that 'the Jews persecute the Christians because they always persecute the true followers of the divine will, and that it is the Jews who incite the Gentiles to harass the believers'.[3] Milligan's and Frame's views did not settle the difficulties. Milligan's conclusion about the indubitable nature of the persecutions has been challenged, as we shall see in Chapter 3; Frame's view that there were charges in Thessalonica of Christianity being a false religion cannot be substantiated from the letter.

The debate as to whether one ought to look to the past for a referent for God's 'wrath' or to the near or distant future (the destruction of Jerusalem or the final judgment) remained unsettled. No events of the

---

1. Frame, *Thessalonians*, pp. 115-16; M. Dibelius, *An die Thessalonicher I, II* (Tübingen: Mohr, 1937), p. 12.

2. Milligan, *Thessalonians*, p. 30.

3. Frame, *Thessalonians*, p. 109; cf. D.E.H. Whiteley, *Thessalonians* (Oxford: Oxford University Press, 1969), pp. 46-47.

past or present seemed substantial enough for the judgment in v. 16. Events in the future were possible, but no suggestion won a consensus.

Summary

Paul's statements against the Jews in 1 Thess. 2.14-16 conflict with his views in Romans 9–11. Some scholars in the nineteenth and early twentieth centuries suggested that the problem passage could not have been written by Paul. Neither the question of the authenticity of the passage nor the debate about its meaning was settled in that period. In the next chapter I shall consider some recent debates regarding authenticity.

Chapter 2

THE QUESTION OF AUTHENTICITY REINTRODUCED

Questions about the authenticity of 1 Thessalonians arose again with the introduction of computer analysis to New Testament studies in the early 1960s. The discussion of these questions was short-lived. Studies based on comparisons of sentence lengths and frequency of words used[1] concluded that the letter was inauthentic; however, these conclusions were successfully challenged by others[2] who also used statistical analysis but decided in favour of the letter's authenticity because the vocabulary of major terms is Pauline. In this period Walter Schmithals[3] proposed that the two letters to the Thessalonians are really segments of four different letters. For our purposes it is enough to note that by the early 1970s, the multiple letters theory had been left behind[4] in favour of one asserting the authenticity of 1 Thessalonians itself.

This short period of renewed doubt about Paul's authorship and the integrity of 1 Thessalonians led to a general consensus among New

---

1. A.Q. Morton and J. McLeman, *Christianity and the Computer* (London: Hodder & Stoughton, 1964).

2. K. Grayston and G. Herdan, 'The Authorship of the Pastorals in the Light of Statistical Linguistics', *NTS* 6 (1959), pp 1-15; H.H. Somers, 'Statistical Methods in Literary Analysis', in J. Leed (ed.), *The Computer and Literary Style* (Kent, OH: Kent State University, 1966).

3. See W. Schmithals, 'Die Thessalonicherbriefe als Briefkompositionen', in E. Dinkler (ed.), *Zeit und Geschichte: Dankesgabe an Rudolf Bultmann zum 80. Geburtstag* (Tübingen: Mohr [Paul Siebeck], 1964), pp. 295-315. Robert Jewett has an excellent summary of the arguments of Schmithals and others. See R. Jewett, *The Thessalonian Correspondence: Pauline Rhetoric and Millenarian Piety* (Philadelphia: Fortress Press, 1986), pp. 33-46.

4. E. Best, *A Commentary on the First and Second Epistles to the Thessalonians* (London: A. & C. Black, 1972), pp. 31-35. See also R.F. Collins, 'A propos the Integrity of I Thes', *ETL* 55 (1979), pp. 67-106.

Testament scholars that the letter was written by Paul and is complete as it stands. The discussion moved on to the question of whether Paul could have written the problem passage. Karl-Gottfried Eckart reintroduced the issue of the authenticity of the passage in 1961 by arguing that it was foreign to the rest of the text:

> Therefore we will not go amiss, if we regard 2.13-16 as a foreign body in the letter on the basis of objective, technical arguments.[1]

In 1971 Birger Pearson re-opened the question; this development has led to appreciable discussion.[2] Noting the theological disparity between 1 Thess. 2.14-16 and Romans 9–11, Pearson asked, 'Could Paul have written such a statement [v.16]?'[3]

Pearson's assessment that the problem passage was not by Paul's hand rested upon several points to be discussed below. For now we should note Pearson's concern for the theological incongruence with Romans 11 and the importance of that incongruence on his judgment. He concluded that the harsh remarks against the Jews in 1 Thess. 2.14-16 were not like Paul at all.

In addition, Pearson questioned the historicity of the view implied by the problem passage that there was significant persecution during the 40s and 50s CE. While his query recalls Baur's, Pearson advanced some significant new points discussed fully in the next chapter. Here, however, I shall focus upon three different points and an additional case against authenticity from Schmidt[4]. Responses to the arguments will follow.

Arguments against Authenticity

The Historical Difficulty

In addition to the important historical difficulty regarding the question of extensive persecution just mentioned, Pearson posed two additional objections to authenticity. They echo Baur's views. Pearson doubted

---

1. K.-G. Eckart, 'Der zweite echte Brief des Apostels Paulus an die Thessalonicher', *ZTK* 63 (1961), pp. 30-64 (34).

2. B.A. Pearson, '1 Thessalonians 2.14-16: A Deutero-Pauline Interpolation', *HTR* 64 (1971), pp. 79-94.

3. Pearson, '1 Thessalonians', p. 85.

4. D. Schmidt, 'I Thess. 2.13-16: Linguistic Evidence for an Interpolation', *JBL* 102 (1983), pp. 269-79.

that Paul would cite the Judaean churches as examples for his Gentile congregations[1] and that a historical event from the past could be the referent for the 'wrath' that had 'come upon' them.

Using the meaning of the simple past for *ephthasen* ('has come upon'), Pearson turned to the only event which he found convincing for *orgē*: the destruction of the Jerusalem temple. Thus, he proposed a date after 70 CE for the passage, one that could accommodate both the persecution of the Judaean churches and an event of catastrophic proportions to which *orgē* and *eis telos* could refer.

The Structural Difficulty

Pearson's analysis of the structure of the letter advanced the stylistic investigation begun in the 1960s. He examined 1 Thessalonians for internal consistency and concluded that there was an interpolation which extended from v. 13 through v. 16.[2] Verse 13 seemed to be the beginning of a second thanksgiving section (cf. 1.2-3). He was puzzled as to why Paul would have reiterated a thanksgiving section. Verses 13-16 could be deleted from the text, leaving a smoother connection between vv.12 and 17. Further, the 'apostolic parousia' introduced by vv.11-12 could be easily continued in v. 17. This apparent break in thought reinforced his suspicion that the problem passage was an interpolation.[3]

The Terminological Difficulty

Pearson suggested that Paul's assertion that the church at Thessalonica imitates the churches in Judaea (v. 14) differs from his customary use of the theme of imitation. In every other instance Paul urges imitation of Christ or of himself (1 Cor. 4.16; 11.1; Phil. 3.17; 1 Thess. 1.6). According to Pearson, the unusual use of *mimēsis* (imitation) results in theological incongruence[4].

The Linguistic Construction Difficulty

Schmidt[5] pointed to additional evidence confirming Pearson's

---

1. Baur, *Paul the Apostle of Jesus Christ*, pp. 87-88.
2. Pearson, '1 Thessalonians', p. 81.
3. Pearson, '1 Thessalonians', pp. 81-95.
4. Pearson, '1 Thessalonians', p. 87.
5. Schmidt, 'I Thess. 2.13-16', p. 269.

evaluation that the problem passage was an interpolation[1]. He focused upon Paul's linguistic constructions in the undisputed parts of 1.2–3.10 and compared the results with the syntax of 2.13-16. He tried to find a 'syntactical pattern of his [Paul's] style'[2] by analyzing three levels of syntactical relationship: the formation of noun and verb phrases and clauses, the sequence of phrases in a sentence, and the connection between sentences. He looked at 1.2–3.10 (everything before the exhortation section) in order to see 2.13-16 in the structure of the letter, paying special attention to the dependent clauses and to the syntactical devices relating them to the sentence to which they were linked. He was not so much interested in the syntax of each sentence as in the sequence of sentences. He found that 1.2-22 (the opening thanksgiving section) consists of three main clauses connected by *gar* ('for') and many dependent clauses.

For Schmidt, the problem passage differs from the undisputed parts of 1.2–3.10 in several ways:

1.   The first sentence (2.13) uses the conjunction *kai* ('and') to connect two independent clauses rather than Paul's usual use of *gar* or no conjunctions, as in 2.1-12. Schmidt says that nowhere else in 1 Thessalonians is *kai* used to connect two main clauses.

2.   Verse 15 has more dependent clauses than any other sentence in the entire section and more levels of embedding (subordination). All the dependent clauses tend to come last in word order and occur without an embedding device such as *hōste* ('that', 'so that', or 'in order that') or *hoti* ('that' or 'because'). Schmidt calls the abundance of dependent clauses 'a litany' since it contains seven levels of 'embed' compared

---

1.   Schmidt, 'I Thess. 2.13-16', p. 269. Schmidt thinks that the form and content of the verses under consideration were 'peculiar'. He never states that it is the theological incongruence between this passage and Romans which led him to the investigation, but the fact that he relies heavily upon Pearson's assertion that the polemic against the Jews fits well with the historical situation post 70 CE indicates that, for him, Paul's relationship with the Jewish people in the first century was not the one expressed in 1 Thess. 2.13-16. Therefore, he must think that the relationship is best reflected in Romans.
2.   Schmidt, 'I Thess. 2.13-16', p. 271.

to a maximum of five in the other parts of 1 Thessalonians (e.g. 1.4-6)[1].

3. The separation of the nouns 'Lord' and 'Jesus' by a participle is unusual in the Pauline corpus.

4. The noun phrase *tōn ekklēsiōn* ('of the churches') in v. 14 is followed by a genitive noun phrase ('of God'), a prepositional phrase ('being in Judaea'), and 'in Christ'. He says that each of these three constructions is Pauline, but that the combination of them is not.

Schmidt concludes that vv. 13-16 are not 'completely incorporated'[2] into the syntactical pattern of the rest of this larger section.

This concludes a summary of the recent objections raised against the authenticity of the passage. We now turn to the main responses to these objections.

Responses to Arguments against Authenticity

Arguments for the authenticity of the passage are mostly repetitions of those from the early twentieth century.

The Historical Difficulty

While Pearson based his conclusion (that Paul would not have held up the Judaean churches as examples of churches enduring persecution) upon the lack of evidence of persecution in the forties and fifties of the first century, I. Howard Marshall asserts that extreme persecution actually happened. He takes the historical picture in Acts as the key. Marshall says of the Judaean churches that

> they were particularly the object of persecution by the Jews, and it was also the Jews who were responsible for the persecution in Thessalonica (Acts 17.5). It is true that Paul could have referred to other churches in his mission field where the Jews had also been instrumental in causing trouble; the Judean churches may be singled out because they were the first to be persecuted, or perhaps they had suffered intensely, or more probably, because Paul wants to relate the suffering of the Thessalonians to an attitude which stemmed from Palestine and was part of a series of attacks on the prophets, Jesus, and his followers.[3]

1. Schmidt, 'I Thess. 2.13-16', p. 273.
2. Schmidt, 'I Thess. 2.13-16', p. 273.
3. I.H. Marshall, *1 & 2 Thessalonians* (Grand Rapids: Eerdmans, 1983), p. 78.

By using Acts, Marshall could reach a solution for why Paul would elevate the Judaean churches. Yet it was Baur's view that the account in Acts is not historical. The question of sources now enters the fray; it is an important one and will be considered in Chapter 3.

Responding to Pearson's rejection of the passage on the basis of there being no recent historical referent for *ephthasen*, scholars have offered the same list of national disasters which their earlier colleagues had suggested (see Chapter 1). Rather than locating the meaning in a national disaster, George E. Okeke turns to Paul's conception of an imminent parousia where the world is divided into 'the righteous' and the 'foes of God'.[1] As persecutors the Jews were already in the camp of the condemned, while the Thessalonians were in the camp of the saved. In Okeke's view the judgment about the Jews was already decided: they were damned. The fulfilment of this judgment awaited the eschaton. Donald Juel also appeals to an event in the future but explains that the 'wrath' refers to the rejection of Christ as messiah by Jews. It was the 'final line'[2] which had been crossed and would culminate in their certain judgment and the completeness of God's wrath against them at the end of the age.[3]

Just as in the last century, *eis telos* is translated temporally ('at last', or 'finally')[4] or intensively ('to the uttermost').[5] Similarly *orgē* is understood in ways reminiscent of the earlier defence of the authenticity of the passage; it is seen as:

　　1.　　a judgment which came into being with the death of Christ[6]

　　1.　G. Okeke, 'I Thessalonians 2.13-16: The Fate of the Unbelieving Jews', *NTS* 27 (1980–81), pp. 127-36 (130).

　　2.　D. Juel, *I Thessalonians* (Augsburg Commentary on the New Testament; Minneapolis: Augsburg, 1985), p. 233.

　　3.　L. Morris, *The Epistles of Paul to the Thessalonians* (Grand Rapids: Eerdmans, 1984), p. 65.

　　4.　Marshall, *Thessalonians*, p. 81; see also Best, *Thessalonians*, p. 121.

　　5.　See S.A. Cummins, 'Historical Conflict and Soteriological Reflection: An Exegesis of 1 Thessalonians 2.13-16 with Particular Reference to 1 Thessalonians and Romans 9–11' (MA thesis, McGill University, Montreal, 1988), p. 41. Cummins points to the intensive use in Jn 13.1 and 2 Cor. 12.12. For the intensive use 'forever' or 'to the end', see Mt. 10.22.

　　6.　K.P. Donfried, 'Paul and Judaism: I Thessalonians 2.13-16 as a Test Case', *Int* 38 (1984), pp. 242-53. See also J.C. Beker, *Paul the Apostle: The Triumph of God in Life and Thought* (Philadelphia: Fortress Press, 1980), p. 190. So also C. Masson, *Les deux épîtres de Saint Paul aux Thessaloniciens* (Paris: Delachaux &

and would be revealed fully during the events leading up to the parousia;

2.   a historical event which occurred in the recent past. There have been no new suggestions,[1] hence no need to repeat the list from Chapter 1;

3.   an impending event of supreme moment, whether the destruction of the Jerusalem temple predicted by Jesus[2] or some other eschatological event.[3]

One new suggestion has altered the view held by Knowling that the 'wrath' refers to a divine decision against the Jews and was manifested in their hardening against the gospel. Johannes Munck argues that God only *temporarily* hardened the hearts of the Jews against the reception of the gospel because they had rejected the messiah. Munck thinks that early Christian tradition determined that God's judgment was upon the Jews since the crucifixion. He believes that Paul had modified this view by indicating that the hardening was only in operation *until* the end of the age (Rom. 11.25-27).[4] Munck argues that since *to telos* had become a term for the end of the world (Mt. 10.22; 24.13; Mk 13.13), *eis telos* is best understood as meaning 'until the end',[5] indicating that the *orgē* would not be final. He contends that *eis telos*

Niestlé, 1957). In reflecting upon Paul's severe statement in 2.16b, Masson says, 'Comment donc Paul peut-il faire à son sujet une déclaration aussi catégorique? N'oublions pas que pour lui, comme pour les autres écrivains du Nouveau Testament, la mort et la résurrection de Jésus-Christ étaient l'évènement eschato-logique, le salut offert aux hommes pécheurs qui ne sauraient le refuser sans se perdre.' (p. 35). See also A.L. Moore, *1 and 2 Thessalonians* (The Century Bible; Greenwood, SC: Attic, 1969), p. 47.

1.   See E. Bammel, 'Judenverfolgung and Naherwartung', *ZTK* 56 (1959), pp. 294-315; Best, *Thessalonians*, p. 119; Jewett, *The Thessalonian Correspondence*, pp. 37-38.

2.   W. Hendriksen, *Exposition of I and II Thessalonians* (Grand Rapids: Baker, 1975), p. 73. See also R. Schippers, 'The Pre-Synoptic Tradition in I Thessalonians II 13-16', *NovT* 8 (1966), pp. 223-34.

3.   See R. Badenas, *Christ the End of the Law* (JSNTSup, 10; Sheffield: JSOT Press, 1985), p. 72; L. Gaston, *No Stone on Another: Studies in the Significance of the Fall of Jerusalem in the Synoptic Gospels* (Leiden: Brill, 1970), pp. 456-57. Marshall, *Thessalonians*, p. 81.

4.   J. Munck, *Christ and Israel: An Interpretation of Romans 9–11* (Philadelphia: Fortress Press, 1967), p. 62.

5.   Munck, *Christ and Israel*, p. 64; cf. Milligan, *Thessalonians*, p. 32.

had acquired a new meaning in the New Testament, a meaning beyond 'to the uttermost'. This effort to have 1 Thess. 2.14-16 cohere with Romans 11 operates mostly outside the realm of historical events and finds the interpretive key in a theological perspective. This suggestion will be taken up more fully in Chapter 4.

Although it is clear that scholars who have defended the problem passage as authentic have found events—either in Paul's recent past, impending, or flowing from a divine decision—to which 'wrath' could refer, nevertheless they have not agreed on one precise referent. Similarly, they have failed to agree on the translation or the meaning of *ephthasen* and *eis telos*.

The Structural Difficulty

Opposing Pearson, John C. Hurd[1] concludes that the passage is authentic because it can reasonably be maintained within the structure of the letter. Hurd argues that the passage fits with Paul's frequent use of a rhetorical form which Hurd names 'the sonata form ABA'. The main idea is that 'Paul discusses one point, passes to a second and then closes the discussion with a recapitulation of the first point'.[2] Indeed, Hurd points out that Paul uses this pattern frequently and faults the various partition theories for 1 Corinthians because they failed to recognize it. For instance, in 1 Corinthians 8 Paul discusses meat offered to idols then ch. 9 digresses to a different topic and ch. 10 returns to the original topic but with a different approach. Hurd notes that this pattern is standard in Paul's writings.[3]

In the case of our passage, Hurd notes that Paul employs the same sequence of thought there as he uses in 1.2-10. Hurd's outline of the parallels between 1 Thess. 1.2-10 and 2.13-16 follows:[4]

1. we give thanks (1.2; cf. we give thanks, 2.13);
2. constantly (1.2; cf. constantly, 2.13);

---

1. J.C. Hurd, 'Paul Ahead of his Time: I Thess. 2.13-16', in P. Richardson with D. Granskou (eds.), *Anti-Judaism in Early Christianity: Paul and the Gospels* (Studies in Christianity and Judaism, 1; Waterloo: Wilfrid Laurier University Press, 1986), pp. 21-36. See also W.G. Kümmel, *Introduction to the New Testament* (trans. H.C. Kee; Nashville: Abingdon Press, 1973), pp. 255-69.

2. Hurd, 'Paul Ahead of his Time', p. 28. Kümmel also judges the passage to be authentic within the body of the letter.

3. Hurd, 'Paul Ahead of his Time', pp. 28-33.

4. Hurd, 'Paul Ahead of his Time', p. 29.

3. election (1.4; cf. you received 2.13);
4. our gospel came to you (1.5; cf. the word of God which you heard from us 2.13);
5. not only in word (1.5; cf. you accepted it not as the word of humans, 2.13);
6. but also in power (1.5; cf. but as what it really is, the word of God, 2.13);
7. and in the Holy Spirit and with full conviction...(1.5; cf. which is at work in you believers, 2.13);
8. and you became imitators of us and of the Lord (1.6; cf. for you, brethren, became imitators of the churches...2.14);
9. for you received the word in much affliction...(1.6; cf. for you suffered, 2.14);
10. the success of the missionaries (1.7-8; cf. the suffering of the missionaries, 2.14-15);
11. you turned to God from idols (1.9; cf. hindering us from speaking to the Gentiles, 2.16);
12. to serve a living and true God and to wait for his Son (1.10; cf. that they may be saved. 2.16);
13. who delivers us from the wrath (1.10; cf. but God's wrath has come upon them at last, 2.16).

The parallelism as outlined seems sufficiently close to allow the conclusion that 1 Thess. 1.2–2.16 has as its gross structure the ABA pattern with 2.1-12 as the middle member. Each of the three panels of the triptych is marked at the opening by a formal structural signal and each closes with an eschatological climax: 'wrath' (1.10), 'kingdom and glory' (2.12), and 'wrath' (2.16). Hurd shows that although the first passage (1.2-10) in the triptych is similar to the third (2.13-16), the latter is not a slavish imitation of the former.[1] The reception of the gospel in the former passage brought joy, but in the latter it brought suffering.

Hurd finds this pattern in two places in 1 Thessalonians as well as in Paul's other letters. It exists between 1 Thess. 2.17-20 and 3.9-13 with 3.1-8 as the middle member. In addition it is found in 1 Corinthians 12, 13 and 14 with ch. 13 a digression from the theme introduced in ch. 12.[2] We turn now to a lengthy response to the

---

1. Hurd, 'Paul Ahead of his Time', p. 29.
2. Hurd, 'Paul Ahead of his Time', pp. 28-33.

linguistic construction difficulty. The terminological difficulty will be discussed below.

The Linguistic Construction Difficulty

Schmidt's objection to the authenticity of 1 Thess. 2.14-16 on linguistic grounds has already been discussed. Jon Weatherly[1] contends that Schmidt neglected to apply his methodology to Paul's other undisputed letters, and that such an application would suggest that the linguistic patterns of the problem passage are consistent with Paul's style.

1. Schmidt investigated only 1 Thessalonians for the use of *kai* to introduce matrix sentences (the most semantically prominent sentence in a paragraph or sentence cluster). Weatherly found that *kai* does join cola and fuller compound sentences in the undisputed letters (Rom. 1.28; 2.27; 3.8; 5.16; 1 Cor. 5.2; 6.2; 2 Cor. 1.7, 15; 2.3; Gal. 6.16; Phil. 1.9, 25; 1 Thess. 1.6). While it may be argued that these examples are not true matrices but expansions of the former sentence—what Schmidt calls 'embeds'—Weatherly points to 2 Cor. 1.15 as an undisputable example of *kai* introducing a matrix, since it introduces the lead sentence of a new paragraph. He says:

> As is the case in 2.13, the introductory *kai* in this verse is not duplicated elsewhere in the immediate context. But it is undisputably Pauline, thus demonstrating that Paul could, as the occasion demanded, depart from the linguistic pattern he had established in a context and introduce a matrix with *kai*.[2]

2. Concerning embeds, Weatherly notes[3] that 2.14-16 contains only one more embed (cf. Schmidt's view that there are two) than in other parts of 1 Thessalonians, for example, 1.6. The final embed of 2.16, *eis to anaplērōsai* ('so that they fill up'), is not subordinate to *hina sōthōsin* ('so that they might be saved') but rather to *kōlyontōn hēmas tois ethnesin lalēsai* ('[the Jews'] preventing us from speaking to the Gentiles'). Is one more level of embedding sufficient evidence to conclude that the passage is an interpolation? Weatherly observes that Rom. 4.16-17 has nine levels of embeds and Phil. 1.12-15 has seven.[4]

---

1. J.A. Weatherly, 'The Authenticity of 1 Thessalonians 2.13-16: Additional Evidence', *JSNT* 42 (1991), pp. 79-98 (91).

2. Weatherly, 'The Authenticity of 1 Thessalonians 2.13-16', p. 92.

3. Weatherly, 'The Authenticity of 1 Thessalonians 2.13-16', p. 93.

4. Weatherly, 'The Authenticity of 1 Thessalonians 2.13-16', p. 94.

Obviously, Paul sometimes varied his style.

3. With regard to the separation of *kyrion Iēsoun* by the participle *apokteinantōn* (2.15), Weatherly claims that this use is not typical of any extant early Christian writing (thus an anomaly in general) but that there are several instances where Paul separates a noun from an attributive adjective with an intervening verb form (1 Cor. 7.7, 12; 10.4; 2 Cor. 7.5; Phil. 2.20; 3.20). Thus, the style of 2.15a is not un-Pauline.

4. Concerning the modifiers of *tōn ekklēsiōn* (2.14), Weatherly suggests that because these phrases are found nowhere else in the Pauline corpus, it does not follow that they are interpolations.[1] Paul may have employed them for reasons related to the context. The genitive *tou theou* and the geographical designations are not unlike him (1 Cor. 1.2; 2 Cor. 1.1). It was necessary for him to specify *en tē Ioudaia* in this context in order to indicate to which churches the Thessalonians were being compared. The phrase *en Christō Iēsou* probably stresses the unity between the Thessalonian church and the Judaean churches, especially as regards persecution (cf. the suffering of Christ in 2.15a). Thus, the phrases of v. 14a can be explained on the hypothesis of the authenticity of the passage.

Weatherly has shown that it is not feasible to predict Paul's linguistic mode. Schmidt himself acknowledged that vv. 13-14 actually contain Paul's stamp even if not usually in this combination, and he also noted that Paul seems to have a preference for dependent clauses without an embedding device. In the case of vv. 15-16b, perhaps Paul used a 'litany' of dependent clauses for emphasis and therefore his syntactical pattern in these verses differs from that in the rest of the letter. One need only recall Werner Kümmel's caution[2] that since we have so few of Paul's letters to examine, it is difficult to reach reliable conclusions about what he might or might not have written. The style and syntax of 1 Thessalonians are not so dissimilar to what is found in other letters of Paul as are the style and syntax of Colossians and Ephesians. Some scholars, however, still argue for the authenticity of the latter in spite of such evidence. Why then should we relegate three verses in 1 Thessalonians to inauthenticity without trying our best to make sense of them as they stand?

Bearing in mind Kümmel's principle and two important facts—that

---

1. Weatherly, 'The Authenticity of 1 Thessalonians 2.13-16', pp. 95-96.
2. So Kümmel, *Introduction to the New Testament*, pp. 255-69.

Paul's letters address different churches and different problems (which may contribute to differences in style) and that scholars are still trying to make sense of Colossians and Ephesians (whole letters where problems of style are greater than those of 1 Thess. 2.14-16) as possibly authentic—I should find it difficult to be convinced by Schmidt's argument. I think that we should refuse to abandon the challenge to seek a key which can unlock the problem passage.

A Study Illuminating both Structure and Terminology
Karl Donfried's work on *mimēsis* (imitation), also sheds useful light on the structure of 1 Thessalonians. Donfried argues that 1 Thess. 2.14-16 fits into the structure of the whole letter once one recognizes that Paul often moves from the general to the specific in discussing a topic.[1] Donfried argues on the basis of structure that the use of *mimēsis* in this passage is part of Paul's style.

In the first chapter Paul offers a general thanksgiving (1.2-5a) and general references to apostolic integrity (1.5b). The general thanksgiving section continues with the imperative that the Thessalonians became imitators of him and his co-workers because they received the word in much affliction and became an example to all the believers in Achaia (1 Thess. 1.6-8).

Chapters 2 and 3 of 1 Thessalonians are further amplifications of this general thanksgiving, with elaboration on the theme of apostolic integrity occurring in 2.1-12. Verses 13-16 pick up on two themes in the general thanksgiving: imitation and affliction. Donfried thinks that these verses intensify and expand the earlier general references to imitation and affliction. Initial general references to imitation (1.6) are emphasized and made more specific in 2.14 and given a consequence in 5.9: those who imitate Paul, the Lord and the Judaean churches are destined for salvation.[2] If, then, Paul's use of 'imitation' makes sense structurally (even if it is unlike that in any of his other letters), is it not possible that the historical situation Paul faced and to which 1 Thessalonians is addressed differs significantly from these other letters? Donfried's results are compelling and cast doubt upon Pearson's conclusions.

---

1. Donfried, 'Paul and Judaism', pp. 242-53.
2. A similar development can be seen in Paul's treatment of the theme of hope: he makes general mention of it at the beginning of the letter (1.3), then specifies and expands it in chs. 3 and 4 (Donfried, 'Paul and Judaism', pp. 242-53).

Donfried and Hurd have shown that objections to the authenticity of the problem passage on the basis of structural, linguistic and syntactical analyses are not convincing. As a result, these objections have not been supported by a consensus among scholars. In addition, it should be kept in mind that a passage which does not seem to make sense in a particular context is not necessarily inauthentic for that reason. For example, 2 Cor. 6.14–7.1 has frequently been thought to be out of place in the Pauline correspondence. The argument against its present location is that it can easily be removed and that the content of the remainder makes better sense without it. Yet, in spite of the structural difficulties, it is seldom proposed that 6.14–7.1 is a non-Pauline interpolation,[1] even though the passage has some ideas not usually found in Paul's letters.[2] The approach scholars have taken with 2 Corinthians seems to me to be a properly cautious one: it tries to understand the passage in its context, and then, in the face of substantial evidence in favour of its misplacement, it seeks to make sense of it as an authentic piece of Paul's thought without rejecting it as inauthentic. I put forward this example as a model for dealing with the problem passage.

Summary

All but one of the main modern objections to the authenticity of 1 Thess. 2.14-16 have now been reviewed, as have the responses from the chief defenders of the view that it was indeed written by Paul. I shall discuss the most serious objection to authenticity in Chapter 3. Just now, it is necessary to sum up the main points of this chapter.

While the theory of interpolation does away with the theological incompatibilities, it assumes that Paul had to be consistent in his

1.   While Best concludes that the passage is a fragment out of place, Barrett maintains that it makes sense in its present context. See E. Best, *Second Corinthians* (Atlanta: John Knox Press, 1987), pp. 65-68; C.K. Barrett, *A Commentary to the Second Epistle to the Corinthians* (London: A. & C. Black, 1973), pp. 192-93. Günther Bornkamm is an exception to those who maintain its authenticity. See G. Bornkamm, *Paul* (trans. D.M.G. Stalker; New York: Harper & Row, 1971), p. 246. See also R. Bultmann, *The Second Letter to the Corinthians* (trans. R.A. Harrisville; Minneapolis: Augsburg Publishing House, 1985), pp. 175-80.

2.   Bornkamm, *Paul*, p. 246. Bornkamm thought that the language is closer to that of the Dead Sea Scrolls.

thinking on the Jews and on 'imitation'; yet it relinquishes too quickly the task of locating the passage within Paul's own historical situation, and it disregards the function of these verses within the hermeneutical unit of the letter itself.

Further analyses of history, linguistics, structure and style have countered the theories of inauthenticity with strong support for the authenticity of the passage, even though there is no agreement as to what Paul meant in v. 16c. Much stronger structural, stylistic, linguistic, theological and historical evidence needs to be at hand before one can judge what is or is not compatible with Paul's literary structure, style, syntax or theology, and what historical referents to his words are reasonable.

We turn now to Pearson's most serious objection to the authenticity of the problem passage.

Chapter 3

THE HISTORICITY OF SUFFERING IN 1 THESSALONIANS 2.14-15

In this chapter I examine an objection to the Pauline authorship of
1 Thess. 2.14-16 which was reintroduced by Pearson. He pointed to
the historical incongruity between this passage, which suggests that the
persecution of the Judaean churches was so well known that Paul
could use them as an example for his new church at Thessalonica, and
the actual suffering of Judaean churches. He cited Hare's conclusion[1]
that there was no significant persecution of Christians by Jews in
Judaea before the war of 70 CE. Pearson also questioned the notion
that the trouble at Thessalonica resulted in significant suffering for the
Thessalonians. While he did not deny that tribulation occurred there,
he disputed the claim that there was 'thoroughgoing, systematic
persecution'.[2] He argued that the Christians did not have to meet
secretly (see the exhortations of 4.11-12 and 5.14, which would have
been pointless if they had had to hide). Thus, for Pearson, even the
unquestionably authentic parts of Paul's letter do not report empirical
evidence of persecution. Rather, the references to suffering in the
letter serve a theological purpose:

> With respect to the situation in Thessalonica at the time of the writing of
> 1 Thessalonians, Paul speaks generally—this is a theological *topos*,
> revealing his eschatologically oriented theology—about the apostle and his
> congregation undergoing 'tribulation' (*thlipsis*, 1:6, recapitulated at 3:3),
> but that the Thessalonian Christians were actually suffering persecution in
> the apostolic period is very much in doubt.[3]

Supported by Hare's view and the theological *topos* of the authentic

1.   D.R.A. Hare, *The Theme of Persecution of Christians in the Gospel according
to St Matthew* (Cambridge: Cambridge University Press, 1967), pp. 30-35.
2.   Pearson, '1 Thessalonians', p. 64.
3.   Pearson, '1 Thessalonians', p. 87. Earlier, Baur had called the comparison
of the sufferings of the churches 'far-fetched' (*Paul the Apostle*, II, pp. 85-97).

parts of Paul's letter, Pearson concluded that the reference to actual suffering at the hands of the Jews in v. 14 is an intrusion into the text and is therefore inauthentic. The strength of Pearson's argument for the inauthenticity of our problem passage needs to be taken seriously and investigated more carefully. This chapter must now investigate what can be known about the severity of persecution of these churches in the first century. I begin with a consideration of the Greek text.

The verb *paschein* in 1 Thess. 2.14 (*epathete*) is to be understood in the sense of 'suffered'. It can also mean 'experienced', although that meaning is rare in Greek literature of the time. Paul, however, does use it in this way in Gal. 3.4. In all other places in his letters, as in the LXX, it is used in an unfavourable sense meaning 'to suffer' or more frequently 'to endure'. In 1 Cor. 12.26 we read, 'If one member *suffers*, all suffer together...' Paul uses *paschein* in the sense of 'to endure' in 2 Cor. 1.6: 'If we are afflicted, it is for your comfort and salvation; and if we are comforted, it is for your comfort, which you experience when you patiently endure the same sufferings that we *suffer*'.

The evidence from 1 Thessalonians supports Pearson's view that some kind of suffering was indeed being experienced in Thessalonica. We need only examine the abundance of references to tribulation: *hypomonē* (1.3), *thlipsis* (1.6; 3.3; 3.7), *thlibō* (3.4), *paschō* (2.2), *pathēma* (2.14), *ekdiōkō* (2.15), *agonōn* (2.2), *anankē* (3.7). Nevertheless, there is a remarkable absence of words having to do with fear, which may indicate that whatever the difficulties were, the lives of the Thessalonians were not threatened.

When *paschein* is followed by *hypo*, as in 1 Thess. 2.14, it literally means 'to suffer at the hands of someone' (see also Mt. 17.12). Thus, scholars[1] have often accepted Paul's statement 'for you suffered the same things...as they [the Judaean churches] did from the Jews...' as clear evidence of Jewish persecution of the Judaean churches. Munck, for example, stated that 'in 1 Thess. 2.15-16 we get a detailed picture of the Jews as persecutors...'[2] But is the evidence so very clear?

What can be known about the persecution of the Judaean churches

---

1. See Milligan, *Thessalonians*, p. 30, and Chapter 1 of this monograph. See also Munck, *Christ and Israel*, pp. 51-54; J. Munck, *Paul and the Salvation of Mankind* (trans. F. Clarke; London: SCM Press, 1959), pp. 216-17. Munck points to Acts 1–12 as evidence of Jewish persecution of Christianity at its very beginning.

2. Munck, *Paul and the Salvation of Mankind*, p. 202.

in the 50s is connected with the question of sources. The view of the early church in Acts contrasts with the view in Paul's other letters; Acts indicates that there was widespread persecution of the Jerusalem church (for example chs. 6–9; 22.4; 26.9-11).

Is Acts a reliable source for the idea that the Jerusalem church suffered severe persecution? If it is, then perhaps the passage from 1 Thessalonians is authentic. If it is not, and such persecution is improbable, then the passage is more likely inauthentic and should perhaps be relegated to an author after Paul. An alternative possibility, which has already been hinted at and one which I support, is that the statements are exaggerated for some reason.

At the beginning of the twentieth century it was common for scholars of Acts to accept as historically accurate the view that persecution of the earliest church in Jerusalem was extensive and severe and involved the first apostles. Milligan, for instance, expressed this view in his 1908 commentary on 1 Thessalonians. Although he admitted that there was no record of the persecution of the churches of Judaea in Acts (except for the brief period in the Jerusalem church recorded in Acts 8), nevertheless he thought that they were persecuted because 'they were the earliest Christian communities, and had throughout their history been exposed to severe hostility'.[1] Further, their sufferings would 'doubtless consist in excommunication and social outlawry, as well as in actual legal persecution'.[2]

Decades of historical criticism have altered Milligan's view, at least to some extent. Most scholars now generally agree that the writer of Acts had specific theological concerns and moulded the account to promote them. At the same time, however, the view that Acts is historically accurate in its presentation of persecution in the first century still flourishes. For instance, Munck can admit that Luke had a 'tendency or a theology'[3] but at the same time maintain that Luke's portrayal of the severe persecution of the Jerusalem church and its apostles by Jews is accurate.[4] He concludes on the basis of the account of Paul's persecution of the church in Acts 26.10-11 that 'Luke knows from the tradition he took over that punishments and tortures were

---

1. Milligan, *Thessalonians*, p. 29. See also Neil, *Thessalonians*, p. 50.
2. Milligan, *Thessalonians*, p. 29.
3. Munck, *Paul and Salvation*, p. 245.
4. Munck, *Paul and Salvation*, p. 244.

used, and that in several cases a sentence of death was passed'.[1] Futhermore, Munck thought that the church was under 'constant persecution'.[2] He draws upon Acts 1–12 for evidence; but Hare has rightly pointed out that while the early Christian movement was widely disapproved, Acts can produce evidence of only two Christian martyrdoms.[3] Before I discuss the evidence from Acts, the evidence from the Pauline corpus will be reviewed.

The closest possibility of corroborating evidence from Paul's own letters for the view that the Judaean churches were persecuted comes from Gal. 1.13, where Paul says, 'For you have heard of my former life in Judaism, how I persecuted the church of God violently and tried to destroy it'. The verb *ediōkon* is used and it is followed by *kath' hyperbolēn*, which qualifies it. What does *ediōkon* mean in this context? Does it imply that persecution took place? If persecution did take place, was it violent or not? If it was violent, was anyone killed? The verb *ediōkon* means 'to persecute' or 'to seek after' or 'to drive out'. However, *ediōkon* is in the imperfect tense and not the aorist. There is some ambiguity as to whether the event was really completed. It can mean 'I began persecuting' or 'I tried to persecute'.

The qualification *kath' hyperbolēn* should literally be translated as 'according to or bordering on the extreme'. Arland Hultgren[4] has shown that the translations of *kath' hyperbolēn* as 'violently' (RSV) and 'savagely' (NEB) are incorrect: *hyperbolēn* has to do with the intensity of Paul's zeal and not the intensity of violence. To support his view, he points to a parallel passage in Paul's autobiographical remarks about his activities as a persecutor in Phil. 3.6, where he emphasizes his zeal. Thus, Hultgren suggests altering the usual rendering of Gal. 1.13 and proposes the translation 'I persecuted the church of God *to the utmost*'. In this and the parallel passage (1.23) the verb *diōkōn* is followed by the verb *eporthoun* ('to destroy', 'to make havoc of', or 'to pillage'). It is the *church* which was being destroyed. The meaning could be actual deaths or simply harassment. There is no way to know for certain. It may be that Paul harassed the

---

1. Munck, *Christ and Israel*, p. 55. Now see P. Richardson, *Israel in the Apostolic Church* (Cambridge: Cambridge University Press, 1969).
2. Munck, *Paul and Salvation*, pp. 216-17.
3. Hare, *Persecution*, p. 62.
4. A.J. Hultgren, 'Paul's Pre-Christian Persecutions of the Church: Their Purpose, Locale, and Nature', *JBL* 75 (1976), pp. 97-111 (110).

Christians when they were meeting—that is, he destroyed their meetings. Stephen's death may have been an exception.

There is, of course, a tradition that connects the general persecution of the Jerusalem church with Stephen's death (Acts 6–7). Hultgren argues that the view presented by Acts regarding the type of persecution inflicted is quite different from that reflected in Paul's letters, which link it to being reviled and slandered (1 Cor. 4.12-13); being afflicted, perplexed and struck down (2 Cor. 4.9); and being beset with weaknesses, insults, hardships and calamities (2 Cor. 12.10). Hultgren concludes that while physical force was possible, deaths were unlikely. That deaths resulted is a later development, which Acts reflects. While Paul could have been present at the death of Stephen, he was not necessarily there; Paul himself makes no mention of his presence. Even if Paul had been present, Hultgren thinks it unlikely that he was 'consenting' to Stephen's death, which was more likely 'a mob action without judicial procedure and lying outside the meaning of persecution as generally understood'.[1]

Disciplinary response to the Christian movement in the first two decades after Christ was likely conducted on an *ad hoc* basis. It is unlikely that the Sanhedrin or any other Jewish body had the authority to put to death offenders of the law during Paul's lifetime.[2] It is certain that flogging was one form of punishment and imprisonment was another.

Baur was the first to point formally to the theological tendency of Luke and to note that the letters of Paul do not support the view of persecution of the Jerusalem church presented by Acts.[3] In 1950 John Knox, progressing beyond Baur, advanced the principle that one should use Acts only when it is in agreement with the letters of Paul.[4] Recently Lüdemann and Jewett[5] have added their support. However,

---

1. Hultgren, 'Paul's Pre-Christian Persecutions of the Church', p. 111.
2. For bibliography and discussion, see P. Winter, *On the Trial of Jesus* (Berlin: de Gruyter, 1961), chs. 7–8; D.R. Catchpole, 'The Problem of the Historicity of the Sanhedrin Trial', in E. Bammel (ed.), *The Trial of Jesus* (SBT, II/13; London: Allenson, 1970), pp. 47-65; R. Brown, *The Gospel according to John* (AB, 29A; Garden City, NY: Doubleday, 1970), II, p. 797.
3. Baur, *Paul and the Apostle*, the introduction.
4. J. Knox, *Chapters in a Life of Paul* (New York: Abingdon Press, 1950).
5. G. Lüdemann, *Paulus, der Heidenapostel*. I. *Studien zur Christologie* (Göttingen: Vandenhoeck & Ruprecht, 1980). Jewett, *The Thessalonian Correspondence*, pp. 114-32.

the debate over the reliability of Luke for an accurate historical picture of persecution continues. Diverse viewpoints have surfaced, from that of Martin Hengel, who thinks that Acts should be given a rather generous amount of confidence on this point, to that of E.P. Sanders, who is more conservative about what one can learn historically from Acts. The positions of these two scholars will be examined in some detail.

The Position of Martin Hengel

Hengel's position on the historical accuracy of Luke's account is unclear. He seems to believe that Luke is both reporting actual history and not reporting it. He states, 'His [Luke's] account always remains within the limits of what was considered reliable by the standards of antiquity'.[1] Indeed Lk. 1.3 'is more than mere convention; it contains a real theological and historical programme, though this cannot be measured by the standards of a modern critical historian'.[2] According to Hengel, Luke, like many other historians of the time

> rigorously omits everything that does not fit in with his narrative purposes... and elaborates what he wants to stress... combine[s] separate historical traditions to serve his ends, and separate[s] matters that belong together if as a result he can achieve a meaningful sequence of events.[3]

Hengel is admitting that a great deal of shaping by the writer took place. He acknowledges that Luke suppressed and misrepresented elements in which he had no interest and that he exaggerated those which aided his purpose (the healing of the paralysed Aeneas is said to have converted the residents of two entire villages).[4] Hengel claims that the author of Acts shows by his confusing of biographical and geographical details that he was not primarily interested in the church in Jerusalem or Judaea, nor in Peter, who appears and disappears in relation to Paul; instead he is interested in the apostle Paul and his mission as far as Rome. The community in Jerusalem is only the

---

1. M. Hengel, *Acts and the History of Earliest Christianity* (trans. J. Bowden; London: SCM Press, 1979), p. 61.
2. Hengel, *Acts*, p. 61.
3. Hengel, *Acts*, p. 61.
4. M. Hengel, *Between Jesus and Paul: Studies in the Earliest History of Christianity* (Philadelphia: Fortress Press, 1983), p. 116.

connecting link between Jesus and Paul.[1] If Hengel's view of Luke's use of traditions is right, surely Hultgren is likely to be correct that Luke's description of the degree of persecution of the Jerusalem church is tendentious.[2]

Concerning the degree of persecution suffered by the earliest Jerusalem church, Hengel accepts the description in Acts as evidence of severity and regards 1 Thess. 2.14-16 as support for his view. He admits that we do not know the nature of the persecutions to which Paul refers in v. 14, but nevertheless assumes that there were persecutions in Judaea and that Paul was involved in them. Further, he discounts Paul's own statement (Gal. 1.22) that he was not known to the churches of Judaea, and argues that despite Gal. 1.22 we should not doubt that Paul the Pharisee and scholar was involved in this persecution.[3] He then proceeds to an elaborate conjecture.

Hengel proposes that there was a Greek-speaking Christian community and an Aramaic one in Jerusalem. Paul, the Pharisee from the Greek-speaking synagogue, persecuted only the adherents of the Greek-speaking Christian community. As Hengel puts it:

> It is not surprising that the Greek-speaking Diaspora Pharisee Saul of Tarsus was 'personally unknown' to the more conservative Aramaic-speaking community in Jerusalem. However, the Hellenist community was expelled from Jerusalem; Saul had contributed to their 'destruction'.[4]

However, this historical reconstruction disregards, among other things,[5] what Hengel had just noted, namely that Luke 'over-draws the contours of persecution'[6] and exaggerates Paul's role in the death sentences involved (Acts 26.10; 22.4). According to Hengel, Luke presents the persecutions as extreme in order to magnify the miracle of Paul's conversion. Just when Hengel seems about to give up the historical accuracy of the accounts in Acts, he suggests that 'at the urging of the Greek-speaking synagogues, the Sanhedrin in Jerusalem was also involved in the punishment of these "despisers of the law"'.[7]

---

1. Hengel, *Jesus and Paul*, pp. 106-109.
2. Hultgren, 'Paul's Pre-Christian Persecutions', pp. 97-111 (111).
3. Hultgren, 'Paul's Pre-Christian Persecutions', p. 154.
4. Hultgren, 'Paul's Pre-Christian Persecutions', p. 154.
5. See the cogent points of E.P. Sanders in his review of Hengel's *Between Jesus and Paul* in *JTS* 37 (1986), pp. 167-72.
6. Hengel, *Jesus and Paul*, p. 153 n. 145.
7. Hengel, *Jesus and Paul*, p. 153 n. 145.

However, the historical reconstruction of two separate communities in Jerusalem which had little to do with each other creates a rather elaborate picture of churches and synagogues in the first century, a picture of Pharisees like Paul who came to Jerusalem to study and formed Greek-speaking synagogues there. A major piece of evidence for Pharisees establishing Greek-speaking synagogues is a Greek inscription[1] from a synagogue which had an immersion pool. Hengel proposes that it was Pharisees from this or similar Greek-speaking synagogues who were Stephen's opponents and that they involved the Sanhedrin.

A number of Hengel's assumptions seem to be based on silence, for there is no evidence, or only weak evidence. This paucity of evidence raises several questions for his proposal about what was happening in Jerusalem in the early 40s and 50s. Thus, E.P. Sanders asks whether two distinct Christian communities could have existed in Jerusalem yet had nothing to do with each other, and whether Paul, a zealous persecutor, was unknown to one entire group.[2]

It cannot be demonstrated, however, that Hengel's view is completely false. There is a great deal of uncertainty about how Pharisees were educated and whether they formed synagogues, and, if they did, what type they formed. Further, we lack information about the nature of several groups Hengel mentions: that to which Stephen belonged, that which Paul persecuted, and that which was driven out of Jerusalem. When all of these uncertainties are added to Hengel's own conclusion—'We can hardly say anything about the historical situation of the community in Jerusalem and Judea before the persecution by Agrippa I'[3]—I remain unconvinced that the accounts in Acts about the severity of the persecution of the Jerusalem church can be taken at face value.

---

1. The inscription as it exists in Hengel's *Between Paul and Jesus* (p. 17) is: 'Theodotus, Son of Vettenus, priest and archisynagogos, built the synagogue *for the reading of the law and instruction in the commandments*; also the lodging, the guest room and the water system to provide for those in need coming from abroad. The foundation stone was laid by his fathers, the elders and Simonides.' *CII*, no. 1404.

2. Sanders, review of Hengel's *Between Jesus and Paul*, pp. 170-71.

3. Hengel, *Jesus and Paul*, p. 203.

The Position of E.P. Sanders

Sanders is decidedly more restrained concerning the reliability of Luke's portrayal of the early church: he sides with Knox and Lüdemann in asserting that Acts can be used with complete confidence only when it agrees with the letters of Paul. Otherwise, the latter are historically more accurate and should be our basic source.[1] Sanders notes several facts about persecution which can be learned from Paul's letters:[2]

1. Paul persecuted the church in his role as a zealous Pharisee (Gal. 1.13, 23; Phil. 3.6; 1 Cor. 15.9).
2. Paul would have avoided persecution as a Christian if he were still preaching circumcision (Gal. 5.11). The evangelists who preached circumcision seemed to avoid persecution (Gal. 6.12).
3. There is an allegorical reference to the persecution of Christians (possibly only Pauline Christians) by those 'born according to the flesh' (Gal. 4.29).
4. Paul suffered five times from the thirty-nine lashes—persecution from Paul's point of view and punishment from the perspective of Jews.

In summary Sanders says,

> The point which emerges with most certainty from considering these passages is that at least some non-Christian Jews persecuted (that is, punished) at least some Christian Jews in at least some places. The best-attested fact is that Paul himself carried out such persecution. It is less certain that all of the references to persecution refer to Jewish punishment of some in the Christian movement, although that is the most likely assumption. From Galatians (especially 5.11 and 6.12), and from 1 Thess. 2.16, it also appears likely that the issue was circumcision; that is, the admission of Gentiles to the people of God without requiring them to make full proselytization to Judaism.[3]

The situation of other apostles, namely, those who circumcised Gentile converts, appears to be quite different (Gal. 5.11); that is, they

---

1. E.P. Sanders, *Paul, the Law, and the Jewish People* (Philadelphia: Fortress Press, 1983), p. 181.
2. Sanders, *Paul, the Law, and the Jewish People*, pp. 190-91.
3. Sanders, *Paul, the Law, and the Jewish People*, p. 191.

were not punished. Likely the Jerusalem apostles belong in this camp, although we cannot be certain.[1] Sanders says that the reference in 1 Thess. 2.14 to the suffering of the churches in Judaea raises the possibility of the persecution of the Christian movement in Jerusalem,[2] yet it is to be noted that Peter and the others were not driven out of Jerusalem—or if they were, only for a short time.[3] On the whole the church lived there in peace.

Sanders's position here has the advantage of being consistent about the reliability of Acts and in reconstructing the situation using Paul's letters and Acts where they agree. This approach seems to me to be headed in the right direction. In support of Sanders's reconstruction I offer the following observations.

1. In two of the three places where Paul mentions that he persecuted the church as a zealous Pharisee (Gal. 1.13; Phil. 3.6), he seems to tie together his early persecution of the church with the situation of his converts who are being compelled to be circumcised as worshippers of the God of Israel. The entire letter to the Galatians and the reference 'Look out for the dogs, look out for the evil-workers, look out for those who mutilate the flesh' (Phil. 3.2) are concerned with the problem of some people who want to circumcise the Gentiles. In Galatians these people seem to be from Jerusalem while in Philippians their origins are less clear. In any case, the situation reminds Paul of his own behaviour as a persecutor and he affirms that his Gentile converts should stand firm against circumcision because they already are 'the true circumcision' (Phil. 3.3). This evidence supports Sanders's view that people who admitted Gentiles into the people of God without requiring them to be circumcised were in danger of being persecuted. The apostles in Jerusalem seem to have circumcised and therefore did not likely suffer persecution.

2. Sanders's contention that the church in Jerusalem lived in peace is supported by Galatians 2, in which the Jerusalem church does not seem to have been following the practice which led to Paul's being persecuted, namely, admitting Gentiles uncircumcised into the church. Acts supports this view (Acts 15, 16 and 21). According to Acts 15 it

1.   Sanders, *Paul, the Law, and the Jewish People*, p. 204.
2.   Sanders, *Paul, the Law, and the Jewish People*, p. 204.
3.   S.G.F. Brandon, *The Fall of Jerusalem and the Christian Church* (London: SPCK, 2nd edn, 1957), pp. 88-100.

was not the general practice of the Jerusalem apostles to allow the uncircumcised into the people of God without their being circumcised, and the apostles had to write a letter to the Gentiles to let them know of their approval of Paul's practice and of certain other requirements. Thus it seems that there were no Gentiles in the Jerusalem church; if there were, they were circumcised (see Acts 16.3).

3. Rom. 15.31 makes the picture less sunny. Paul asks the Roman Christians to pray for him that he might be delivered from the unbelievers in Judaea. This raises the possibility of some persecution. Furthermore, we have evidence of three members of the Jerusalem church who were killed by Jews in the first century: Stephen, James the brother of John,[1] and James the brother of Jesus.[2] Of the three, Paul could only have known of the first two. James, the brother of Jesus, was martyred in 62 CE and the letter to the Thessalonians (usually dated about 50–51 CE) had already been written before it happened.

Although Paul could not have known about the death of James the brother of Jesus, Josephus's account in *Ant.* 20.200-203 reveals important information about the religious practice of non-believing Jews and the Jerusalem church.

According to Josephus, James was killed after being charged with breaking the Jewish law, but Josephus also tells us that some who were strict in observance of the law (*peri tous nomous akribeis*) opposed this action of the High Priest, Ananus. We cannot be certain if this phrase means that those who complained to the incoming Roman governor were strict in the Jewish or the Roman law. If it is the Jewish law, there is a likelihood that those who were *akribeis* ('strict') were Pharisees (Josephus frequently uses *akribeis* to describe them although not exclusively). If the Pharisees supported James as a strict observer of the law, we have proof that the martyrdom was an isolated incident and that in general the Jerusalem church was seen as an observant assembly within Judaism and remained unmolested. At least we hear nothing of general deaths resulting from persecution. At any rate, in the eyes of some Jewish leaders it appears that James did not offend to the extent of requiring Ananus's high-handed policy.

However, perhaps what is being referred to is the Roman law. Jerusalem was temporarily without a procurator because Festus had

1. James, the brother of John, was killed by Agrippa I. See Acts 12.1-3.
2. See Josephus, *Ant.* 20.200-203.

died and Albinus, the new one, had not yet arrived in Jerusalem. Thus Ananus's execution of James may have broken Roman law because it is probable that execution was beyond his authority. This may be the reason why some religous men of the city sent letters to Agrippa II and complained to Albinus. I think that this possibility is less likely, since Josephus normally uses 'strict in observance of the law' only with reference to the Jewish law (*War* 1.110-11; 2.162). Even if James was killed because he broke the Jewish law, we hear of only such isolated incidents, not large-scale violence, done to Christians in Jerusalem.

Hare's judgment about the passage in Josephus is, I think, correct. He says that it 'would indicate that the Christians in Judea, at least up until 62 AD, were living in harmony with their fellow Jews'.[1] The two killings are significant but not indicative of large-scale persecution of the churches of Judaea.

4. Additionally, there are many times in Paul's letters where reference to the suffering of the Jerusalem church would have created a bond between the Gentile churches and the church from which the gospel began. If Paul could have pointed to specific examples,[2] so much the better. The church in Philippi, for instance, was facing some kind of opposition (Phil. 1.28) which seems to have produced some suffering (1.29-30), although we hear nothing of the form it took. There is more in the letters about Paul's own suffering (1.17; 2.17; 3.10; 4.14). He might have stated the parallel between his suffering and that of the Jerusalem apostles (had he been able to point to examples), especially since the letter to the Philippians reflects upon the servanthood, suffering and death of Jesus, and upon Paul's own potential sacrifice (2.17). The churches in Galatia were facing opposition because of accepting Gentiles without the obligation of circumcision. Had the Jerusalem church been suffering persecution for the same reason, or even if it had been suffering it for another reason,

---

1. Cited in Pearson, '1 Thessalonians', p. 87.
2. The passage in 1 Cor. 4.9-12 is not a record of actual instances of persecution of the Jerusalem apostles. It is a list of general sufferings juxtaposed with boasts of achievement by the Corinthians (3.4-23; 4.6-8). As such, it suggests that a less magnified view of themselves would be more appropriate. Beyond general difficulties we learn nothing about specific experiences of the apostles. We do learn how Paul handles the self-magnification of his churches.

Paul might have found its example useful to support his missionary churches.

There is a parallel point: in making his collection for the saints in Jerusalem, Paul never cites as an incentive for generosity any mention of their having suffered persecution.[1]

5. Finally, Acts itself does not consistently depict major persecution. It provides us with conflicting evidence. In 8.1-3 we hear about a persecution which arose after the martyrdom of Stephen and scattered the church in Jerusalem except for the apostles who, curiously enough, escaped. Could the Jews not find them? Why would the leaders of the movement escape persecution? At any rate, if the apostles left Jerusalem, it was only for a brief time. The text in Acts 9.31, a typical summary by Luke, indicates that at least part of the community is back in Jerusalem, and the picture is serene: 'So the church throughout all Judea and Galilee and Samaria had peace and was built up; and walking in the fear of the Lord and in the comfort of the Holy Spirit it was multiplied'.[2]

Summary

I agree with Hengel that not much can be known about the extent of persecution of the church in Jerusalem. I also agree with Sanders that what can be known does not point to extensive persecution, nor does it lead us to think that the Jerusalem church admitted Gentiles into it, or if it did, that they were allowed in without circumcision. If the Jerusalem church was being persecuted regularly, Paul for some reason mentioned it only once (1 Thess. 2.14) and avoided mention of it in other letters, even those where it might have brought moral support to his congregations.

There is little external or internal evidence to support Paul's statement about the suffering of the Judaean churches in 1 Thess. 2.14.[3] When associated with the killing of the Lord Jesus and the prophets, this seems to suggest that the suffering included physical violence. Stephen was persecuted, and although one cannot rule out the possibility that the Jerusalem church itself may have experienced some

---

1. Brandon, *The Fall of Jerusalem* cited by Hare, *Persecution*, p. 63.
2. See Brandon, *The Fall of Jerusalem*, pp. 88-100.
3. Hare, *Persecution of Christians*, pp. 30-35.

persecution, on the basis of the findings discussed in this chapter, the extent of it was not severe.

Nor is it likely that the Thessalonians suffered severe persecution. As Hare concludes, it would be easy to exaggerate their sufferings but their real experience is more likely to have been 'public insults, social ostracism and other kinds of non-violent opposition'.[1] How then should we proceed?

We need to recall Pearson's comment about Paul's references to suffering in 1 Thess. 1.6 and 3.3 cited at the beginning of this chapter: 'Paul speaks generally—this is a theological *topos*, revealing his eschatologically oriented theology',[2] and not historical reality. Pearson thus rejected 1 Thess. 2.14-16 as being written by Paul because the latter verses, implying extreme persecution in Thessalonica, contradict Paul's general perspective on suffering in view of the end of the age (1.6; 3.3). What Pearson thought was a contradiction was in fact straightforward. He pointed to Paul's theological *topos* with regard to his view of the end of the age. This view might have propelled him into a new line of inquiry for the problem passage: namely, a rhetorical one. This is the direction we shall explore.

Paul does imply something about the severity of persecution in 1 Thess. 2.14-16. He says that the Thessalonians 'suffered the same things' as did the Jerusalem Christians and then describes the Jews as having 'killed' Jesus and the prophets and 'driven out' Paul or 'persecuted' him or others. There is an association with what had happened to the Judaean Christians. As the sentence runs, their suffering at the hands of the Jews is mentioned just before 'killed... the Lord Jesus'. Although, strictly speaking, this does not say that the Jews *killed* any Judaean Christians, mention of their suffering leads into the killing of Jesus and the prophets, so as to associate the two in the mind of the reader, and probably in that of the original hearers. The close connection of the statements implies that some violence had been endured. That scholars have argued about the issue of persecution for more than a century demonstrates the effectiveness of Paul's rhetoric here. What we really know about the Judaean Christians is that they were driven out for a short time (Acts 8.1).

---

1. See Hare, *Persecution of Christians*, p. 63; cf. A.J. Malherbe, *Paul and the Thessalonians: The Philosophic Tradition of Pastoral Care* (Philadelphia: Fortress Press, 1987), p. 46.

2. Pearson, 'I Thessalonians', p. 87.

To say that the Thessalonian Christians had suffered the same things as their Judaean counterparts is probably exaggeration: the vagueness of the other references to suffering in 1 Thessalonians indicates that no Thessalonian Christians had been 'driven out' of their city or forced to hide from violent persecutors (1 Thess. 4.11-12; 5.14).

It is my view that in 1 Thess. 2.14-16 Paul's polemic is based on real opposition he faced when writing the letter or very recent opposition; it is a polemic which required exaggeration in order to support and brace his church. But before I can undertake a rhetorical examination of Paul's statements, I must show why it is important to focus upon the passage in its own right.

I turn therefore to an important investigation of how theological harmonization of Paul's views about the Jewish people in 1 Thess. 2.14-16 and Romans 9–11 prevents scholars from focusing on the problem passage itself and skews the historical picture. I propose that the best approach tries to understand the passage in its own right. What is gained are new insights into the interpretation of the passage, the historical situation, and a better understanding of the apostle.

Chapter 4

From Theological Harmonization to Interpreting the Passage in its Own Right

In the first chapter we examined the serious difficulties with
1 Thess. 2.14-16: Paul's elevation of the Judaean churches as
examples seems strange; his statement about the sufferings of the
Judaean churches is unusual; and his castigations of the Jews and his
judgment against them contrasts with his more positive attitude of
them in Romans 9–11. We also reviewed the main late nineteenth and
early twentieth century positions on the question of the authenticity of
1 Thessalonians and of the problem passage. Chapter 2 reviewed
more recent arguments for and against the acceptance of the problem
passage as by Paul's hand. We saw that historical, structural, stylistic
and theological considerations were mustered against authenticity but
effectively countered by other arguments. Chapter 3 investigated the
most serious challenge to the passage's authenticity: that there is little
proof of severe persecution of the Judaean churches in the early
decades of the first century. It was suggested that this lack does not
require us to reject the problem passage, but rather to acknowledge
that Paul may have had certain intentions in making these statements,
and to investigate them with an alternative approach. However, before
employing that new approach, I must examine a tendency which I
hinted at in the earlier chapters and which in my own approach I shall
try to avoid: the tendency towards the theological harmonization of
Paul's apparently contradictory statements about the Jews in
1 Thess. 2.14-16 with those in Romans 9–11.

The Tendency towards Theological Harmonization

Scholars who wish to see Paul's thinking about the Jewish people as
consistent often resolve the contradiction in one of two ways:

1.   They reject 1 Thess. 2.14-16 as not being by Paul because the passage does not concur with what Paul says about the Jewish people in Romans. We saw this approach in both Chapters 1 and 2 when discussing scholars of the early and late twentieth century who rejected the passage as inauthentic.

2.   They accept the passage as authentically by Paul and by harmonizing it with what he says about the Jews in Romans 9–11. One of the clearest, most intriguing examples of how this theological harmonization is achieved is seen in Johannes Munck's equation of *orgē, ephthasen* and *eis telos* in v. 16c with selected passages from Romans 1 and 9–11.

Theological Consistency: Equation of Terms

To what event could *orgē* in 1 Thess. 2.16c refer? While the most natural translation for *ephthasen* is 'has come upon' (indicating an event in the recent past), for Munck no recent historical event was significant enough. While the verb *ephthasen* could be understood as a proleptic aorist and therefore refer to an event in the future like the destruction of Jerusalem, he rejected this possibility on the grounds that *eis telos* makes the pronouncement absolute whereas the devastation of the Jerusalem temple did not eradicate the Jewish people. Further, he thought that *eis telos* could not mean 'completely' or 'utterly' because such a construal 'is not compatible with Romans 11, which presupposes the ultimate salvation of the Jews'.[1] This latter statement explains Munck's assumption that Paul is consistent in what he believes. Because Munck assumed that what Paul really thought about the Jews is found in Romans, he decided that *eis telos* cannot be read 'completely'. Instead, by translating it as 'until the end' (that is, the wrath was *temporary* and would cease just before the end of the age, thereby allowing time for the conversion of the Jews) he could maintain theological consistency between 1 Thess. 2.16 and Rom. 11.25-27.

Munck opposed translating *ephthasen* as a proleptic aorist because 'such an application of the aorist is not found elsewhere in the New Testament'.[2] He is surely correct here. It is true that the aorist is sometimes translated as a proleptic, but in the examples which

1.   Munck, *Christ and Israel*, p. 63.
2.   Munck, *Christ and Israel*, p. 63.

Robertson[1] gives, each one involves a conditional clause. For instance, 'If it is by the finger of God...then the kingdom of God has come upon you' (Mt. 12.28). The use of *ephthasen* in 1 Thess. 2.16c is not in a sentence with a conditional clause; rather, it stands on its own, and to translate it as a proleptic would be an anomaly in the New Testament.

Although Munck admitted that *ephthasen* is best understood in its simple past sense ('has come') he preferred the poorly attested[2] secondary reading *ephthaken*.[3] In this perfect tense the meaning is that something had come upon the Jews in the past and continued to be upon them. When determining to what *orgē* referred, Munck seems to have had his eye on the letter to the Romans. His starting point was theological, that is, the theology of Paul's view of the Jewish people in that book: they would be saved when the full number of the Gentiles had come into the people of God and before the end of the age (Rom. 11.25-27). Munck was able to achieve theological consistency between the problem passage and Romans 9–11 by equating the *orgē* of 1 Thess. 2.16 with God's 'hardening' of the Jews in Rom. 9.17-22 and 11.7-12. He maintained that the 'wrath' had begun with 'the rejection of the gospel of the crucified Messiah';[4] it was manifest in a divine decision to harden the Jews. Munck thought that the hardening continued in the present persecuting behaviour of the Jews towards the messengers of the gospel. He explained,

> It is probably most reasonable to assume that the wrath, namely the hardening of the Jews, set in when they rejected the gospel of the crucified Messiah, before their attempts to prevent the Christian preachers from addressing the Gentiles. The persecution carried on by the Jews is therefore a symptom of their hardening, and this hardening is radical *eis telos*. In this case the 1 Thessalonians passage is compatible with the view in Romans 11, where the hardening has already taken place, and no reference is made to the future.[5]

1.   A.T. Robertson, *A Grammar of the Greek New Testament in the Light of Historical Resaerch* (New York: Hodder & Stoughton, 2nd edn, 1915), p. 846. The examples Robertson gives include Mt. 12.26, 28; 18.15; 1 Cor. 7.28; Rev. 10.7; and Jn 15.6.

2.   Okeke, 'I Thessalonians 2.13-16', p. 130.

3.   B.F. Westcott and F.J.A. Hort, *The New Testament in the Original Greek* (Chicago: F.H. Revell, 1902).

4.   Munck, *Christ and Israel*, p. 63.

5.   Munck, *Christ and Israel*, p. 64.

At first glance it seems that Munck has succeeded in making 1 Thess. 2.16 cohere with Paul's views about the Jews in Romans 9–11. On closer examination, this explanation of the wrath appears forced. Is it accurate to equate terms as Munck does (*orgē* = 'hardening', as in Rom. 9.18, 22; *ephthasen* = divine decision to harden as in Rom. 9.18; *eis telos* = 'until the end' as in Rom. 11.25)? Can *orgē* in 1 Thess. 2.16 be equated with the 'hardening' of the Pharaoh and the Jews in Rom. 9.18-22? If the earliest manuscripts attest *ephthasen*, does it make sense to prefer *ephthaken*, a poorly attested secondary reading? One suspects the choice of the secondary reading is made for the sake of a theological preference (in order to show the 'wrath' as a divine decision made at the crucifixion).

Romans itself calls into question the equation of a temporary 'hardening' and 'wrath'; the latter often possessing an eschatological sense. In Romans as elsewhere Paul uses this particular meaning for wrath (see Rom. 2.5, 8; 5.9; 9.22; 1 Thess. 1.10; 5.9). Although Rom. 1.18 shows wrath in the present, it is obvious that the manifestation is reserved for the judgment in the future (2.8). Rom. 3.5 and 4.15 are more complicated. In 3.5 the present tense is generalizing and the sense of the verse is something like 'Can a God who brings wrath be fair?' The wrath, however, will come in the future, at the judgment (3.6). In 4.15 'the law works wrath' indicates wrath in the present, but punishment is in the future. The sense is that the wrath stirs up transgressions which *will* be punished, not 'the law *worked* wrath, which *has now already come* upon the people utterly, finally, and decisively'. Thus, the historical referent 'wrath = temporary hardening' is inadequate to explain the entire clause 'wrath has come upon them…'

'Wrath' comes to expression in an event which punishes. For Munck the 'hardening' *is the punishment*, but according to Rom. 9.22 God *refrains* from expressing wrath and exercises patience. According to 1 Thess. 2.16c God has sent some punishment upon the Jews either 'at last' or 'utterly'. One would have to force the meaning of the passages in Romans in order to achieve an equation between the wrath of 1 Thess. 2.16c and Rom. 9.17-24.

We can observe a similar forcing of the evidence in Munck's translation of *eis telos* as 'until the end' (meaning that the punishment was temporary and that just before the end of the age Jews would be saved). By this translation he could remove the sense of finality of *anaplērōsai autōn tas hamartias pantote*[1] ('so as to fill up their sins always') and the usual sense of *eis telos* as 'utterly' or the alternative 'at last'. The use of this latter term in the Gospels and in other letters of Paul (Mt. 10.22; 24.13; Mk 13.13; Lk. 18.5; Jn 13.1; 1 Cor. 10.11) shows that Munck's interpretation of it as temporary is most unusual. My reading of each of these passages is that 'right to the end' is the proper sense, for example, from the synoptics, the one who endures right to the end will be saved (Mt. 10.22; 24.13; Mk 13.13) and from Jn 13.1, Jesus loved the disciples to the end—not temporarily, but right to the end or completely. In 1 Cor. 10.11 Paul says *eis hous ta telē tōn aiōnōn katentēken* ('unto whom the end of the ages has come'). To be sure, here the *eis* does not go with *telos*; it refers to 'us' (*hēmōn*) which just preceded the preposition and relative pronoun. Nevertheless, the sense of *eis* here is 'unto' in a decisive sense and not temporarily: the end of the ages has come to us!

Munck derived his view of wrath as the hardening of the Jews from Rom. 9.18. But according to Paul, God's hardening of Pharaoh's heart had nothing to do with God's wrath or punishment for sin. On the contrary, Paul is arguing there that God's action of hardening had *nothing* to do with good or evil actions. Equations based upon theological consistency do not do justice to any passage on its own merits. Munck was able to harmonize passages, but his solution seems to me unsatisfactory for an adequate understanding of our particular passage.

Theological Consistency: Augmentation of Negative Statements
Donfried took a slightly different tack from Munck and investigated the literary tradition for negative judgments against the Jews similar to those expressed in 1 Thess. 2.16. He noted that in Lk. 11.47-52/Mt. 23.29-36 as well as in Wis. 19.3-5 there were such judgments. He suggested that Paul used a pre-synoptic tradition which he found appropriate for the situation in Thessalonica.[2]

---

1. Okeke, 'I Thessalonians 2.13-16', p. 132.
2. Donfried, 'Paul and Judaism', p. 249; see also Koester, *Early Christianity*, p. 113; see now I. Broer, '"Der ganze Zorn ist schon über sie gekommen" Bermerkungen zur Interpolationshypothese und zur Interpretation von 1 Thess. 2,14-16', in R.F. Collins (ed.), *The Thessalonian Correspondence* (Leuven: Leuven University Press, 1990), pp. 137-59. Broer concludes that Paul used this tradition to shock his people and that the use of v. 16 indicates Paul's love for them.

Whereas the references to wrath in Matthew, Luke and Wisdom have a strictly future eschatological context, the one in 1 Thess. 2.16 seems to refer to something which has already happened ('has come'). Only the death of Christ through which God's judgment and wrath expressed themselves seemed to Donfried an appropriate referent.[1] According to him, what triggered Paul's use of the statement in 1 Thess. 2.16 was hostility by Jews in Thessalonica: they hindered him, as he says in v. 16. Pointing out that the relationship between 1 Thessalonians and Romans is one of consistency, Donfried argues that in Romans (9.22-24; 10.3, 21) Paul does not alter his negative judgment against the Jews from his first letter but augments it by adding the new information that at the end of time God's mercy would be mysteriously extended to Israel and would lead to their inclusion.[2]

Donfried also tried to find a historical referent for wrath and took *ephthasen* in its simplest meaning ('has come'), which led him to look for an event in the past to which v. 16c could refer. Unfortunately, his explanation of the referent of the wrath as the death of Jesus is not fully convincing. It may be helpful to recall D.E.H. Whiteley's view that such an explanation of wrath is 'over-subtle'.[3] Since Donfried looks within the verses preceding the statement for the referent, why did he overlook the other components of v. 15? The charges of killing the Lord Jesus and the prophets, and of driving 'us' out, displeasing God, and opposing all humanity push beyond the death of Jesus as the historical referent for *orgē*. Further, I cannot understand how Paul's statements in 1 Thess. 2.16 can be said to have been augmented by those in Romans. There are in fact significant differences.

In Romans 9–11, Paul's negative comments notwithstanding, the source of Jewish blindness is God. Paul's discussion of the Jewish people underscores how their rejection of the gospel fits into God's plan for the salvation of Gentiles (11.11-12); indeed, in Rom 11.17-24 Paul warns the Gentiles that the natural branches can be readily grafted back into the root, and the grafted branches easily cut off. In other words, Paul emphasizes here the positive place of the Jewish

---

1. See also C.E.B. Cranfield, 'A Study of 1 Thessalonians 2', *IBS* 1 (1979), pp. 215-16.

2. Donfried, '1 Thessalonians', p. 252. See also H.-M. Lübking, *Paulus und Israel im Römerbrief: Eine Untersuchung zu Römer 9–11* (Bern: Peter Lang, 1986), pp. 129-31.

3. Whiteley, *Thessalonians*, p. 81.

people in God's plan, which ends with their salvation (11.26). This is in sharp contrast to 1 Thessalonians, where the Jewish people are said to be filling up the measure of their sins as they always do and to be the recipients of God's wrath without reversal. Thus, instead of claiming that Paul 'augmented' what he had said in 1 Thess. 2.14-16, I contend that he 'revised' it.

It is curious that Donfried overlooks these differences. I suspect, therefore, that he uses the theology of Romans to harmonize 1 Thessalonians with the former letter. He concedes that 'Only when the coherent theology of Paul is understood can the contingent situation of each Pauline letter be comprehended'.[1] But to which coherent theology is he referring? On what basis is this judgment made? On other instances of Paul's polemic? For example, 2 Cor. 11.13 or Rom. 2.17-23? It does not seem so; rather, it is the Paul of Romans 9–11 who is in mind.

Donfried is partly correct: there does seem to be a central coherence to Paul's thought. Nevertheless, like so many others he errs in setting up a false construct called 'Paul's theology' which he assumes to have been immune to change. More plausibly, Beker[2] and Sanders[3] discuss a coherent core that Paul applied in non-uniform ways in diverse circumstances, but they maintain that the immediate context affected what he wrote. Thus, we need not choose between 'theologically unharmonious with what Paul wrote elsewhere and therefore inauthentic' and 'able to be theologically harmonized and therefore authentic'. We should examine the passages themselves to see whether or not we can explain them as authentic in their immediate context; that is, one passage might *differ* from another because of different circumstances. Difference or sameness does not necessarily establish authenticity or inauthenticity.

Theological Consistency: Equation of View, Allowance for Mood
Neil's interpretation depended heavily upon Romans for its core. The historical referent for 'wrath' was God's rejection of the Jewish people because of their unbelief. Paul's statement in 1 Thessalonians reflects his temporary angry mood, caused by persecution,[4] laid aside

1. Donfried, 'Paul and Judaism', p. 253.
2. Beker, *Paul the Apostle*, p. 362.
3. Sanders, *Paul, the Law, and the Jewish People*, pp. 4-6, 144-48.
4. Neil, *Thessalonians*, pp. 52-54; Hendriksen, *New Testament Commentary*,

in favour of his actual view, which is expressed best in Romans.[1] Neil thought that Paul's view[2] at the time he wrote 1 Thessalonians was the one he revealed in Romans, that is, that the rejection of the Jews was not permanent but would last until the fullness of the Gentiles came in (Rom. 11.25). To Neil's credit, his solution allows for differences in Paul's mood. One is reminded of Frame's observation, 'The letters of Paul reveal not a machine but a man; his moods vary...'[3] Nevertheless, Neil's conclusions are excessively dependent upon the theology of Romans and a relatively static view of what Paul thought in his lifetime.

Summary
There is a tendency to harmonize passages by defenders of the Pauline authorship of 1 Thess. 2.14-16. The rejectors, as we have seen in Chapters 1, 2 and 3, assume that Paul could not have made such vitriolic statements about his own people, that the severity of persecution in v. 14 does not reflect the historical reality of Paul's time, and that no catastrophe other than the destruction of the Jerusalem temple could account for his statement in v. 16c that the wrath had come upon them to the uttermost. Support for the rejector's position comes from trying to understand 1 Thess. 2.14-16 in the light of Romans 9–11 and deciding to give the latter passage precedence. Similarly, for the defenders of authenticity, proof comes from giving precedence to Romans. Munck explains away differences between the letters by equating Paul's terms; Donfried equates the negative statements in the letters and explains that Paul's positive attitude towards the Jews in Romans merely augments what he had said earlier. The implication is that when he wrote 1 Thess. 2.14-16 Paul already held the positive views found in Romans 11 but simply had not expressed them. Neil also equates Paul's views in the two letters and explains the differences by appealing to a change in his mood.

p. 73. Hendriksen appeals to Mt. 21.43; 23.38; 24.15-28; 27.25; Mk 11.14,20; Lk. 21.5-24; 23.27-31 (p. 73). Now see also U. Schnelle, 'Der erste Thessalonicherbrief und die Entstehung der paulinischen Anthropologie', *NTS* 32 (1986), pp. 207-24.
  1.   Neil, *Thessalonians*, p. 53.
  2.   Neil, *Thessalonians*, p. 51.
  3.   Frame, *Thessalonians*, p. 111.

Such solutions, in the face of repeated indications of serious difficulty, illustrate an unjustifiable tendency towards theological harmonization. The recognition of a difference in Paul's mood or a revision of his thought between two letters should make us pause before assuming that what he said in the early letter was 'really' the same as in the later one. The assumption of consistency is the core of the problem in interpreting the text, and equations based on this assumption do not give the letter to the Thessalonians its rightful place in the interpretation.

It comes as no surprise that contemporary scholars are troubled by Paul's offensive view in v. 16 (the final destiny of the Jews is wrath) compared to that of Rom. 11.26 (the Jews will be brought into the reign of God by a Deliverer from Zion, presumably Christ). The resolution of Paul's attitude towards the Jewish people bears increased weight because of the holocaust in this century.

Certainly, one can resolve the theological incongruence either by declaring 1 Thess. 2.14-16 inauthentic and recommending that we excise it from our texts[1] or by harmonizing its view of the Jewish people with that of Romans by judging the latter to be the actual view, but both solutions rest upon a 'sanitized picture of Paul'.[2] My investigation proposes that we begin neither with the events of this century nor with the theology of Romans in order to understand Paul's views on the Jewish people in 1 Thessalonians. Rather, we must start by examining the material as given before eliminating or rearranging passages.

Interpreting the Passage in its Own Right

Even among scholars who refuse to accept that Paul always had the same viewpoint on the Jewish people, there is no interpretive consensus on 1 Thess. 2.14-16. One of the best analyses of the problem has been done by Okeke, who focuses clearly upon the situation of the letter to the Thessalonians.[3] Instead of harmonizing passages, he contrasts Paul's thoughts about the salvation of the Jews:

---

1. Beck, *Mature Christianity*, p. 46.
2. Jewett, *The Thessalonian Correspondence*, p. 39.
3. Okeke, '1 Thessalonians 2.13-16', p. 136.

> Paul is writing from the background of the conception of an imminent
> parousia which does not permit of a long-term process of rebellions and
> opportunities for repentance... if now is the hour of decision and the Jews
> have opted to be on the side of the foes of God, it seems exegetically
> improper to evaluate 1 Thessalonians on the basis of Romans...[1]

The lurid picture of what would happen to the enemies of the people
of God is meant to encourage members of the new Thessalonian
church by assuring them that their persecutors would get the deserved
punishment. The letter to the Romans addresses a different issue: the
fate of the Jews, given the successful mission to the Gentiles.[2] Okeke is
right to focus upon the date and occasion of the letters as the proper
starting point. This principle avoids the necessity to harmonize or
delete contradictions within the Pauline corpus.

Having located Paul's statements within the context of the eschatological thinking which he had acquired from his Jewish heritage,
Okeke emphasizes that for Paul the world was divided into the sphere
of salvation and the sphere of the damned. Thus Paul's statements in
v. 16c fit rather well in the letter of a man who expected the parousia
and came from a tradition of thinking that the fate of the enemies of
God was the coming wrath.[3]

Hurd's view is similar but more developed. He emphasizes that
Paul's apocalyptic expectations included the belief that all non-
Christians would perish in the Last Day, and he thinks that the wrath
referred to in v. 16c did not need to be of catastrophic proportions
for Paul to have spoken of it. As he puts it,

> Those who are familiar with the mentality of apocalyptic sects know that it
> takes no very special occasion to convince the believer that the end of the
> age is at hand and that the apocalyptic woes have begun.[4]

According to Hurd, Paul's statements in 1 Thess. 2.14-16 are his
attempts to work backwards from his premise about what would
happen at the end of the age and to explain the circumstances which
would justify it, namely, the sins of the Jews.[5] Hurd is able to set the
passage into its own context.

1. Okeke, '1 Thessalonians 2.13-16', pp. 30-131.
2. Okeke, '1 Thessalonians 2.13-16', p. 135.
3. Okeke, '1 Thessalonians 2.13-16', p. 132.
4. Hurd, 'Paul Ahead of his Time', p. 45.
5. Hurd, 'Paul Ahead of his Time', p. 35.

Sanders's view adds another dimension to Hurd's and Okeke's views and, like them, he chooses the letter itself as his starting point. Only secondarily did he bring to bear information from other letters.

Sanders proposes that the problem passage reflects a situation of conflict with the Jews because of Paul's preaching to Gentiles. His view is based upon v. 16 about the Jews' 'hindering' of Paul's preaching and upon what we know from elsewhere about their persecution of Paul (2 Cor. 11.24; Gal. 5.11; 6.12). Just what form this 'hindering' took is not clear. Sanders suggests that the Jews may have been hindering Paul because he was admitting the Gentiles without demanding that they be circumcised. We cannot be certain about the reason, and while some have proposed that the hindering had to do with the Jews' unbelief, 1 Thessalonians does not indicate that the sins of the Jews include hindering of his preaching *to Jews* or their maintaining their unbelief.[1] Their sins have to do with their behaviour in preventing Paul's work with the *Gentiles*, behaviour understood as persecution by the victim and as punishment by the initiator.[2]

Summary

Scholars who try to interpret the passage in its own context are able to find a historical situation to which Paul is responding. However, that situation has not yet been adequately described. Does the eschatological world-view completely explain all the statements in vv. 14-16? It does not explain why Paul emphasized the suffering of the Judaean churches when there is little evidence to support such an emphasis. It overlooks the effect of Paul's association of the suffering of the Judaean churches with the death of Jesus, the prophets and the messengers. Further, it does not illuminate why Paul wrote in precisely the rhetorical way he did. Was he in conflict with the Jews over his not requiring his Gentile converts to be circumcised? Did he change his mind about the destiny of the Jews by the time he wrote Romans? There are still many unanswered questions, and so the fresh approach announced at the end of Chapter 3 has even more relevance. The approach will concentrate on the rhetorical functions and attributes of Paul's remarks and accordingly will shed light on all of these questions.

1. Sanders, *Paul, the Law, and the Jewish People*, pp. 181, 190-92.
2. Sanders, *Paul, the Law, and the Jewish People*, p. 190.

Chapter 5

TOWARDS A FRESH APPROACH

In Chapter 3 I argued that by associating 'suffered the same things' (1 Thess. 2.14) with 'killed the Lord Jesus and the prophets and drove us out' (v. 15), the first statement is strengthened and may even imply that some Judaean Christians had been killed. This implication has led many scholars to judge Paul's statement about the Judaean churches to be an exaggeration and not a reflection of the period of the 40s and 50s. We recall Baur's view that the statement in v. 14 about the suffering of the Judaean churches was 'far-fetched'[1] and, more recently, Pearson's contention that Paul's statements in vv. 14-15 do not appear to describe historical reality.[2] These views point to an alternative approach which may be helpful: perhaps Paul did not intend to describe historical reality. Whiteley saw clearly the rhetorical nature of Paul's statements against the Jews:

> The attack on the Jews, though understandable under the circumstances, is exaggerated. It was the Romans who crucified Christ at the instigation of the Jewish authorities. The Jews killed some prophets, not all, as these words might lead us to suppose.[3]

Whiteley's observation will be taken up below and expanded in subsequent chapters. What scholars have not noted about the charges against the Jews in 1 Thessalonians is that they are part of a larger rhetorical piece.

I shall argue that Paul used hyperbole in a polemical context to help his congregation to stand firm in the face of their historical circumstances, which involved conflict with compatriots who saw the *ekklēsia* in Thessalonica as a dangerous movement. Both the opponents of the

---

1. Baur, *Paul the Apostle of Jesus Christ*, p. 87.
2. Pearson, '1 Thessalonians', p. 87.
3. Whiteley, *Thessalonians*, pp. 46-47.

churches and the churches themselves are treated hyperbolically. The
former are castigated without reserve, the latter are given inflated
praise.

Paul's statements against the Jews contain five or maybe six points,
with the apparent sixth defining the fifth (or the fourth and fifth). I
shall list the items for convenient discussion. The Jews:

1.   killed both the Lord Jesus
2.   and the prophets
3.   and persecuted us (or drove us out *ekdiōxantōn*)
4.   and displease God
5.   and oppose all people
6.   by hindering us from speaking to the Gentiles that they may
     be saved so as always to fill up the measure of their sins.

The six points can be divided into two groups. The first three points
have aorist participles referring to events in the past; the last three
have present participles referring to events in the present (the present
participle *ontōn* is understood in number 5 above).

The Triad about the Past

The first group contains events of the past. The Jews 'killed both the
Lord Jesus and the prophets and drove us out'. Before examining the
content of this triad, I shall comment upon its technical points of
order of phrases and proper nouns separated by a participle.

While the order of the phrases can be changed to read 'both killed
the Lord Jesus and drove out the prophets and us', this order is
unlikely since I have already noted that the statement that Israel 'killed
its prophets' seems to be part of a traditional formula of accusation
within Judaism. It is better to accept 'both killed the Lord Jesus and
the prophets and drove us out'.

In Greek there is a separation of 'the Lord' from 'Jesus' by means
of the participle *apokteinantōn*. One can either translate the phrase
'killed the Lord Jesus' or 'killed the Lord even Jesus'. The latter
translation brings both terms into prominence,[1] which seems to be the
purpose of separating the nouns. By making prominent who Jesus was,
the religious stature of Jesus and the grossness of the act is underlined.

We turn now to an investigation which is generated because of the

1.   Plummer, *Thessalonians*, p. 32.

clue Whiteley's work underlined, namely, that the historicity of the content of the phrases is questionable.

The Jews Killed the Lord Jesus

Against 1 Thess. 2.15, Whiteley observed that the Jews did not kill Jesus.[1] In another place Paul says that the rulers of this world were responsible (1 Cor. 2.8), indicating that he knew that the Romans had executed Jesus. It is true that 'rulers of this age'[2] may be parallel to 'the god of this age' (2 Cor. 4.4) or the *stoicheia* of this world' (Gal. 4.3), rather than being a reference to Pilate. These statements do not preclude Paul's knowing which earthly power had killed Jesus.[3] He certainly knew that Jesus' death was by crucifixion. It was common knowledge that crucifixion was a distinctively Roman means of execution,[4] and such knowledge would have provided the information that the local authorities were not permitted to execute. Paul doubtless knew enough Jewish law to know that crucifixion was not a Jewish mode of execution. These observations support Whiteley's view that in 1 Thess. 2.15 Paul exaggerates the role of the Jews in the death of Jesus.[5]

The Jews Killed the Prophets

Whiteley's assertion that Paul exaggerated when he says that the Jews killed the *prophets* is also correct. In this case, however, he follows a rhetorical tradition of exaggeration. The charge that Israel always killed the prophets is standard rhetoric in Jewish polemical writing, as many have observed.[6] Steck[7] argued that Paul here inserts an early

---

1. Whiteley, *Thessalonians*, pp. 46-47.
2. Käsemann's view is that Paul in this verse is referring to a Wisdom tradition (see also Rev. 12.1) in which Wisdom is persecuted by the worldly powers. In 1 Cor. 2.8, according to Käsemann, Paul emphasizes that the crucifixion is ascribed to demonic worldly powers which use people as their tools, but which are used in turn by God for salvation purposes. E. Käsemann, *Exegetische Versuche und Besinnungen* (Göttingen: Vandenhoeck & Ruprecht, 1965), pp. 272-73.
3. R. Scroggs, 'Paul: *Sophos* and *Pneumatikos*', *NTS* 14 (1967), pp. 33-55 (43).
4. M. Hengel, *Crucifixion* (Philadelphia: Fortress Press, 1977), chs. 6–11.
5. Whiteley, *Thessalonians*, p. 47.
6. Moore (*1 and 2 Thessalonians*, p. 45) notes the parallels in 1 Kgs 19.10; Neh. 9.26; Jer. 2.30. He thinks that Paul was referring to the slaying of John the Baptist. See also H.-J. Schoeps, 'Die jüdischen Prophetenmorde', in his *Aus*

Hellenistic Christian view which built upon the Jewish tradition that
Israel always killed the prophets. He cites the parable of the wicked
tenants (Mk 12.1-12) as an example. It is much more likely that early
Hellenistic Christian ideas such as the rejection of Israel developed
significantly after the destruction of the Jerusalem temple in 70 CE.
Note the development in the rejection motif in Mt. 21.33/Lk. 20.9-
19[1] (parallel passages to Mk 12.1-12), Stephen's speech in Acts 7.51-
52 and Mt. 23.34-37. In any case, Rom. 11.3 repeats the standard
Hebrew tradition. It may indicate a common method of denigrating
one's opponents. Which prophets did the Jews kill? Amos? Elijah?
Elisha? Ezekiel? Isaiah? Perhaps Jeremiah. The statement was an
exaggeration.

I have discussed the first two terms of the triad —'the Lord Jesus',
'the prophets'—and now must try to determine the identity of the last
term, 'us'.

The Jews Drove us out/Persecuted us

What is meant by *ekdiōxantōn* (from the root *diōkō* which has two
meanings: 'to persecute' or 'to drive out') and to whom does 'us'
refer?

The Verb ekdiōxantōn. It is unclear whether the aorist participle
ekdiōxantōn refers to one act or to a series of acts taken collectively.
The use of *diōkō* with *ek* is common in LXX (e.g., Deut. 6.19 and Joel
2.20) where it is best translated 'drive out'. However, we hear nothing
explicit from Paul's own letters of his having been driven out of
places. In 1 Thess. 2.2 Paul mentions that he was shamefully treated
in Philippi (2.2) and that the Thessalonians had received the word 'in
much affliction' (1.6), but he does not specify to what this affliction
refers. Nothing is said about his having been driven out, and the
account in Acts 16 concurs. Further, according to Acts, those who
treated him shamefully in Philippi were not Jews. Let us turn, then, to

---

frühchristlicher Zeit (Tübingen: Mohr, 1950), pp. 126-43.

    7.   O.H. Steck, *Israel und das gewaltsame Geschick der Propheten:
Untersuchungen zur Überlieferung des deuteronomistischen Geschichtsbildes im
Alten Testament, Spätjudentum und Urchristentum* (Wageningen, Netherlands:
H. Veenman & Zonen, 1967), pp. 274-79.

    1.   J.T. Sanders, *The Jews in Luke–Acts* (Philadelphia: Fortress Press, 1987),
pp. 211-13.

the possibility of translating this phrase '[the Jews] *persecuted* us'.

At the time of the writing of 1 Thessalonians it is unlikely that Paul had experienced the persecution/punishment (the thirty-nine lashes) by Jews to which he refers in 2 Cor. 11.24. At least we do not hear of severe punishment of Paul in 1 Thessalonians. The situation in Galatia was quite different. Someone is 'compelling' Gentiles to be circumcised as a part of their entry into the Christian movement. In Gal. 5.11 Paul says that he is experiencing persecution because he is not preaching circumcision. Paul's explanation coheres with Smith's conclusion that peculiarity of practice was the reason for persecution.[1] Paul experienced punishment/persecution (in contrast to Jewish Christians, cf. Gal. 6.12) because his practice was at odds with Judaism.

The situation in Thessalonica does not seem to be the same. There is no mention of circumcison and no discussion of Jewish law. Apparently the Jews in Thessalonica (or elsewhere) were hindering Paul in some way from preaching to the Gentiles, but we are not told what form this hindering took. He does not seem to have been *punished* although we cannot be certain. In any case, placed next to the phrase about the killing of the Lord and the prophets, whatever is meant by *ekdiōxantōn* is heightened. I propose that the word be rendered 'persecuted' because of the intensification by association. The proposal can be substantiated from yet a different perspective. Ernest Best[2] makes a good case for the translation 'persecuted' because at this time the preposition *ek* in combination had lost much of its value and should be understood as intensifying the meaning of *diōxantōn*. To say that Paul had been *persecuted* (with the thirty-nine lashes by the synagogue) by the time of the writing of this letter is likely an exaggeration. In Chapter 3 I argued that we cannot assume that the accounts in Acts are historically reliable. The many colourful statements in Acts about the motivation and behaviour of the Jews in

1. M. Smith, 'The Reason for the Persecution of Paul and the Obscurity of Acts', in E.E. Urbach, R.J. Zwi Werblowsky and C. Wirszubske (eds.), *Studies in Mysticism and Religion* (Jerusalem: Magnes, 1967) '... the persecutions cannot be explained solely by reference to the peculiar Messianic beliefs of the Christians, since peculiarities of Messianic belief seem to have been matters of comparative indifference in the first century, provided they did not lead to pecularities of practice' (p. 262).

2. E. Best, *Thessalonians*, p. 116.

the persecution of Paul (jealousy, 13.45; 17.5; stirring up crowds, 13.50; 14.2; 17.13; 21.27; poisoning minds, 14.2; plotting, 20.19; molesting, 14.5; stoning, 14.19; attempted murder, 23.12; 26.19) reveal the attitudes of the author of Acts more than historical reality. Paul says nothing of these things, only that the Jews hindered him from preaching to the Gentiles.

The 'us' of '...and Persecuted us'. It is easy to slide over 'us' in 1 Thess. 2.15 without noticing it and yet I think that it might have a significant function in the triad about the past. What is the referent of 'us' in v. 15a? No certainty is possible. In its ambiguity, 'us' has the elasticity to be an encompassing term.

There are two occurrences of 'us' in 1 Thess. 2.14-16 and they are placed among a number of participles. The first 'us' in v. 15a ([the Jews] persecuted us) is part of the triad of happenings in the past, while the second 'us' in v. 16 (the Jews hinder 'us' from preaching to the Gentiles so that they might be saved) is part of happenings in the present.

Best applies the 'us' in v. 15a to Paul and his companions,[1] but Neil suggests that perhaps it is to be taken as applying to the apostles in general.[2] There is also the possibility that Paul had in mind some of the people from the church in Thessalonica. There seem, then, to be three main possibilities for the meaning of 'us':

1. Paul (and his co-workers, e.g., Silvanus and Timothy).
2. The apostles in general, including Paul (and perhaps co-workers).
3. 'Us Christians', meaning some of the members of the church at Thessalonica[3] and perhaps Paul and his co-workers.

First it is important to note that Jews generally punished their own people but not Gentiles for defying the Jewish law. Paul's Gentile co-workers are then likely not included in the 'us'—unless Paul is exaggerating. As we learned in Chapter 3, Paul was persecuted/punished because he was still considered to be within Judaism.[4] In the last chapter it was noted that the letter to the Galatians indicates that Paul

---

1. E. Best, *Thessalonians*, p. 116.
2. Neil, *Thessalonians*, p. 51.
3. Rigaux, *Thessaloniciens*, pp. 78-79.
4. Sanders, *Paul, the Law, and the Jewish People*, pp. 190-92.

was persecuted because he did not preach circumcision (Gal. 5.11; 6.12). For a Jew, circumcision was part of obeying the law. To deliberately defy the law, as Paul was doing by not demanding circumcision of Gentiles before accepting them into the people of God, led to a punishment of the thirty-nine lashes (2 Cor. 11.24). However, that would not be true of one of Paul's co-workers, Timothy, a Gentile according to Acts 16.1. While the Paul of Acts has Timothy circumcised, it is doubtful that the Paul of the letters would have done so (Gal. 2.3; 5.11; Phil. 3.3; 1 Cor. 7.18-20). Therefore, if Paul is implying that Timothy is part of the group being persecuted, he was exaggerating: as far as we know, the synagogue did not go about persecuting Gentiles for not obeying the Jewish law. Further, from the letter to the Galatians, it appears that punishment was given to disobedient *leaders* (Gal. 5.11; 6.12) and therefore, when Paul says 'us' he likely did not have in mind people from the church at Thessalonica either. Also, according to v. 14, it was not the Jews but the Gentiles—the *symphyletōn* in Thessalonica—who were disturbing the church.

I have already mentioned that there is no clear evidence in the Pauline corpus that Paul and his companions were 'driven out' of any diaspora city by Jews. If this is what Paul is implying, he is exaggerating again.

Since the first two parts of the triad—killed 'the Lord Jesus' and 'the prophets'—are related to activities in Judaea, it seems natural to consider the third as also having taken place there. Thus, perhaps the 'us' refers to the apostles in general. This interpretation would be probable if it could be shown that the Jerusalem apostles endured persecution to the point of being 'expelled'. We have seen that in the one recorded instance when there was a driving out of members of the early Christian movement from Jerusalem, the apostles were not all driven out or were driven out only for a brief period of time, and the Jerusalem church appears to have led a relatively peaceful existence.[1] This information from Acts counts against taking 'apostles' as the referent of 'us'.

In contrast, Paul's own letters suggest that he may mean 'us' in the sense of 'us apostles'. His statement in 1 Thess. 2.6 that he has the right of a Christian apostle to demand payment from the Thessalonians,

---

1. See Chapter 3.

though he did not exercise this right, may be an indirect association with the apostles in Jerusalem who availed themselves of such support (cf. 1 Cor. 9.3-14). By referring to what he is entitled to as an apostle, he aligns himself with the apostles in Jerusalem. Not criticizing their practice, he simply notes that he did not exercise the full extent of his authority as apostle. If an association with the other apostles is intended in 2.6, the 'us' of v. 15a may continue the implication of common experiences of 'apostles' in general. As was noted above, the Jerusalem apostles seem to have lived in relatively peaceful circumstances and therefore (assuming that 'us' includes the Jerusalem apostles) for Paul to suggest that they were persecuted like the Lord and the prophets is another exaggeration.

Whether Paul is implying that 'us' refers to the apostles in general or to himself and his co-workers, or to some members of the Thessalonian church, his placing of 'persecuted' alongside the killing of Jesus and the prophets makes it seem that some of the 'us' have been killed. The identity of those meant by 'us' is probably not as important as the word's rhetorical function.

We may be able to determine something about the function of 'us' in 1 Thess. 2.15a from a tradition recorded in Matthew and Luke. Matthew's version of it states that those who are killed and persecuted from city to city are 'prophets', 'wise men' and 'scribes' (Mt. 23.34-36). Lk. 11.49 has Jesus make the accusation 'I will send to them [Israel] prophets and apostles, and some of them they will kill and persecute...' In the first case there is a sequence of 'prophets' and 'wise men' and 'scribes' (Matthew). In the second the sequence is from 'prophets' to 'apostles' (Luke). While it is impossible to prove, it appears that there is a diminishing religious hierarchy at least in Matthew's terms. In the case of Luke, 'apostles' may stand second to the 'prophets' because of chronology. And in the case of our passage the sequence is 'the Lord Jesus, the prophets, and us'. This appears to me to be a diminishing hierarchy. Paul regarded the prophets as the authors of 'Scripture', and though he thought highly of the apostles, he would not rank them as highly as the biblical authors.

Leaving aside the question of the possible dependency of Paul on an earlier tradition,[1] and taking our cue from the parallels in Matthew

---

1. See Schippers, 'Pre-Synoptic Tradition', pp. 232-33, who proposed that Paul depended upon a presynoptic tradition. See also the earlier work of J.B. Orchard, 'Thessalonians and the Synoptic Gospels', *Bib* 19 (1938), pp. 23-42,

and Luke, the broader meaning of 'us', namely, 'us apostles' (the leaders of the Christian movement), gives more rhetorical force to the triad of the victims of suffering in the past: 'the Lord Jesus, the prophets, and us'. It is the religious leaders who are persecuted and so the church can expect to imitate them.

The three items in the triad are united by *persecution* (the direct statement of violence with regard to the Lord and the prophets and by association and implication the 'us'). By associating the 'us' with the Lord Jesus and the prophets, the triad becomes unified as persecuted religious leaders: the Lord Jesus, the prophets and 'us'. If I am correct, we can understand why Paul did not elaborate the participation of the Romans in the death of Jesus or specify which prophets were killed or specific occasions when he was persecuted: his point was to say that all righteous religious leaders endure persecution. Here 'the Jews' function as a foil for the list of the righteous ones. The function of 'us' is one of legitimization and elevation of status. The association of past and present sufferings gives support to the readers who are facing difficulty: the righteous have always faced opposition.

The Triad about the Present

When we move on to the fourth, fifth and the apparent sixth point in the list of accusations against the Jews in 1 Thess. 2.15-16, we note that Paul says that the Jews displease God and oppose all humanity by hindering him and others from preaching to the Gentiles so that they may be saved so as always to fill up the measure of their sins; but he does not cite cases. Nor does he gives qualifiers, for example, 'Some Jews displease God' or 'Jews displease God some of the time'. He implies that all the Jews displease God all of the time (note especially *pantote*). This is another of the exaggerations in this passage. Further, to say that the Jews oppose all humanity (*pasin*) is still another exaggeration. Some Jews certainly opposed some Gentiles, but to say that the former opposed all of the latter is simply not true. Even if

and Pearson, '1 Thessalonians', p. 83. Arguing against dependency is F. Nierynck, 'Paul and the Sayings of Jesus', in A. Vanhoye (ed.), *L'apôtre Paul: Personnalité, style et conception de ministère* (Leuven: Leuven University Press, 1986), pp. 265-321, who maintains that there is no certain trace of a conscious use of the sayings of Jesus; there are allusions but no explicit quotations. See also B. Rigaux, *Saint Paul les épitres aux Thessaloniciens* (Paris: Gabalda, 1956), p. 445.

Paul means that the Jews oppose the people to whom he is preaching, he has implied something more than that they are hindering him. The implied 'all Jews' of v. 15 followed by the repetitive and explicit 'all' of v. 15 and 'always' of v. 16 leads me to agree with Whiteley's suggestion that if Paul were experiencing opposition, the violent outburst would be understandable. However, it was also exaggerated.[1] A study of the exaggerated language can help us to understand Paul's rhetoric in the context of polemical situations as necessarily extreme but probably not his final and absolute judgment.

Summary

In each of the clauses of 1 Thess. 2.14-16 (except 'by hindering us from speaking to the Gentiles that they may be saved'), Paul exaggerated a kernel of historicity. Rather than relegate the passage to the category of inauthenticity, we can better understand the statements in these verses by looking for their rhetorical function within the passage and later within the letter.

Thus, we can now move forward with what I think is a more fruitful approach, one which assumes authenticity and tries to determine the significance of the passage in the literary context of the letter. Further, it assumes that Paul wrote in a nuanced fashion giving his words colour and force. In the next chapter literary material approximately contemporary with Paul will be examined for evidence of the use of exaggeration when polemicizing against opponents. That the use of exaggeration or hyperbole to castigate one's opponents was common enough in the first century will also be observed. We turn now to representative material from both Jewish and Graeco-Roman writings.

---

1. Whiteley, *Thessalonians*, p. 47.

Chapter 6

1 THESSALONIANS 2.14-16 IN THE CONTEXT OF
GREEK AND ROMAN RHETORIC

The statements about the Jews in 1 Thess. 2.14-16, although perhaps
containing some historical basis, are misconstrued if we approach
them as observations of actual deeds of the Jews. My hypothesis is that
Paul's rhetoric implies a severity of persecution greater than that
actually experienced by the Judaean and Thessalonian churches and
deliberately exaggerates the characterization of the Jews for the
purpose of denigrating them. He does so because they oppose his work
with the Gentiles, and he sets them up as foils for the Thessalonian
church. They are the persecutors whereas the church is the suffering
righteous. I have termed such exaggeration 'polemical hyperbole'.
The first half of the phrase denotes the fact of real opposition which
led to the statements; the second half alerts us to their exaggerated
nature.

This hypothesis raises some questions. What do we know about the
use of exaggeration in the ancient world to denigrate opponents? Why
and how is it used? What are its elements?

Because most of us no longer study rhetoric formally, it is difficult
to appreciate fully the role that exaggeration played in rhetoric in the
ancient world. It has, however, been employed in communication
from the beginning of time and is not the domain only of experts. In
Bernard Shaw's *Pygmalion*, Higgins and Pickering, those experts at
rhetoric, accuse Eliza's father of coming to Higgins's residence to
blackmail him. Although it becomes clear that this is indeed the case,
her father denies it. To prove to Higgins that he has nothing to hide
and is straightforward, Alfred Doolittle exaggerates his willingness to
reveal why he has come:

> I'll tell you, Governor, if you'll only let me get a word in. I'm willing to
> tell you. I'm wanting to tell you. I'm waiting to tell you.

Higgins turns to Pickering and says:

> Pickering: This chap has a certain natural gift of rhetoric. Observe the
> rhythm of his native woodnotes wild. 'I'm willing to tell you: I'm
> wanting to tell you: I'm waiting to tell you.' Sentimental rhetoric! that's
> the Welsh strain in him. It also accounts for his mendacity and
> dishonesty.[1]

Higgins was not the first to observe that exaggeration was part of
natural rhetoric. Quintilian, the first-century Roman rhetorician,
observed it and had this to say:

> Hyperbole is employed even by peasants and uneducated persons, for the
> good reason that everybody has an innate passion for exaggeration or
> attenuation of actual facts... (*Inst.* 8.6.75).

While some uneducated people had the good fortune to have a
predisposition to effective communication and eloquence, the ancients
taught their students to improve their speeches by the study of the
natural rhetoric of great authors like Homer. In fact, only through the
systematic study of such writers as Homer were the elements and
devices of rhetoric categorized by the Greek and Roman rhetors.
Rhetoric was defined by Aristotle as 'the faculty of discovering the
possible means of persuasion in reference to any subject whatever'
(*Rh.* 1.2.1).

As a result of the ancients' study of exaggeration in natural speech,
formulations were developed about the means of persuasion. Thus, we
can learn how one used exaggeration to vilify an opponent whether in
the courts or in speeches of blame. We can use these formulations as
clues to how Paul exaggerates in his writings against opponents,
without having to sort out whether or not he studied rhetoric
formally.[2] As may be expected, he was influenced by the general

---

1. G.B. Shaw, *Pygmalion*, in *Androcles and the Lion, Overruled, Pygmalion*
(London: Constable, 1916), p. 135.
2. See E.A. Judge, 'St Paul and Classical Society', *JAC* 15 (1972), pp. 19-
36, and 'Paul's Boasting in relation to Contemporary Professional Practice', *AusBR*
10 (1968), pp. 37-50; also P. Marshall, *Enmity in Corinth* (Tübingen: Mohr,
1987), p. 400.

rhetorical principles current in the culture of the time, a point that has been well documented.[1]

The Use of Rhetorical Principles in Letters

That we have only Paul's letters is not a hindrance in the study of his rhetoric. Letters were substitutes for the physical presence of a person, though obviously not a perfect substitute because the reader might more easily misinterpret the writer without having the benefit of tone of delivery.[2] Apparently Paul's letters were known to be more effective than his speeches (2 Cor. 10.10). While this judgment seems to originate from his opponents, it is a backhanded compliment for his skill as a writer. Since his letters were collected and copied we know that they were valued and therefore were persuasive.

Frank W. Hughes argues for the connection between rhetoric and letters by noting that of the twenty-one epistolary types cited in the handbook of Pseudo-Demetrius,

> several of them are named with technical terminology from Graeco-Roman rhetoric. For example, the 'blaming' (*memptikos*) type and the 'praising' (*epainetikos*) type seem to be clearly related to epideictic rhetoric because the standard topics of this *genus* of rhetoric are praise and blame. In Aristotle's *Ars rhetorica*, epideictic rhetoric is described as a *genos* of rhetoric in 1.2.3, and then in 1.3.5 and 1.3.7 the phrase 'those who praise or blame' (*tois epainousi kai psegousi, hoi epainountes kai hoi psegontes*) is employed as a synonym for those who do epideictic rhetoric. The *psektikos* ('vituperative') kind of rhetoric, which along with 'enkomiastic' (*egkōmiastikon*) rhetoric seems to constitute the *genus* of epideictic rhetoric in the *Rhetoric to Alexander*. It appears, therefore, that

1. Judge, 'St Paul and Classical Society', pp. 19-36. F.W. Hughes, 'The Rhetoric of 1 Thessalonians', in Collins (ed), *The Thessalonian Correspondence*, pp. 94-116; B.C. Johanson, *To All the Brethren: A Text-Linguistic and Rhetorical Approach to 1 Thessalonians* (Stockholm: Almqvist & Wilksell, 1987), pp. 34-35. G.A. Kennedy, *New Testament Interpretation through Rhetorical Criticism* (Chapel Hill: University of North Carolina Press, 1984); for a summary of the use of rhetoric to study the New Testament, see Jewett, *The Thessalonian Correspondence*, pp. 63-68, and H.D. Betz, *Galatians: A Commentary on Paul's Letter to the Churches in Galatia* (Philadelphia: Fortress Press, 1979), pp. 14-25.

2. See S.K. Stowers, *Letter Writing in Greco-Roman Antiquity* (Philadelphia: Westminster Press, 1986), pp. 23-26; Malherbe, *Thessalonians*, pp. 71-78. See also F.W. Hughes, *Early Christian Rhetoric and 2 Thessalonians* (JSNTSup, 30; Sheffield: JSOT Press, 1989), p. 29.

some of the technical terminology of rhetorical style, topics, and *genera* became part of the terminology of the relatively little we know of systematic teaching about letters.[1]

The categories of the praising and blaming[2] letters are particularly interesting, since Paul in 1 Thess. 2.14-16 blames the Jews for their many sins. According to Stowers, the types of letters used in the Graeco-Roman world were directly related to the genera of speeches, and most types were associated with the epideictic division of rhetoric.[3] While rhetorical principles were intended for oral discourse, it is not unreasonable to believe that they were used directly or indirectly for the composition of letters as well. Although among the classical rhetoricians there were differences of opinion as to the purpose, occasion and audience for the types of rhetoric,[4] they did agree that judicial, deliberative and epideictic are the three genera of all speeches.

The Epideictic Speech

In general, the judicial (forensic) speech was used in the courts in order to drive home or refute a charge. The deliberative speech was

1. Hughes, *Rhetoric*, p. 27; Hughes notes that Aristotle uses *psegein* for 'blame' rather than *memptein* but the point still holds that there is a connection between letter writing and rhetoric (p. 27 n. 66).

2. Stowers noted that an 'accusing' letter seems to be 'blame' with a forensic style, that is, common legal procedures are reflected although the technical methods of judicial rhetoric are not employed (p. 166). The accusing type castigates things which are said to have been done beyond the bounds of propriety. Stowers, *Letter Writing*, p. 167.

3. Stowers, *Letter Writing*, pp. 27-28, 51.

4. Aristotle thought that judicial speeches had to do with the past and were concerned about the just; deliberative ones, the future and the expedient; and epideictic ones, the present and the honourable. See Aristotle, *Rh.* 1.3.1-8; See also Cicero, *To Gaius Herennius*, book 3. This author believed that the epideictic *genus* is not usually practiced as a separate *genus* but used in conjuction with deliberative or judicial speeches (3.8). Cicero concerns himself with the social setting of the three *genera*: the court room, the assembly, and the ceremonial gathering. See Cicero, *On Invention* 1.5.7; *On the Making of an Orator* 1.31.141. Quintilian focuses upon speeches to audiences for certain purposes such as giving judgment, advice and pleasure, respectively. See *Inst.* 3.4.6-8. Quintilian denied that the epideictic speech is concerned with the honourable, the deliberative with the expedient, and the forensic with the just. He emphasized that each *genus* may be concerned with any of these affairs.

used to persuade or dissuade people regarding a future course of action. The epideictic genus, sometimes also called demonstrative or encomiastic, is particularly relevant to this study because its main concern is to praise, to vituperate, or both in a ceremonial setting, and we note that Hughes has argued that 1 Thessalonians is an epideictic letter.[1] Aristotle discusses the epideictic speech in the context of the differentiation of the three genera by their proper occasion:

> Further, to each of these a special time is appropriate: to the deliberative the future, for the speaker, whether he exhorts or dissuades, always advises about things to come; to the forensic the past, for it is always in reference to things done that one party accuses and the other defends; to the epideictic most appropriately the present, for it is the existing condition of things that all those who praise or blame have in view. It is not uncommon, however, for epideictic speakers to avail themselves of other times, of the past by way of recalling it, or of the future by way of anticipating it (*Rh.* 1.3.4).

According to Aristotle, in terms of chronological time the epideictic speech was used to deal mainly with the concerns of the present, although the past could be recalled and the future anticipated.

In discussing the goal of each of the three genera, Aristotle has this to say:

> The end of the deliberative speaker is the expedient or harmful; for he who exhorts recommends a course of action as better, and he who dissuades advises against it as worse; all other considerations, such as justice and injustice, honour and disgrace, are included as accessory in reference to this. The end of the forensic speaker is the just or the unjust; in this case also all other considerations are included as accessory. The end of those who praise or blame is the honourable and disgraceful, and they also refer all other considerations to these (*Rh.* 1.3.5).

The goal then of the epideictic speech is to praise or blame in order to bring honour upon some and disgrace upon others. Accordingly, Hughes's view that 1 Thessalonians is focused upon issues of the present rather than those of the past or future seems to me to be correct. In any case, it is not the primary purpose of this work to decide which type of speech most suitably fits the letter. It is enough to note that in the problem passage and its context of 1.2–2.18, panegyric and censure permeate Paul's communication. These contents

---

1. Hughes, 'The Rhetoric of 1 Thessalonians', p. 97; see also Jewett, *The Thessalonian Correspondence*, p. 71.

are part of nearly every type of letter. As Stowers noted, 'Letters of praise and blame, then, are perhaps the most basic and most ideal of the types. Praise and/or vituperation is used in virtually every type of letter that the theorists isolated.'[1]

The most helpful technique in the style of the epideictic speech is amplification[2] and hyperbole is part of it. The Greek and Roman rhetors provide us with the tools necessary for understanding the nature of amplification and hyperbole and their uses in denigrating an opponent. Subsequently, a comparison will be made with 1 Thess. 2.14-16 in order to determine how Paul's statements about the Jews may be exaggerations and to see what light might be shed upon their function in the passage and within the letter in general. Thinking about the passage from a rhetorical perspective necessarily involves a movement back and forth between the theories of rhetoric and the passage.

Amplification

In Quintilian's view, the power behind the art of speaking well was knowing the methods of 'enhancing or attenuating the force of words'.[3] This power was connected with devices that would 'elevate or depress the subject in hand'.[4] Strategies to elevate the subject were called amplification (*auxesis*) while those to depress it were named attenuation (*meiosis*). In general, amplification elevates or depresses one side of a topic. The author of Cicero said that it was used 'to increase the importance of a subject and to raise it to a higher level, but also to diminish and disparage it'.[5] Although amplification was used in all forms of speech,[6] it was employed especially in the case of eulogy (praise) or vituperation (censure or blame).[7] An early rhetorician described the method as applied to eulogy, which employs

1. Stowers, *Letter Writing*, p. 77.
2. Aristotle, *Rh.* 1.9.40-41; 2.28.5.
3. *Inst.* 8.3.89.
4. *Inst.* 8.3.90.
5. Cicero, *On the Making of an Orator* 3.26.104.
6. See Aristotle, *Rh.* 2.18.2-5.
7. Quintilian, *Inst.* 3.7.1-4. According to Seneca (*Ep.* 94.39, 49; 95.34, 65) at the time of the empire, praise and blame were considered types of exhortation which transcend the three rhetorical categories of judicial, deliberative and epideictic. See also Stowers, *Letter Writing*, p. 93.

the amplification of creditable purposes and actions and speeches and the attribution of qualities that do not exist, while the vituperative species is the opposite, the minimization of creditable qualities and the amplification of discreditable ones (*Rh. Al.* 3.1425b.35-40).

In order to blame, one must know which topics to choose, that is, the opposite to praiseworthy things: the unjust, unlawful, inexpedient, ignoble and the unpleasant.[1] Humble origin, poverty, mean appearance, distinction or natural advantages, if such are said to have led to more vices, are also used. The judgment of an opponent by others[2] is useful as are matters of incidental result (e.g., loss of health because of a neglect of exercise or destitution because of inattention to one's affairs), things done as a means (e.g., unconcern for others in order to gratify the person one is in love with) and indispensable conditions (eg., the act of drinking as necessary for intoxication).[3] Thus, we learn that by pointing out ignoble actions, background and character, one castigates opponents.

After one has in mind the topics to use in vituperation, one must know how to amplify them. A list of how the amplification of the topics is to be conducted according to *Rhetoric to Alexander*[4] follows, with notes appended providing examples from the problem passage.

1. *Actions*: Show that 'the actions of the person in question have produced many bad, or good, results'. (Paul: the Jews' actions of persecution, killing and harassing have incurred the wrath upon them.)

2. *Previous Judgment*: Introduce 'a previous judgment'—an 'unfavourable one if you are blaming—and then set your own statement beside it' and compare the two, 'enlarging on the strongest points of your own case and the weakest ones of the other and so making your own case appear a strong one'. (Paul: 'The Jews oppose all humanity', a standard Gentile charge against the Jews. Paul sets other accusations alongside this one.)

3. *Compare Two Things Contrasting in Size*: '...set in comparison with the thing you are saying the smallest of the things that fall into

1.   *Rh. Al.* 2.1426a.1-20.
2.   Quintilian, *Inst.* 3.7.19-22.
3.   *Rh. Al.* 2.1426a.1-20.
4.   *Rh. Al.* 3.1426a.20-1426b.20. See also the ten commonplaces listed in *To Gaius Herennius* 2.30.48-49 and the section on *indignatio* from Cicero, *On Invention* 1.53.100–1.54.105.

the same class, for thus your case will appear magnified...'

4. *Compare Two Things Contrasting in Quality*: 'Supposing a given thing has been judged a great good, if you mention something that is its opposite, it will appear a great evil; and similarly supposing something is considered a great evil, if you mention its opposite, the latter will appear a great good'. (Paul's associations of the Jews who persecuted the churches of Judaea with the *symphyletai* who are harassing the Thessalonians; the suffering of the churches of Judaea with that of Thessalonica; the sufferings of the Lord, the prophets, and us.)

5. *Prove the Intentions of the Person*: '...prove that the agent acted intentionally, arguing that he had long premeditated doing the acts; that he repeatedly set about doing them; that he went on doing them a long time; that no one else had attempted them before; that he did them in conjunction with persons whom no one else had acted with or in succession to persons whom no one else had followed; that he was acting willingly; that he was acting deliberately; that we should all be unfortunate if each of us acted like him'. (Compare Paul's portrayal of the Jews as consistently and intentionally hostile to their religious leaders [Jesus and the prophets], the churches, Paul, and all people.)

6. *Build your Case*: '...Building up one point on another...if you prove a person responsible for many things, whether good or bad, they will bulk large in appearance. You must also consider whether the matter bulks larger when divided up into parts or when stated as a whole, and state it in whichever way it makes a bigger show...' (Compare Paul's list of completely negative activities of the Jews.)

Quintilian discusses amplification under four principal methods: augmentation, comparison, reasoning and accumulation.[1] These conventions, although categorized differently, are in content essentially the same as those of the author of *Rhetoric to Alexander* above. However, he gives examples which are helpful to understand how amplification works. This is important as we prepare to assess 1 Thess. 2.14-16 later in this chapter.

Quintilian did not list all the possible methods of amplification, omitting the most frequent and obvious ones, but including the most general ones. Further, he did not want to give a rigid set of rules[2] for rhetoric. He wanted to indicate the direct path without restricting the

1. *Inst.* 8.4.3.
2. *Inst.* 2.13.1.

orator to 'the ruts made by others'.[1] He recognized that part of the art of rhetoric was the distinctive stamp of the orator's personality and the circumstances.[2] Still, the guidelines he laid down give us insight into the general principles followed by those wishing to enhance what they wanted to say. Quintilian emphasized that amplification could be achieved through augmentation, comparison, reasoning and accumulation.

Augmentation

Quintilian categorizes augmentation in three main ways.

1. One can choose a stronger word to describe a thing, a person, or an action:

> ...we may say that a man who was *beaten* was *murdered*, or that a *dishonest* fellow is a *robber*, or, on the other hand, [in attenuation] we may say that one who *struck* another merely *touched* him... (*Inst.* 8.4.1)

Through the words one chooses one can give 'grandeur even to comparative insignificance'.[3] The increase of the power of a word, then, is amplification. We shall see below that the increase of several words in a series is hyperbole.

2. One can amplify by building words upon words, proceeding step by step 'to the highest degree or even beyond it'.[4] Quintilian cites Cicero:

> It is a sin to bind a Roman citizen, a crime to scourge him, little short of the most unnatural murder to put him to death; what then shall I call his crucifixion? (*Inst.* 8.4.4)

The steps are easily perceived. The writer moves from the actions of binding to scourging to murdering, designates the first term 'a sin', and asks what the last action should be called. The reader or audience is moved along by the craft of the orator to wonder what appellation could possibly be given to something surpassing murder. Truly, this must be an outrageous act. Quintilian observed that one might linger over each step or proceed with speed.

3. The third method of augmentation does not involve gradation,

1. *Inst.* 2.13.16.
2. *Inst.* 2.13.2.
3. *Inst.* 8.4.3.
4. *Inst.* 8.4.3.

but rather simply reiterates that which cannot be surpassed. 'You beat your mother. What more can I say? You beat your mother.'[1]

Comparison

Amplification through comparison rises from the lesser to the greater. Quintilian gives this example from Cicero: 'In truth, if my slaves feared me as all your fellow citizens fear you, I should think it wise to leave my house'.[2] By comparing an example of lesser significance (slaves and household) one amplifies the situation of ruler and city.

Reasoning

Reasoning is described by Quintilian in this way:

> One thing is magnified in order to effect a corresponding augmentation elsewhere, and it is by reasoning that our hearers are then led on from the first point to the second which we desire to emphasize. (*Inst.* 8.4.15)

Cicero, about to reproach Antony for his drunkenness and subsequent vomiting, says: 'You with such a throat, such flanks, such burly strength in every limb of your prize-fighter's body'.[3] The reference to throat and limbs enables the listener to estimate the quantity of wine which would have to be consumed in order for it to exceed Antony's great body's ability to absorb it. The reference also prepares one for later events (the violence and necessity of the bursting forth of the wine)[4] and predisposes the audience to revulsion.

Accumulation

Accumulation involves a gathering of words and sentences which are identical in meaning but instead of being presented as a series of steps, are executed as a 'piling up' of words.[5] Quintilian gives an example to illustrate:

> What was that sword of yours doing, Tubero, the sword you drew on the field of Pharsalus? Against whose body did you aim its point? What meant those arms you bore? Whither were your thoughts, your eyes, your

1. *Inst.* 8.4.7.
2. *Inst.* 8.4.10.
3. *Inst.* 8.4.16.
4. *Inst.* 8.4.16-17.
5. *Inst.* 8.4.26.

hand, your fiery courage directed on that day? What passion, what desires were yours? (*Inst.* 8.4.27)

Obviously the speaker amplifies with the purpose of judging Tubero's intentions. In the example the accumulated details have one reference, Tubero. At other times a number of separate things are accumulated. The heightening of this effect may also be produced by having the words rise to a climax:

> There stood the porter of the prison, the praetor's executioner, the death and terror of the citizens and allies of Rome, the lictor Sextius. (*Inst.* 8.4.27)

The climax is produced by listing different ways of referring to the same person, the lictor Sextius. However, each item in the piling up of words is not in itself amplified as in hyperbole, as we shall see. What constitutes the amplification is the gathering of the items into a force of words. Increasing the power of words, piling words upon words in a series, comparisons, augmentation in one area which leads to augmentation in another area, the accumulation of words and phrases which are piled up and mean the same thing—all are involved in amplification. We now turn our attention to hyperbole, a more extreme form of amplification. We shall learn from Quintilian's examples how hyperbole is to be understood.

Hyperbole

Amplification is fundamental to the art of persuasion, and hyperbole is the servant of amplification. It is used to make a point still more prominent. Says Quintilian:

> It means an elegant straining of the truth, and may be employed indifferently for exaggeration or attenuation. It can be used in various ways. We may say more than the actual facts...exalt our theme by the use of simile...produce the same result by introducing a comparison...or by the use of indications...or we may employ a metaphor... Sometimes again, one hyperbole may be heightened by the addition of another. (*Inst.* 8.6.68-72)[1]

We can see that the various methods of employing hyperbole parallel

1. See also *To Gaius Herennius* 4.33.44: 'Hyperbole is a manner of speech exaggerating the truth, whether for the sake of magnifying or minifying something. This is used independently or with comparison'.

those of employing amplification. The 'straining of the truth' is surely parallel to calling a dishonest fellow a robber.[1] As an example of pushing augmentation beyond the highest degree, Quintilian cites Virgil: 'there was not one more fair saving Laurentian Turnus'.[2] Here Laurentian Turnus exceeds the superlative.

When Quintilian gives an example for 'saying more than the actual facts', he uses a quotation from Cicero: 'He vomited and filled his lap and the whole tribunal with fragments of food'.[3] The hyperbole points up the extent of Antony's drunkenness and the indecency of his behaviour. In magnifying Antony's body parts, Cicero amplifies his case about how much wine Antony had consumed; by employing the hyperbole about his vomit filling the whole tribunal, the point is made even more prominently, thus revealing his real purposes, to discredit Antony and, perhaps indirectly, to give credit to himself.

In enhancing what one wants to say, a certain proportion must be observed, for if hyperbole is taken too far it leads to extravagant affectation:

> It is enough to say that hyperbole lies, though without any intention to deceive. We must therefore be all the more careful to consider how far we may go in exaggerating facts which our audience may refuse to believe. (*Inst.* 8.6.74)

Quintilian emphasizes that if the hyperbole is too exaggerated it causes laughter.[4] If this is the author's intent, well and good, but if not, such excess leads to being called a fool.

Further, although hyperbole strains the truth, there should be no deliberate intention to deceive; but if necessary to prove a point, it is appropriate to substitute falsehood for truth; and if the speaker's motives involve the pursuit of truth, Quintilian thought there was no vice in the practice.[5] 'For judges are not always enlightened and often have to be tricked to prevent them from falling into error.'[6]

The function of hyperbole in the lawcourts was to move the judges. Quintilian asserted that if all judges, senators and those assembled were philosophers one could get straight to the truth, but the orator

1. See above and Quintilian, *Inst.* 8.4.1.
2. Virgil, *Aeneid* 7.649-50, quoted by Quintilian, *Inst.* 8.4.6.
3. *Inst.* 8.6.68, in which he cites Cicero, *Philippics* 2.25.63.
4. *Inst.* 2.17.27-30.
5. *Inst.* 2.17.28.
6. *Inst.* 2.17.29.

was engaged in the difficult task of swaying hearers who were 'fickle of mind' and therefore thought that the art of rhetoric must be called in to

> aid us in the fight and employ such means as will help our case. He who has been driven from the right road cannot be brought back to it save by a fresh détour. (*Inst.* 2.17.29)

When the subject was abnormal, it was expected that hyperbole would be employed:

> For we are allowed to amplify, when the magnitude of the facts passes all words, and in such circumstances our language will be more effective if it goes beyond the truth than if it falls short of it. (*Inst.* 8.6.76)

Although Quintilian noted that exaggeration could go beyond the truth, there was no intention to deceive. On the contrary, he assumed that rhetorical principles would be employed by the good person speaking well.[1]

Exaggeration was found in all of the rhetorical categories, as Quintilian notes:

> conciliation, narration, proof, exaggeration, extenuation, and the moulding of the minds of the audience by exciting or allaying their passions, are common to all three kinds of oratory. (*Inst.* 3.4.15)[2]

Although pervasive in all oratory, exaggeration was used most in speeches of vituperation and eulogy. In due course I shall investigate how Paul vituperates against his opponents.

The rhetors noted that whether in a judicial speech for the law courts or in one of vituperation for a ceremonial occasion, the judge and/or audience formed a third party to the speaker and the person spoken about. In order to ensure a favourable hearing, a speaker often began with some words of praise to the audience and the judge.[3] This

---

1. See *Inst.* 2.15.33-34; 6.2.18. Aristotle anticipated the criticism that rhetoric could be used to deceive and responded by saying that one could make that objection about everything except virtue itself (*Rh.* 1.1.12).

2. It is noteworthy that there is an exaggeration of things unjust, cruel or hateful which was called *deinosis* (*Inst.* 6.2.24). It awakened emotions which did not naturally arise from the case or were stronger than the case would suggest. In this case ills generally regarded as tolerable are made to seem endurable. This is not the device in 1 Thess. 2.14-16 since the activities of the Jews could in no way be seen to be tolerable.

3. Quintilian, *Inst.* 83.7.23-25; *On Invention* 1.15.20-22.

method (*captatio benevolentiae*) included setting forth one's good qualities, lamenting one's own or the client's misfortune, and working up hatred of the opponent.[1] Knowing one's audience was important, because one could be assured that the denunciation would be well received if it was certain that the audience would disapprove of the behaviour and characteristics of the one blamed.[2]

In summary, classical writers on rhetoric argue that amplification is the augmenting of a word, or a heightening of a point by comparison with another point. It can be attained by the development of a series of words and ideas or a piling up of synonymous points. Amplification is the method of increasing the power of words. It is a method of amplification involving the straining of the truth in order to make a point clearer in the mind of the judge or listener. Hyperbole can be a metaphor or a series of or a piling up of exaggerations which do not, however, strain credulity. It can be employed in all of the methods of amplification such as augmentation, comparison, reasoning and accumulation.

Examples of Hyperbole in Paul's Letters

General hyperbole in Paul's letters is not our main concern, yet, because it is connected to polemical hyperbole, I offer a few examples of it to prepare for the discussion in the next chapter.

We can find a large number of examples of hyperbole in the letters of Paul. Sanders has argued convincingly that Paul's assertions that in his mission from Jerusalem to Illyricum he had completed a full circle (Rom. 15.19) and that he had become all things to all people in order to win some (1 Cor. 9.22) are hyperbolic.[3] Paul's missionary journey was not a full circle, and Paul could not be a Jew to Jews and a Gentile to Gentiles in a mixed church. More recently, the hyperbole in 1 Cor. 4.13 (Paul as the refuse of the world and the offscouring of all things) has been noted,[4] and A.B. Du Toit has pointed to 'hyperbolical contrasts' in the letters of Paul.

---

1. See *To Gaius Herennius* 1.4.7-1.5.8; 6.2.6-7; *On Invention* 1.15.22-1.17.25.
2. Quintilian, *Inst.* 3.7.23-25.
3. See Sanders, *Paul, the Law, and the Jewish People*, pp. 186-88.
4. K.A. Plank, *Paul and the Irony of Affliction* (Atlanta: Scholars Press, 1987), p. 85.

Since one of Du Toit's examples is from 1 Thessalonians, it is of particular interest. I cite him directly, beginning with the quotation from 1 Thess. 4.8:

'Therefore whoever rejects this (teaching which I have delivered to you— *vide* v.1-2) is not rejecting man but God...' Undoubtedly anyone who rejected Paul's teaching by implication also rejected Paul the apostle and Paul the man. The semantic level of his statement therefore indicates that whoever rejects Paul's teaching rejects not so much the apostle as God who gave him his commission. But this is not expressed in a bland comparative. Paul applies the technique of verbal shock in order to counter the possibility of unholy living.[1]

Du Toit's case can be made even clearer. He did not note both the singular form of the noun *anthrōpon* (4.8) and the lack of a definite article before it. Thus, 'whoever disregards this, disregards not *a man* but God...' Earlier in the letter (2.13) Paul had asserted that what he preached was not of human origin but from God; note there the plural form of *anthrōpōn*. The contrast of a singular person and God implies the person's singular authority. Thus, what is implied is not that the word of the Christian tradition is God's but that *Paul's* is. What Du Toit described as a 'verbal shock', the rhetors might have said was hyperbole to the highest point: he equated his views with God's.

Now, according to 1 Cor. 4.4, Paul knew that some of his work could conceivably be judged negatively by God at the end of the age. Further, when giving advice about relationships between men and women (1 Cor. 7) he closes by stating, 'And I think that I have the Spirit of Christ' (7.40), thereby indicating at least a hint of doubt about whether his word was the Lord's. Thus, it is not unreasonable to speculate that Paul in 1 Thess. 4.8 is not certain that his exhortations are God's. While from a human perspective Paul thought that he was preaching God's word, he leaves open the possibility that from the divine perspective things might look different.

Gal. 1.11-17 presents an extremely confident Paul who believes that the gospel he preaches is from God. However, there he is defending his gospel against other leaders who differ from his views. The situation is quite different in 1 Thessalonians. No leader appears to be challenging Paul's exhortation for sexual restraint. Thus by bringing

1. A.B. Du Toit, 'Hyperbolical Contrasts: A Neglected Aspect of Paul's Style', in J.H. Petzer and P.J. Hartin (eds.), *A South African Perspective on the New Testament* (Leiden: Brill, 1985), pp. 178-86.

together his word and God's as an equation, and by implying that his perspective was God's, 1 Thess. 4.8 is, as Du Toit has quite rightly judged, a hyperbolical contrast.[1]

Lawrence L. Welborn's note about 'hyperbolic praise'[2] in 1 Cor. 1.5 leads us to an important distinction between hyperbole and amplification. Paul tells the Corinthians that through God they have *all* speech and knowledge. Without going into the concrete difficulties at Corinth, we can easily detect at least rhetorical amplification here. Paul does not say that the Corinthians have *only* speech and knowledge, nor *outstanding* speech and knowledge, nor *uncommon* speech and knowledge, but *all* speech and knowledge (*en panti logō kai pasē gnōsei*). The statement on its own is amplification. Hyperbole would demand repetition or a series of statements with non-restrictive qualifiers.

There is a similar type of exaggeration found in 1 Thess. 1.8, where Paul says that the Thessalonians' faith in God was such that they 'became an example to *all* the believers in Macedonia and in Achaia'. He might have said that news of their faith has travelled to the churches he visited in Macedonia and Achaia (1.7), but instead he makes a sweeping statement with non-restrictive qualifiers. On its own this example, like Welborn's, is amplification, but when Paul adds that news of their faith has travelled not only throughout Macedonia and Achaia but *everywhere*, it is surely hyperbolic praise. We shall see that in 1 Thess. 2.16 Paul uses *pantote* ('always') together with a series of hyperbolic statements to exaggerate the sins of the Jews.

Paul used negative hyperbole as well. Compare his statement in

---

1. Compare the alternate interpretation of H. Kruse, 'Die "dialektische Negation" als semitisches Idiom', *VT* 4 (1954), pp. 385-400. He argued that 1 Thess. 4.8 is a 'semitic negation' like that found in Exod. 16.8 where, when the people complain about the lack of food in the wilderness, Moses says, 'Your murmurings are not against us but against the Lord'. The pattern consists of a denial of the first statement, and an affirmation of the second, for the purpose of emphasizing the latter statement. Thus, according to Kruse, what is meant is *not*: not statement A, rather statement B; rather: less so A and more so B. Kruse's view does not invalidate the point that even if Paul means something like 'Whoever disregards this, disregards less so a man but rather more so God', there is still an implication that Paul elevates his teaching to the highest level through an equation or near equation with God. Therefore it is reasonable to affirm that 1 Thess. 4.8 is hyperbolic.

2. L.L. Welborn, 'On the Discord in Corinth: 1 Corinthians 1–4 and Ancient Politics', *JBL* 106 (1987), pp. 85-111 at 108.

1 Cor. 15.30-31 where he says, 'Why am I in peril every hour?...I die every day'. This example needs no explanation.

Paul's exaggeration appears to have led to confusion in some of his churches. According to 1 Cor. 5.9-13, Paul had written to the Corinthians about not associating with sexually immoral people, but the Corinthians were puzzled as to his exact meaning. Apparently they thought he meant the non-Christian people in Corinth but he really only meant immoral followers of Christ (1 Cor. 5.11). Within 1 Cor. 5.9-13 there is a long list of derogatory words that cover every kind of unsavoury person: *pornoi* ('sexually immoral persons'), *pleonektai* ('coveters'), *harpagai* ('swindlers' or 'rogues'), *loidoroi* ('revilers'), *methysoi* ('drunkards') and *eidololatrai* ('idolaters'). Paul advises his converts not to associate with a Christian who is such a person. Once he starts a list of vices, rhetorical momentum takes over, and a form of exaggeration results. The list seems to imply that there may have been members of the Christian community who were guilty of such transgressions. This is doubtful. How many swindlers, revilers and idolaters were actually in the church? These verses are indicative of Paul's generalizing tendencies which, in this case, misled the Corinthians.

In some cases it can be shown that Paul was immediately conscious of having gone too far, or at least of having appeared to do so. In Romans 6–7 he parallels and so virtually equates the law with sin and the flesh (7.5-6). Subsequently, he asks whether or not he has implied that the law is sin. He denies it (7.7). *Mē genoito*[1] as the reply to a rhetorical question frequently signals an overstatement, or at least a possible misinterpretation of his position.

Sometimes, it can be shown, Paul had greatly assisted in the over-interpretation. The vice lists indicate that those who commit various sins and remain in an unrepentant state will not inherit the kingdom of heaven (1 Cor. 6.9-11; Gal. 5.19-21). But when he had to deal with individuals like the man in Corinth who was living with his stepmother, Paul softened his rhetoric. Perhaps the man in Corinth took Paul's view that 'All things are lawful' (1 Cor. 10.23) to its logical conclusion.[2] Perhaps the man thought that Christians were

1. A.J. Malherbe, '*Mē Genoito* in the Diatribe and Paul', *HTR* 73 (1980), pp. 231-40.
2. Apparently some had taken his over-statement as his actual view, and he had to qualify it later.

already living in the eschaton, and as such they were new creations; the old had passed away (2 Cor.5.17); and all things done unto the Lord were good (1 Cor. 10.23-31).[1] Paul had contributed to the misunderstanding of what was appropriate behaviour.

We also see exaggeration when Paul describes his ethical theory. Those in Christ are a new creation (2 Cor. 5.17; Gal. 6.15). As such, they experience the indwelling Spirit who leads them to demonstrate the fruits of the Spirit (Rom. 8.1-13; Gal. 5; Phil. 1.11) and to fulfil the law through love for people (Rom. 8.4). But in actual fact his letters are filled with exhortations to live better lives, to be blameless for the day of Christ (Phil. 1.10; 1 Thess. 3.13). Thus, although some of Paul's rhetoric sounds as if the fruits of the Spirit automatically follow the indwelling of the Spirit, he knew better.

Categorizing Paul's Polemical Hyperbole in 1 Thessalonians 2.14-16

By definition, a hyperbolic statement is amplification. However, amplification is not necessarily hyperbole. In the case of polemical situations, amplification is achieved through such means as accumulation and inflation of discreditable statements about actions or characteristics of an opponent while the latter has the function of making the former more prominent. The difference is a matter of degree. At most we can attempt to line up Paul's statements along a continuum and offer the following judgments.

Hyperbole

The Suffering of the Judaean Churches (2.14). If Paul had used a more extreme word such as persecute (*diōkein*) to describe the experiences of the Judaean churches and if one could be certain that the Jerusalem church suffered no difficulty from the Jews, there would be no doubt about the statement being hyperbolic. Since there is evidence that the church experienced suffering from the Jews at least some of the time, we should proceed with caution. As was argued in Chapter 3, it is not likely that the Judaean churches were chosen for comparison with the Thessalonians because of the severity of persecution experienced by them. Rather, it is likely their prominence

---

1. Jewett has noted that millenarian groups frequently violate traditional sexual mores on the grounds that the new age is present. He gives several examples. See *Thessalonian Correspondence*, p. 172.

at the beginning of the Christian movement and the fact that they did experience some disapproval which makes them a significant example for comparison.

Further, the letter is addressed to the Thessalonians who are experiencing actual opposition. By comparing the suffering of the Judaean churches with the suffering of the Thessalonians and by following it up with statements about the Jews' killing the Lord Jesus and the prophets, Paul implies a greater suffering than that of the Thessalonians. Through mutual association the afflictions of the Judaean Christians are amplified as is the status of those in Thessalonica. The Thessalonians in suffering are on an equal basis with the earliest and most prominent church. We recall that the author of *Rhetoric to Alexander* had advocated just such a method in raising the status of one party through association with another.[1] Placing the Thessalonians' suffering alongside that of a larger church and a list of serious and dangerous activities of that church's opponents (the Jews) makes the sufferings of the Thessalonians loom larger than the evidence supports (see 1 Thess. 4.11). The force of the initial statement is increased to the point of straining the truth through association with the other phrases and, therefore, is hyperbole.

The Jews Killed the Lord Jesus (2.15). This assertion is an exaggeration of the role that the Jews played in the death of Jesus: the Romans killed him. A more accurate statement would have been that the Jews 'opposed' or 'made to suffer' or 'took legal steps against him', but Paul uses the categorical 'killed' (*apokteinein*). Even if this is part of a tradition, Paul nevertheless accepts it. It is also true, however, that Paul did not raise the charge to the highest possible degree—'murder' (*phoneuein*)—as did the later tradition (Acts 7.52). Nevertheless, a statement may be hyperbolic without being raised to the highest degree possible: it need only strain the truth, which this assertion does.

The Jews are 'hostile to', 'opposed to', 'contrary to', 'against' (enantiōn) all Humanity (2.15). This statement is hyperbolic because there are no limits to the judgment. Even if v. 16 is intended as the reason—'they hinder us from preaching to the Gentiles so they may be saved'—the assertion that they oppose or are hostile to *all* humanity

1. *Rh. Al.* 3.1426a.25-30.

is extreme beyond amplification. That they oppose *all* humanity (presumably both Jew and Gentile) by hindering Paul's preaching *to all Gentiles* may be an instance in which Paul hyperbolically glorifies his own mission (cf. Romans 11, where he assigns universal significance to it). Did he seriously think that his mission would determine the fate of humanity, both Jew and Greek? I take Romans 11 to be an assertion to that effect, but his argument there (that his mission to the Gentiles will incidentally save the Jews) to be new. Thus, the statement in 1 Thess. 2.15 may reasonably be called hyperbolic.

Amplification would require a generalizing list of people to whom the Jews were hostile—for example, a list of names or even 'the Gentiles'. Further, that Paul appeals to a charge which was standard in the Gentile world[1] shows that he is amplifying what has always been said of the Jews, which was in itself an exaggeration of the facts. This charge was generally made of Jews because they kept separate from Gentiles and did not eat with them. Thus, it was said that they were hostile to outsiders.[2]

The Jews Fill up Always the Measure of their Sins (2.16). This statement is pushed to the limit. There are no qualifiers; indeed, there is no extension possible. This statement forms the climax of other exaggerations and so is hyperbolic.

The Wrath Has Come upon the Jews to the Uttermost (2.16). From this verse we do not know what manifestation the envisaged wrath has taken. The speaker must have some historical event in mind. If it did not have an actual referent, and the Jews were living in serenity, the statement would be laughable. Paul would not likely have risked being made a fool. As to what the historical event was, it is really impossible

---

1. Josephus, *Apion* 2.121. Josephus, referring to the works of Apion, says, '...[he] would have it appear that we [the Jews] swear by the God who made heaven and earth and sea to show no goodwill to a single alien, above all to Greeks'. See Tacitus, *Hist.* 5.5.

2. J.G. Gager, *The Origins of Anti-Semitism: Attitudes toward Judaism in Pagan and Christian Antiquity* (Oxford: Oxford University Press, 1983). Gager has shown that the view of Jews as isolationist is based upon selective evidence and does not reflect historical reality.

to say. It has been noted that any large disaster would have sufficed.[1] Paul's statement that the extent of the wrath was 'to the uttermost' (*eis telos*) is extreme. There is nothing beyond 'uttermost' and therefore the assertion is hyperbolic. Even if we give *eis telos* a temporal reading 'at last', the statement is still excessive. This was not the first time that God's wrath had come upon the Jews. According to Jewish history it had happened many times before.

Probable Hyperbole
The Jews Killed the Prophets (2.15). In accord with the tradition that the Jews killed the prophets, Paul amplifies the 'some' who may have been killed into '*the* prophets' who were killed, implying that all of them had been killed. Since Paul's amplification is implied but not directly stated, we can regard this statement as an instance of probable hyperbole.

The Jews Displease God (2.15). This unqualified assertion within a list of castigations does not take into account the pleasing acts of the Jews, for example, their prayers, their worship and so forth. There is neither a qualifying statement (e.g. 'Some Jews displease God...') nor a list of actual observed sinful behaviour of the Jews that is the direct cause of God's displeasure.

How were the Jews displeasing God? One might argue that the statement refers to the killing of the Lord and the prophets. But Paul here switches from a past participle to a present. For that reason one might argue that God's displeasure has to do with the Jews' preventing Paul from speaking to the Gentiles. This is possible, but it could also be that Paul is using a series of participles in order to create a list of sins of the Jews.

Each phrase mentioning a sin is joined by a connecting *kai*. After the two past participles there is a present participle, *areskontōn* ('[the Jews] displease God'), followed by an adjective (*enantiōn*) which is used like a quasi-participle in this sentence ('[the Jews] who oppose all humanity') followed by another present participle, *kōluontōn* ('[the Jews] hinder us'). In favour of the last participle's qualifying the quasi-participle one need only note that there is no connecting *kai*, unlike in the preceding phrases. However, the result is still a list of

---

1. Hurd, 'Paul Ahead of his Time', p. 35; Jewett, *The Thessalonian Correspondence*, pp. 37-38.

sins, so that '[the Jews] displease God' is best understood as one of a series and not dependent upon the quasi-participle and the final participle.

Since the generalization '[the Jews] displease God' follows several other sweeping statements (v. 15a) and is followed by the generalization 'and oppose all humanity', the accumulating effect strains the truth.

Thus, as it appears in context, I judge the phrase to be an instance of probable hyperbole. The whole statement may be part of a response to the accusation that Paul was a people pleaser, a standard rhetorical charge against philosophers at that time.[1] Paul emphasizes that he does not please people, but rather God (1 Thess. 2.2-4). His assertion that the Jews displease God presupposes that he knows what pleases God and exaggerates, by generalization and association with other sweeping statements, in order to put the opposition by Jews into a theological framework useful to his purposes. By saying that God is at work in the Thessalonians (2.13) but the Jews displease God, Paul reassures the Thessalonians of God's support in the midst of their suffering from opponents.

Possible Hyperbole
The Jews Persecute 'us' (2.15). The ambiguity of 'us', already discussed in Chapter 5, serves to elevate Paul and others to the status of the prophets and the Lord. This comparison of someone of lower status with those of higher status is typical of both amplification and hyperbole. The comparison here with the religious elite, and the fact that nowhere else does Paul mention his having been persecuted or driven out at this time, suggests that the statement is hyperbolic and not simply amplification.

However, Paul's being punished by the Jews, referred to in 2 Cor. 11.25 may already have happened before he wrote 1 Thessalonians. About this we cannot be certain. If the reference is to an activity in the past, the statement may not be hyperbolic. We know that he endured the thirty-nine lashes. But, if the statement refers to activities current in Thessalonica, it is likely hyperbolic. While the Jews could have opposed his acceptance of Gentiles without circumcision, their opposition does not seem to have precipitated a

---

1.   Malherbe, *Thessalonians*, p. 3.

full-blown conflict at this time as it would later in Galatia. These uncertainties lead me to suggest that this phrase should be placed in the category of possible hyperbole.

The Jews are Hindering us from Speaking to the Gentiles that they may be Saved (2.16). 'They hinder' (or 'they are attempting or intend to hinder', as is conceivable,[1] though not likely) by itself is not necessarily an exaggeration, since it could be a generalization on the basis of a certain number of individual occurrences. But in this context the generalizing present tense, the lack of qualification, and the preceding heightened statements lend themselves to the exaggerated tone of the passage. This statement, then, also falls into the category of possible hyperbole.

In the preceding discussion we have seen that most of the statements in 1 Thess. 2.14-16 can be seen as hyperbole and that all of them involve at least some amplification. While there is some difficulty in distinguishing hyperbole from amplification, I have taken the view that hyperbole is a straining of the truth beyond amplification. Since what is extreme depends upon the situation one is describing, I noted the continuum along which Paul's statements fall. Tools for this task include taking historiography into consideration, noting the words used and the presence or absence of qualifiers. There are cases where a generalization can be made on the basis of a number of cases. These would not be instances of hyperbole but of amplification. However, if there is a set of sweeping statements one after the other, the effect is to exaggerate the facts and, therefore, the statements are hyperbolic.

Polemical Hyperbole, Invective and Slander

How does Paul's choice of past and present sins of the Jews compare with the range of possibilities available to him from rhetorical convention? We have seen that Quintilian mentioned that one might criticize humble origin, poverty, mean appearance, vices, vices of progeny, negative qualities, and activities to amplify one's case against an opponent.[2] We have noted, too, that hyperbole is a straining of the

---

1. H.W. Smyth, *Greek Grammar* (Cambridge, MA: Harvard University Press, 1968), p. 421 §1878a.
2. *Inst.* 3.7.19-22. See also *Rh. Al.* 2.1426a.1-20.

truth without the intention to deceive.[1] How is hyperbole like invective or slander?

Invective

According to Quintilian invective, which can be described as a violent verbal attack on an opponent, can be true or untrue, the chief motivation being the applause of the audience. As he says:

> there are some who, if all else fails, fill up the gaps in their case with abuse of their opponents, true if possible, but false if necessary, the sole consideration that weighs with them being that it affords exercise for their talents and is likely to win applause during its delivery. (*Inst.* 12.9.8)

In any case, Quintilian thought that a good orator makes sparing use of invective, overuse often leading to the opposite effect to that desired. He discusses such a result with regard to a judicial case:

> Such conduct seems to me so unworthy of our perfect orator that, in my opinion, he will not even bring true charges against his opponents unless the case demand. For it is a dog's eloquence, as Appius says, to undertake the task of abusing one's opponent, and they who do so should steel themselves in advance to the prospect of being targets for the like abuse themselves, since those who adopt this style of pleading are frequently attacked themselves, and there can at any rate be no doubt that the litigant pays dearly for the violence of his advocate. (*Inst.* 12.9.8-9)

Despite the Greek and Roman rhetors' counsel that one ought to use restraint in employing invective,[2] it is nonetheless evident that in practice much abuse took place. R.G.M. Nisbet has shown that 'invective came easily to the Romans' and that their invective often 'showed more regard for literary convention than for historical truth'.[3] He lists the stock themes as criticisms of social background, physical appearance, immorality, avarice or pretentiousness. Further, according to Nisbet one could use abusive vocabulary, for example, animal names; use favourite catch words, for example, *carnifex* (Cicero, *In Pisonem* 5), *tyrannus* (Cicero, *Pro Sestio* 109), *crudelitas*

---

1.   *Inst.* 8.6.68-74.

2.   See H.F. North, 'The Concept of Sophrosyne in Greek Literary Criticism', *Classical Philology* 43 (1948), pp. 1-17. Even in the grand style of oratory, *sophrosyne* (moderation, good taste and restraint) was the ideal.

3.   R.G.M. Nisbet, 'The *In Pisonem* as an Invective', Appendix 6 in his edition of Cicero, *In L. Calpurnium Pisonem: Oratio* (Oxford: Clarendon Press, 1961), pp. 192-98.

(Cicero, *In Pisonem* 7), *furor* (*In Pisonem* 21, 26, 91); or give an account of the activities of one's enemy which, in spite of a wealth of circumstantial detail, was largely or completely fictitious (Piso's return from his drinking-den in *In Pisonem* 13 or Cicero's handling filthy clothes in the family laundry [Dio Chrysostom 46.5.1]). Most of these themes were employed to cause pain or laughter, not to be believed.

J.R. Dunkle has demonstrated how exaggeration of certain qualities in a ruler coupled with the pejorative term 'tyrant'[1] was a type of political invective designed to undermine a Roman emperor. The ruler was charged with being power hungry and arrogant, despotically capricious, and cruel. This type of invective was used not only by Cicero but was characteristic of the period, and while it had some basis in fact, it was often the result of political prejudice and personal antagonism.[2] The sameness of the vocabulary and the frequency of its use show that some rhetors were more interested in 'arousing the indignation of their audience than being completely truthful'.[3]

It was a commonplace for an orator to give 'prejudiced interpretations of behaviour, exaggerations and irrelevant charges, not to present clear facts but to arouse the indignation of the audience against one's opponent'. Dunkle says that 'rhetorical invention and coloring has much more effect than unadorned truth'.[4] In order to make a political enemy into a tyrant in the eyes of one's audience, an orator had to fulfil certain of their expectations and used negative stereotypes of behaviour to describe an opponent's acts. Dunkle notes that, to Romans, 'personalities were more important than political programs'.[5] Thus, an orator more frequently defamed the character of an opponent than attacked his political principles. Further, when acts were castigated, it was often in order to show the corruption of the person.

The denunciation of political figures for political gain was not only the domain of the Romans. Josephus besmirched his opponents in one

---

1. See J.R. Dunkle, 'Study of the Rhetorical Tyrant in Rome of the First Century BC' (PhD dissertation, University of Pennsylvania, 1965), pp. 1-4.

2. See J.R. Dunkle, 'The Greek Tyrant and Roman Political Invective of the Late Republic', *TAPA* 98 (1967), pp. 151-71. See also Dunkle, 'Rhetorical Tyrant', pp. 13-46.

3. Dunkle, 'The Greek Tyrant', p. 166.

4. Dunkle, 'The Greek Tyrant', p. 167.

5. Dunkle, 'The Greek Tyrant', p. 171.

context while giving praise to them in another. Recently Goodman has pointed out that in the Jewish war with Rome an important leader like Simon ben Gioras was portrayed in mid 67 CE by 'his enemies as little more than a bandit...while in October 66 he was a leading and successful general with the rebel forces'.[1] On the basis of the above survey, what we have in 1 Thess. 2.14-16 can be fairly described as invective, since it is a violent verbal attack on opponents. Paul's statement that the Jews kill the truly righteous, displease God, and oppose all humanity defames the very character of Jews and 'justifies' the judgment that they have received God's wrath. We hear nothing of the Paul of Romans where the gifts of the covenant, law, worship and promises are a glorious part of Jewish life (Rom. 9.4). However, since invective can be true or completely false, 'polemical hyperbole' more accurately characterizes Paul's language: he exaggerated some kernels of truth.

Some of Paul's accusations are stereotyped charges not unique to him. That the Jews killed the prophets is one such charge, as is the accusation that the Jews displease God. The contention that they oppose all humanity is also a stereotyped charge originating with Gentiles.[2] He may have taken over some of these standard charges from Jewish and Gentile traditions, but he placed them in serial order and in context.

Although Paul's statements are harsh, they are not as violent as some of those by Roman orators like Cicero. For example, Paul did not say that the Jews handled dirty laundry or that the Jews were immoral, lovers of money, or power hungry. Assertions which have some basis in reality but are exaggerated for the purpose of besmirching one's opponents are polemical hyperbole, while statements which are a complete fabrication are slander, as we shall see below.

Slander

A recent article by Luke Johnson supports some of my views. Arguing that obviously polemical language in the New Testament should be studied in the context of the rhetorical conventions of the time, he focuses on slander in the ancient world, specifically its

1. M. Goodman, *The Ruling Class of Judea: The Origins of the Jewish Revolt Against Rome, AD 66–70* (Cambridge: Cambridge University Press, 1987), p. 163.
2. See Tacitus, *Hist.* 5.5.

common usage,[1] its employment against those who were most threatening to a group or person,[2] and its primary purpose of edification of one's own school.[3] All of these features are shared by polemical hyperbole, but the latter differs from slander in some important ways. For an understanding of slander, we look to Lucian of Samosata:

> Slander, then, is a baseless accusation, made without the cognizance of the accused and sustained by the uncontradicted assertion of one side....
> (*Slander* 6)

In describing how slander is expressed, Lucian says that 'they [the slanderers] make their charges credible by distorting the real attributes of the man they are slandering. Thus, they insinuate that a doctor is a poisoner...'[4] In other words, a false accusation is made for the purpose of completely discrediting a person. In his discussion of how to slander, Lucian suggests that slanderers pay attention to the weaknesses of the person whose ear they want to gain.[5] Thus, if a man is jealous, one could whisper in his ear that a certain person (the one to be slandered) was gazing and sighing at his wife during dinner; if a man is religious, one could tell him that a particular person was irreligous and disrespectful of the gods.[6] Slander, then, primarily involves a complete distortion of the facts, whereas polemical hyperbole is an exaggeration of someone's actual behaviour or characteristics. Slander and polemical hyperbole may overlap, but motives are difficult to assess, and it is difficult to determine what is completely untrue. I shall postpone detailed discussion of Johnson's examples of slander until Chapter 8 where we shall note the overlaps with seemingly parallel passages from Paul's letters.

Johnson's study focuses mainly on the Gospels of Matthew and John,

---

1. L. Johnson, 'The New Testament's Anti-Jewish Slander and the Conventions of Ancient Polemic', *JBL* 108 (1989), pp. 419-41 (430-41). See also B. Vickers, *In Defense of Rhetoric* (Oxford: Clarendon Press, 1988).

2. Johnson notes that while the moderate Plutarch is quite gentle in his criticism of Jews, he calls Socrates a 'charlatan' and some Epicureans 'bufoons' and 'assassins' and prostitutes. 'What this proves is simply that their [the Jews'] version of philosophy was unimportant to him' (Johnson, 'Anti-Jewish Slander', p. 431).

3. Johnson, 'Anti-Jewish Slander', p. 433.

4. Johnson, 'Anti-Jewish Slander', pp. 14-15.

5. Johnson, 'Anti-Jewish Slander', p. 19.

6. Johnson, 'Anti-Jewish Slander', pp. 14-15.

but also discusses our passage briefly. The statements in vv. 13-15 are understood by him as indicating that the early Christian movement blamed the Jews for the killing of Jesus and for the carrying out of the Palestinian and diaspora persecutions. On the one hand, Johnson argues that slander is a convention which does not depend upon the facts;[1] on the other, with regard to our passage he argues that its content is true.[2] He disagrees with Hare's conclusion that persecution in the 30s and 40s was not as severe as Matthew and Acts would have us believe.[3] As proof, Johnson cites four statements from Paul about persecution,[4] including 1 Tim. 1.12-13 (!), and gives a long list of passages from Acts[5] and a long list from Josephus.[6] The evidence from Josephus is used to support the notion that the Jews of the early decades were 'fanatics and violent'.[7]

I have dealt with the statements about persecution from Paul's letters and Acts in Chapter 3. Johnson overlooked the conventional way that the author of Acts describes the Jews: they are uniformly jealous of the success of Christian preachers, and they go about stirring up the rabble. Further, Acts needs to be set within its historical context in which the situation vis-à-vis Judaism and the early Christian movement had changed from the time of Paul's letters. In respect of the evidence from Josephus we need to be cautious. His account of the role of the Jews in the war with Rome is highly tendentious.[8] It must be remembered that Josephus had the Roman emperor as patron and so he exaggerated the role of the Jewish rabble in provoking the war. More importantly, the activities of Jews in the war with Rome are not reliable evidence for the behaviour of Jews regarding a nascent religious movement in the 30s and 40s.

---

1.   Johnson, 'Anti-Jewish Slander', p. 433.

2.   Johnson, 'Anti-Jewish Slander', p. 422 n. 9.

3.   Johnson, 'Anti-Jewish Slander', p. 424 n. 16. See also Hare, *Persecution of Christians*, and Chapter 3.

4.   Gal. 1.13; Phil. 3.6; 1 Cor. 15.9.

5.   Acts 5.17-18; 6.12-13; 7.58; 8.3; 9.1-2, 23; 12.1-2; 13.50; 14.19; 17.5; 18.12; 23.12-15.

6.   *War* 1.89; 1.150; 1.571; 2.8-13; 2.42; 2.65; 2.169-70; 2.223; 2.229-30; 2.264-65; 2.408-409; 2.417; 2.466; 4.135; 4.197-207; 4.310-18; 4.378; 4.509; 7.367; 7.409; 7.437-41.

7.   Johnson, 'Anti-Jewish Slander', p. 422 n. 9.

8.   See S. Cohen, *Josephus in Galilee and Rome: His Vita and Development as a Historian* (Leiden: Brill, 1979).

Is 1 Thess. 2.14-16 really slander if, as Johnson argues, persecution was rampant and Jews were violent? In that case, what Paul says is a clear reporting of facts rather than slander. But Johnson has singled out these statements for discussion, thereby indicating that he (at least initially) judged them as something more than that. In this we are in agreement.

Johnson did not notice the one clear example of slander in the passage: that the Jews hate all humanity. The statement is simply untrue and is therefore slander. It is also an exaggeration. I think, however, that the study of hyperbole is a more appropriate and productive approach to the passage and its function within the context of the letter, one which can take us beyond the acknowledgment that Paul was not just reporting facts or using slander.

While similarities have been noted between Paul's hyperbole and that of the trained rhetors, there seem to be closer parallels between Paul's polemic and that of the Cynic preachers.

Polemical Hyperbole and the Cynic Preachers

Cynic preachers also attacked their opponents.[1] Rather than investigating the extent and directions of their influence, I shall be content with gaining an awareness of the use of polemical hyperbole in letters written by philosophers possibly contemporaneous with Paul. I shall cite examples from the pseudonymous epistles of Heraclitus to Hermodorus (second century CE) and from a letter purported to be by Diogenes of Sinope (whose 'letter' has been dated in the period from 28 BCE to 200 CE).

Heraclitus says that he hears that the Ephesians are about to introduce a new law against him:

> They know, Hermodorus, that I helped you draft the laws, and they want
> to drive me out, but they will not before I have refuted them for having
> decreed unjustly that 'The man who does not laugh, and every
> misanthrope, must leave the city before sundown.' They want to make
> this a law. But there is no one who does not laugh, Hermodorus, except
> Heraclitus; consequently, they can drive me away. O you men, don't you
> want to learn why I never laugh? It is not because I hate men but because I

---

1. Malherbe has shown parallels between Paul's view of his ministry and conceptions of Cynics about their work. See A.J. Malherbe, '"Gentle as a Nurse" The Cynic Background to I Thess. ii', *NovT* 12 (1970), pp. 203-17.

hate their wickedness. Write your law in this way: 'If anyone hates wickedness, he must leave the city' and I shall be the first to leave. I shall gladly be banished, not from my homeland, but from evil. (Heraclitus, *To Hermodorus* 7.2)[1]

Heraclitus criticizes the Ephesians for more than their wars:

A land is denuded of trees, is sacked, old age is treated with contempt, women are seduced, children are snatched from their arms, bedrooms are corrupted, virgins are made concubines, young men become effeminate, free men are clapped into irons, temples of the gods are pulled to the ground, shrines of the heroes are dug up, paeans are offered for profane deeds, and thank offerings are made to the gods for injustice. (Heraclitus, *To Hermodorus* 7.7)

This invective is filled with the type of vehemence that is encountered in 1 Thess. 2.14-16. The facts are strained beyond truth and yet contain some kernel of historical reality. Surely the land was not totally denuded of trees, nor every woman seduced, nor was every Ephesian thanking the gods for injustice. Perhaps several trees were cut down and a few women were seduced. Yet the piling up of generalizations has the effect of amplifying each individual charge and implying widescale and general degradation. Each generalization by itself is not hyperbole, but the accumulation of generalizations implies widespread corruption because there are no qualifiers given to delimit the accusations. The letter by 'Pseudo-Diogenes' confronts his compatriots for killing their citizens instead of educating them:

Diogenes the Dog to the so-called Greeks, a plague on you! And this is already beginning to infect you, even if I should say nothing more. For although to all appearances you are men, you are apes at heart. You pretend to everything, but know nothing. Therefore nature takes vengeance of you, for in contriving laws for yourselves you have allotted to yourselves the greatest and most pervasive delusion that issues from them, and you admit them as witnesses to your ingrained evil... You know nothing as your ancestors did not... It is not only the Dog that hates you; nature itself does too... Look at the number and quality of the men you killed... But, you blockheads, should one not attempt to educate such people rather than kill them?... But nothing is enough for you, for you are lovers of glory, irrational, and ineptly brought up. (Diogenes the Cynic 28)[2]

1. A.J. Malherbe, *The Cynic Epistles* (Missoula, MT: Scholars Press, 1977), pp. 201-207.

2. Malherbe, *The Cynic Epistles*, p. 121.

The use of exaggeration in this passage is obvious. Diogenes is really agitated. Some of the passage is clearly invective. For example, he calls his compatriots 'apes'. They 'pretend to everything but know nothing... as their ancestors did not...' These statements are polemical hyperbole: a straining of the truth to denigrate opponents. Both Heraclitus and Diogenes use standard Graeco-Roman accusations such as 'lovers of glory, irrational, and ineptly brought up' to defame their opponents. In social terms these Cynics were more similar to Paul than were the Graeco-Roman rhetors: they were street preachers too.[1] Paul differs from them in his use of religious language to castigate antagonists.

Diogenes' reference to the Greeks' killing their citizens rather than educating them sounds similar to what Paul says in 1 Thessalonians about the Jews killing the prophets. Yet, there are distinct differences. Paul is not addressing the Jewish people directly. He uses them as examples to instruct his church on the outcome of those who threaten the church. Whereas Diogenes has a concern about city politics and the penal policy, Paul is concerned about God's final wrath and punishment for opponents, including the Thessalonians should they not turn out to be blameless at the day of the Lord (1.10; 5.5-10; 5.23). Paul's deep, eschatological concern is evident throughout Thessalonians. The intensity of the issues is quite different for Diogenes and the apostle. The former has to do with inappropriate public policies in the present, the latter with inappropriate behaviour in the present in view of the coming divine judgment (5.2-10). For that reason we must look beyond pagan to Jewish writings for further elucidation of Paul's polemic.

The Eschatological Dimension of Paul's Polemic

There are many parallels between the rhetorical conventions of castigating one's opponents and Paul's exaggeration of the sins of the Jews in 1 Thess. 2.14-16, but Paul's case is distinct in that his polemic has a religious dimension with eschatological overtones. The Jews killed the Lord Jesus and the prophets, displease God, and hinder Paul from preaching to the Gentiles, thereby preventing them from

---

1. See A.J. Malherbe, 'Antisthenes and Odysseus and Paul at War', *HTR* 76 (1983), pp. 143-73; F.G. Downing, 'Cynics and Christians', *NTS* 30 (1984), pp. 584-93.

salvation. In other words, for censure Paul selects religious themes. Perhaps he uses topics which may arouse the hostility of the audience or uses a Jewish tradition,[1] amplifying with a standard Gentile accusation in order to accord to his situation in Thessalonica.

The first letter to the Thessalonians is usually dated at about 51 CE. It is set against the backdrop of eschatological concerns. Paul begins and ends on the note of the wrath (*orgē*) to come. After praising the Thessalonians for turning from idols to the living God (1.9), he assures them that Jesus, whom they await from heaven, will deliver them from the 'wrath to come' (1.10). Obviously the Thessalonians were awaiting the parousia of the Lord (1.10; 3.13; 4.15; 5.2; 5.23).[2] That the parousia was expected soon is apparent from the concern about those who had already died (4.13). Paul assures them that they are not destined for wrath (5.9) and that both the living and the dead (4.16) will live with the Lord when he returns. Paul's images demonstrate that he expected that return very soon (2.19; 3.13; 4.15; 5.2-4). The present passive participle in 4.15b, *perileipomenoi*, indicates that the entire drama has begun and is being worked out now.

If any of the situations Bammel[3] mentions was the reason behind Paul's conclusion in 1 Thess. 2.16, it was not because the event had international renown. Rather, as Jewett has shown, groups which expect an imminent end to the age and various catastrophes to signal that impending event, would interpret any fateful happening, however small, as part of the beginning of the end.[4] Whatever the event was, it is portrayed by Paul as a sign that God's wrath has come upon the Jews and also serves as a warning that the end is near; God's final wrath will surely come, and the Thessalonians had better be 'blameless' 'on that day'.

When one considers the eschatological tone of this letter to the Thessalonians and Paul's concern for the suffering they are enduring and may yet have to endure before being judged 'blameless' on the 'day of the Lord', the passage in 1 Thess. 2.14-16 fits the context of the letter very well.

---

1. Donfried, 'Paul and Judaism', p. 249.

2. The word *parousia* is used more times in 1 Thessalonians than in any other book in the New Testament.

3. Possibly the expulsion of the Jews by Claudius. Bammel, 'Judenverfolgung', pp. 294-95.

4. Jewett, *The Thessalonian Correspondence*, pp. 37-38.

For parallels to Paul's religious concerns and his eschatological preoccupation in 1 Thessalonians, the *Psalms of Solomon* and the Dead Sea Scrolls provide a rich source.

Polemical Hyperbole in the Context of Jewish Eschatology

The Psalms of Solomon

The *Psalms of Solomon* are not fully eschatological. *Psalm* 17, on the hoped-for arrival of the Son of David, is truly eschatological but the others are not. They do, however, see recent events as 'climactic', and the general air of climax makes them suitable for comparison. The general theme is the activities of the wicked, the suffering of the righteous, and the hope for vindication in the future.

Ps. Sol. 8.11-13 reveals the concern of a pious Jewish group trying to extend to the general populace obedience to the purity laws observed by priests in the Jerusalem Temple in the first century BCE.[1] In castigating the priests, the author says,

> They committed adultery, every man with his neighbour's wife. They concluded covenants with one another with an oath touching these things; they plundered the sanctuary of God, as though there was no avenger. They trod the altar of the Lord, (coming straight) from all manner of uncleanness; And with menstrual blood they defiled the sacrifices, as (though these were) common flesh.

The religious language is striking in its concern for purity and holiness. As to the accusations, obviously no one can verify their accuracy. Gross exaggeration of opponents' faults was a tradition in Jewish internecine polemic already grey with age. Paul's statements in 1 Thess. 2.14-16 are pale by comparison.

The Dead Sea Scrolls

The Dead Sea Scrolls, written in view of an impending end to this world, denigrated opponents of the community, as in the interpretation of Nah. 3.4 which follows:

> Interpreted, this concerns those who lead Ephraim astray, who lead many astray through their false teachings, their lying tongue, and deceitful

---

1. G.W.E. Nickelsburg, *Jewish Literature Between the Bible and the Mishnah* (Philadelphia: Fortress Press, 1981), p. 203.

lips—kings, princes, and people, together with the stranger who joins them.[1]

The charges are general and are not helpful as to specific content. Being a charlatan (*goēs*) and engaging in lying and deceitfulness are standard denunciations used against one's opponent.[2] Which teachings are false? What do the false teachers say that are lies? The effect of the series of charges is to amplify the defaming of the opponents and to make them appear a great evil. Further, to associate this interpretation with Scripture gives the charges more force.

In the *Covenant of Damascus* the writer's aim is to 'encourage the sectaries to remain faithful, and with this end in view he sets out to demonstrate from the history of Israel and the Community that fidelity is always rewarded and apostasy chastised'.[3] In this writing we notice his eschatological heightening in order to exhort his hearers. That the author intends the piece as an exhortation is evident at the beginning of the book:

> Hear now, my sons, and I will uncover your eyes that you may see and understand the works of God, that you choose that which pleases Him and reject that which He hates, that you may walk perfectly in all His ways and not follow after thoughts of the guilty inclination and after eyes of lust. (CD 2)

Those who falter in their responsibilities are on the side of Satan. They will be condemned to darkness. The writer says that just as the children of Seth in Num. 24.17 were smitten with the sword,

> so shall it be for all the members of His Covenant who do not hold steadfastly to these [MS B to the curse of the precepts]. They shall be visited for destruction by the hand of Satan... For they shall hope for healing but He will crush them. They are all of them rebels, for they have not turned from the way of traitors but have wallowed in the ways of whoredom and wicked wealth. They have taken revenge and borne malice, every man against his brother, and every man has hated his fellow and every man has sinned against his near kin, and has approached for unchastity, and has acted arrogantly for the sake of riches and gain. And

---

1. *The Dead Sea Scrolls in English* (ed. and trans. G. Vermes; Harmondsworth: Penguin Books, 3rd edn, 1987), p. 281.

2. Johnson, 'Anti-Jewish Slander', pp. 434-36. He tells us that Josephus called a fellow Jew, Justus of Tiberias, a 'charlatan and a demagogue and a deceiver' (p. 436), and Josephus's opponents called Moses a 'charlatan' (p. 434).

3. Johnson, 'Anti-Jewish Slander', p. 96.

every man has done that which seemed right in his eyes and has chosen the stubbornness of his heart. (CD 8)

The rhetoric is designed to heighten eschatological awareness and to encourage obedience to the covenant. The charges are likely exaggerated. Those who are vilified are called rebels and accused of the standard charge of whoredom and seeking after gain.[1] The list of accusations is hyperbolic because every non-sectarian Jew surely did not hate other people, did not sin against near kin, was not unchaste, and did not act arrogantly in order to become wealthy. Some people may have done some of these things some of the time, but not everyone did all of these things all of the time. The list is designed to gain the assent of the reader against those charged, but the charges are extreme in that there are no qualifiers. Although the rhetoric sounds as if the judgment is absolute, a more moderate view is presented later in the document:

> But all those who hold fast to these precepts, going and coming in accordance with the Law, who heed the voice of the Teacher and confess before God, (saying), 'Truly we have sinned, we and our fathers, by walking counter to the precepts of the Covenant, Thy judgments upon us are justice and truth'; who do not lift their hand against His holy precepts or His righteous statutes or His true testimonies; who have learned from the former judgments by which the members of the Community were judged; who have listened to the voice of the Teacher of Righteousness... God will forgive them and they shall see His salvation because they took refuge in His holy Name. (CD 8)

Just as this writer exhorts the insiders to be among the true Israel and attacks opponents with both conventional means and polemical hyperbole, all within the context of the expected end of the age and its consequent judgments, so Paul nurtures his church and vituperates its opponents, all the while having his eye on the coming drama of eschatological significance.

Summary

The content of Paul's polemical hyperbole bears some resemblances to the works of the Greek and Roman rhetors and the Cynic preachers. However, in religious language and in eschatological framework, it is

---

1. Johnson, 'Anti-Jewish Slander', p. 432.

closer to the sweeping generalized hyperbole of the Dead Sea sect. These comparisons show Paul to be, not surprisingly, a person steeped in Jewish tradition but also permeated by the rhetorical conventions of the day.

In Chapter 5 I noted the kernels of exaggeration in each phrase of the problem passage and in Chapter 6 I investigated the conventions of exaggeration in the writings of the classical rhetoricians and in the religious language of eschatologically minded sects. We must now re-examine the problem passage using the principles of amplification and hyperbole to determine how Paul sought to persuade the church to stand fast in the face of persecution.

Chapter 7

THE RHETORIC OF 1 THESSALONIANS 2.14-16 REVISITED

This chapter explores key aspects of 1 Thess. 2.14-16: the rhetorical movement among its phrases, its structure within the plan of the letter, and its employment of polemical hyperbole.

Hyperbole as Amplification to a Climax

Many purely formal patterns in written expression can awaken an attitude of expectancy in us. Once the shape of the pattern is grasped, the participation of the audience or reader is invited regardless of the subject matter or whether they agree with the proposition being presented in that particular form. Where there is deep resistance to the proposition, it is not as likely that they will surrender to the pattern. But in situations where a decision is still to be reached, 'a yielding to the form prepares for assent to the matter identified with it'.[1] Burke cites an example from 1948: 'Who controls Berlin controls Germany; who controls Germany controls Europe; who controls Europe controls the world'. He argues that as a set of propositions it may or may not be true and that most people may not want to control the world, but regardless of one's doubts about the propositions stated,

> by the time you arrive at the second of its three stages, you feel how it is destined to develop—and on the level of purely formal assent you would collaborate to round out its symmetry by spontaneously willing its completion and perfection as an utterance. Add, now, the psychosis of nationalism, and assent on the formal level invites assent to the proposition as doctrine.[2]

---

1. K. Burke, *A Rhetoric of Motives* (Berkeley: University of California Press, 1969), p. 58.
2. Burke, *A Rhetoric of Motives*, p. 59.

Similarly, the symmetry of Paul's statements, the urgency of the current opposition the Thessalonians were facing, and the eschatological nature of the letter would incline readers to assent to the climax of the passage. To gain such assent serves to denigrate the opponents and to lead to the identification of the readers with the writer as among the suffering 'righteous'.

Although Paul's rhetoric may function to win assent, not all of the amplification and hyperbole is carefully designed to lead to a clear and uninterrupted climax. This becomes evident upon examination of the various directions of rhetorical movement in the passage.

Rhetorical Movement in the Verbs

Paul does not place all of the charges against the Jews in the present tense and begin with 'hinder' and end with the climactic 'kill'. He might have done, if it had been possible to do so without producing laughter from his audience, but presumably the opposition in Thessalonica had not led to martyrdom. There is, however, some climactic movement in the force of the actions mentioned: 'killed', 'persecute', 'displease', 'oppose' (although the latter word in Greek is not actually a verb [*enantiōn*], it does have an active sense to it) and 'hinder' (or 'prevent' or 'stop'). The words descend in force from the strongest, 'kill', to the weakest, 'displease', but the latter is associated with the strongest noun ('God'), which gives it greater force. From 'displease' the words move from the general 'opposing' of everyone to the specific 'preventing us' ('from speaking to the Gentiles'). This latter movement focuses attention on the present after reinforcing the idea that what is happening now is a common pattern of behaviour by the opponents.

Rhetorical Movement within the Series of Accusations

We have seen in Chapter 5 that there are five main charges against the Jews with an apparent sixth which defines the fifth (or the fourth and fifth). The series is divided grammatically into a triad of past activities ('killed the Lord Jesus and the prophets and us') and a doublet of contemporary activities of the Jews in which the first element has a present participle ('displease God'), and the second element contains a quasi-participle ('and oppose all humanity') followed by an explanatory clause having another present participle ('by hindering us from preaching to the Gentiles'). Grammatically, it does not appear that the last participial clause is a separate element, yet the present participle and extended new explanation do have the effect of a separate charge. Thus, I term it the third element of a triad of contemporary charges against the Jews.

In the triad of past activities of the Jews (against the Lord, the prophets, and us) the arrangement does not focus upon the death of Jesus but moves rapidly and cumulatively to the third term, 'us'. Then Paul advances into another triad of charges, one which sweeps out to the view of God and humanity, and then back to the difficulties in the present ('hindering us from speaking to the Gentiles that they may be saved'). This latter element amplifies the fifth and possibly the fourth and fifth phrases ('who are displeasing God and opposing all humanity').

There are two movements. In the first case the movement is from the most truly righteous one to other lesser righteous ones from the past, then to the contemporary righteous ones, 'us'. In the second case the movement is from God to humanity to the specific 'us'. The result of this double direction is the climax which justifies Paul's judgment upon the Jews: 'the wrath has come upon them to the uttermost'. The sweeping charges in the present tense ('displease God', 'oppose humanity by hindering us') justify the sweeping condemnation.

Rhetorical Movement of the Phrases

In order to facilitate the discussion of the phrases in question, each one is numbered beginning with v. 15 after the article *tōn*.

1. *kai ton kyrion apokteinantōn Iēsoun*
2. *kai tous prophētas*
3. *kai hēmas ekdiōxantōn*
4. *kai theō mē areskontōn*
5. *kai pasin anthrōpois enantiōn*
6. *kōluontōn hēmas tois ethnesin lalēsai hina sōthōsin*
7. *eis to anaplērōsai autōn tas hamartias pantote*
8. *ephthasen de ep' autous hē orgē eis telos*

Each of the series of phrases 1-5 is preceded by the conjunction *kai*.[1] The function of the clauses which begin with the conjunction *kai*

---

1. The placement of *kai* at the beginning of successive clauses is called *epanaphora*.

and end with a similar sound *tōn*[1] (except for number 2) is to move
the audience along with the symmetry, thereby encouraging their
assent. Even number 6 seems to follow the pattern, at least with
regard to the sound of the beginning and ending consonants, while the
content explains by means of a specific grievance the charge which is
asserted in number 5. Paul amplified what he wanted to say by the
symmetry of hyperbolic phrases and the accumulation of charges,
charges which move from the past to the present concerns of the
readers or listeners, amplify the topic, and culminate in the climax.
When Paul's statements against the Jews in vv. 14-16a are followed
by 'so as to fill up *pantote* (always) the measure of their sins' (v. 16b)
and are followed by the judgment 'But the wrath has come upon them
to the uttermost' (v. 16c), the climax is reached.

Such a build-up of amplified charges or *gradatio* to a climax was a
commonplace. The symmetry of the series was broken with a 'sudden
let-down' or *bathos*, as Burke[2] points out. In the passage being
discussed this is the statement of judgment in v. 16c.

Beginning with 'kill the Lord Jesus' the list of sins moves symmet-
rically to a climax. The overall effect is to lead the reader to think
that Paul has succeeded in proving the content of the climax: that the
Jews are always filling up the measure of their sins. Logically, this
does not happen at all. Paul's assertions are sweeping generalizations
in quick succession (except for his explanation of the result of the
Jews' hindering his speaking to Gentiles). Thus when he implies that
he has proved the complete measure of the Jews' sins, it is the force of
his terse statements and not the logic of his arguments which moves
us.

There are at least three different movements occurring simultane-
ously in the passage. Compared with the rhetors discussed earlier Paul
sets up his exaggeration in an unrefined way, as becomes evident on
closer examination. Here we should examine a passage from Cicero
which Quintilian uses and which was noted in the discussion of
amplification (Chapter 6). I shall analyse its movement to a climax.

---

1.   The similar sound at the end of each phrase (especially the four participles in
phrases 3-6) is called *homoioteleuton*.
2.   Burke, *A Rhetoric of Motives*, p. 66.

It is a sin to bind a Roman citizen, a crime to scourge him, little short of the most unnatural murder to put him to death; what then shall I call his crucifixion? (Quintilian, *Inst.* 8.4.4)[1]

Printing the passage in vertical form (see below) makes it easier to observe the ascent of the rhetoric, beginning with 'a Roman' and ascending to the climax.

> *civem Romanum* (a Roman)
> *Facinus est vincire* (a sin to bind)
> *scelus verberare* (a crime to scourge)
> *prope parricidium necare:* (almost parricide to put to death)
> *quid dicam in crucem tollere?* (what then is crucifixion?)

The ascension of the sequences (sin…crime…parricide *and* bind… scourge…put to death…crucifixion) and the formal symmetry of the phrases constructed on the same pattern and ending with a similar sound is clear and proceeds in a definite, precise amplification. Each phrase has two main terms and each is intensified step by step to its climax.

As we have seen, Quintilian cited this passage for its amplification.[2] Subsequent to it in his discussion is the hyperbolic statement that Antony had vomited and filled his lap and the whole tribunal.[3] It offers a good example of symmetry of phrases and their movement to a climax.

> You with such a throat, such flanks, such burly strength in every limb of your prize-fighter's body…[4]

> *Tu, inquit,* (You, he asks)
> *istis faucibus,* (your throat)
> *istis lateribus,* (your flanks)
> *ista gladiatoria totius corporis firmitate* (your prizefighter's body)

Quintilian, quoting Cicero, shows the symmetry and accumulation of phrases which moves one's attention to ever larger anatomical areas

1. This is a quotation from Cicero, *Verrine Orations* 5.170.
2. *Inst.* 8.4.16.
3. *Inst.* 8.4.68; see above, Chapter 6.
4. The rest of this sentence in Cicero reads, '…had swallowed so much wine at Hippias' wedding that you were forced to vomit in the sight of the Roman people the next day' (*Philippics* 2.25.63). Quintilian does not quote the entire sentence in illustrating amplification. However, even if he had, it would still be evident that the argument ascends in force to the climax.

so that the audience can estimate the quantity of wine Antony must have imbibed before he reached the point of not being able to absorb any more. Another of the Ciceronian passages that Quintilian cites is similar:[1]

> What was that sword of yours doing, Tubero, the sword you drew on the field of Pharsalus? Against whose body did you aim its point? What meant those arms you bore? Whither were your thoughts, your eyes, your hand, your fiery courage directed on that day? What passion, what desires were yours?

> *Quid enim tuus ille, Tubero, destrictus in acie Pharsalica gladius agebat?* (What was your sword doing, Tubero, the sword you drew on the field of Pharsalus?)
> *cuius latus ille mucro petebat?* (Against whose body did you aim its point?)
> *qui sensus erat armorum tuorum?* (What meant those arms you bore?)
> *quae tua mens, oculi, manus, ardor animi?* (Whither were your thoughts, eyes, your hand, your fiery courage?)
> *quid cupiebas?* (What were you longing for?)
> *quid optabas?* (What were you desiring?)

This passage displays a clear continuous ascension to the climax in its use of questions, each one more pointed than the last. There is movement in the terms mentioned—sword, body, arms, thoughts, eyes, hand, fiery courage, longing, desires—and similarity of sound at the beginning of each question. Quintilian emphasizes the importance of 'a continuous and unbroken series in which each word is stronger than the last'[2] or an 'accumulation of words and sentences identical in meaning...'[3]

As we have observed, Paul's use of language is effective but differs from the guidelines of the experts. His polemic moves back and forth in a way which has direction, but it is not so polished in symmetry and movement as theirs.

1 Thessalonians 2.14-16 and the Structural Plan of 1 Thessalonians

If we look at 1 Thess. 2.14-16 in the context of the letter as a whole, we see a significant number of triads.[4] Stanley B. Marrow observed a

---

1.	Cicero, *For Ligarius* 9, cited by Quintilian, *Inst.* 8.4.27.
2.	*Inst.* 8.4.8.
3.	*Inst.* 8.4.26.
4.	S.B. Marrow, *Paul: His Letters and his Theology* (New York: Paulist Press,

triadic pattern in what he called the thanksgiving section of 1 Thess. 1.3–2.12 and organized in sets A through F below:

A. Remembering before God our Father
1. your work of faith,
2. your labor of love
3. and steadfastness of hope in our Lord Jesus Christ (1 Thess. 1.3).

B. For our gospel came to you,
1. not only in word
2. but also in power
3. and in the Holy Spirit and [in] full conviction (1 Thess. 1.5).

Manuscripts Sinaiticus and Vaticanus include the preposition *en*. If it is accepted as part of the passage, this set is quadratic rather than triadic. The overall result would be to weaken the rhetorical effect of the sets of triads. It would not, however, detract from Marrow's assertion that Paul made use of many triads.

C. [no preamble to the triad]
1. You turned to God from idols,
2. to serve a living and true God,
3. and to wait for his son from heaven, whom he raised from the dead, Jesus who delivers us from the wrath to come (1 Thess. 1.9-10).

D. For our appeal does not spring
1. from error
2. or uncleanness,
3. nor is it made with guile... (1 Thess. 2.3).

E. For we never used
1. either words of flattery, as you know,
2. or a cloak for greed, as God is witness;
3. nor did we seek glory from men, whether from you or from others (1 Thess. 2.5).

F. [no preamble to the triad]
1. We exhorted each one of you
2. and encouraged
3. and charged you to lead a life worthy of God, who calls you into his own kingdom and glory (1 Thess. 2.11-12).

1986). The rhetorical term is 'tricolon' (a three-member phrase) and the members in Greco-Roman rhetoric are often of increasing length (a favourite of the author of *To Gaius Herennius* 4.19.26; Quintilian, *Inst.* 9.3.77).

The triadic patterns which Marrow discerned are followed by a double triadic pattern in 2.14-16:

G. the Jews who
    1. killed both the Lord Jesus
    2. and the prophets
    3. and persecuted us

and

    1. displease God
    2. and oppose all humanity
    3. by hindering us from speaking to the Gentiles that they may be saved.

It appears that in the first two chapters Paul employs several different patterns of triads:

1. Chronological: sets A and C.
2. Intensifying (greater intensity with each phrase): set B and possibly E (see below).
3. Synonymous (a series of synonyms): sets D, E and possibly F.
4. Diminishing: set G.

As far as I can tell, the triads of sets D and E do not have a specific direction of intensity. More information as to the nuances of meaning behind these words is needed before a direction can be detected. Because the terms within each triad appear to be interchangeable, these triads have a synonymous pattern.

Set F can be interpreted as a series of synonyms ('exhort', 'encourage', and 'charge' are similar in meaning, although the first and last terms appear stronger than the middle one), as rising in intensity, if the other meaning of *martyromenoi* is considered as in the intense statement of Gal. 5.3: '*I charge* again to every man who receives circumcision that he is bound to keep the whole law', or as diminishing in intensity if *martyromenoi* is understood to mean 'to exhort'.

It is impossible to be certain about the movement of intensity with triad F, but the first interpretation of the triad appears to be the better one because of the force of the statement after *martyromenoi*. The Thessalonians are charged to lead a life worthy of God, who calls them into his own realm and glory. For Paul, the Jew, this charge is similar to his reasoning in Galatians: those who count themselves part of God's people are required to act in certain prescribed ways, ways which Paul explains in 5.1-2. Thus, I have placed set F together with the intensifying pattern of set B.

Set G has the effect of a set of double triads. As noted above, the first triad encompasses two aorist participles and the second has two present participles and a quasi-participle. In both cases there are three elements. The movement passes from the divine realm to the human. Moving from the righteous of the past to those of the present and from the most truly righteous one to other lesser righteous ones is apparent in the first triad. In the second triad there is also an order of diminishing power: from God and the general world to Paul and his specific experience.

The result of this dual movement has a theological component. It places Paul's activities in the context of the faithful historical figures through whom God has always worked and still is working. This double theological direction leads the audience to assent to Paul's view that the atrocious activities of the Jews are habitual, as expressed in 'so as always to fill up the measure of their sins' which is the climax of the charges, and to agree with his judgment upon them: 'the wrath has come upon them to the uttermost'.

If Paul's intention was, as he states, to show that the Jews filled up the measure of their sins, his list of specific recent sins does not very successfully prove his point. The section is filled with generalizations and judgments but not actual situations which would prove the unrelenting tendency of the Jews to sin. There is really only one specific charge in the present (they prevent Paul from speaking to the Gentiles). As we shall see in the next section, the rhetorical movement of the passage also places the persecution in Thessalonica and the opposition to Paul by Jews (whether within or outside Thessalonica) into a typical framework of end-of-the-age opposition to the divine plan.

One might consider this double theological direction ingenious on the part of Paul. The Greek and Roman rhetors did not, to my knowledge, advocate such a procedure. Yet Paul's various movements are effective. His readers are swept along with the pattern of a series of participles with short phrases and predisposes them to assent to the content.

This examination of triads reveals Paul's use of a variety of patterns: the chronological, intensifying, synonymous and diminishing. Unlike the trained rhetors, for whom a series of eight triads in twenty-six verses would be considered unimaginative, Paul moves from one pattern to the other with ease.

If I am correct in perceiving the double triadic pattern, then the triadic pattern extends further than the thanksgiving section of the letter as Marrow has described it. In Jewett's structure of 1 Thessalonians[1] the triadic pattern is found both in the exordium and in the narratio, but not throughout the latter. Perhaps it is best to say that Paul often makes use of the triadic pattern without trying to fit it into one or the other sections of the letter exclusively.

The Function of Polemical Hyperbole in 1 Thessalonians 2.14-16

In this passage Paul distinguishes the church in Thessalonica off sharply from its opponents. He uses polemical hyperbole to do so. I shall enumerate the rhetorical ways in which he moves his readers to his side and against his and their opponents.

The Effects of Paul's Use of Polemical Hyperbole
Elevation of Status. The comparison of the Thessalonians with a more elite group, the Jerusalem church where the Christian message began, elevates and makes more prominent the experiences of suffering of the Thessalonians than if they were mentioned alone. It sets them against opponents of the movement. We have seen that the ancient rhetors supported this method for amplifying something of lesser degree.[2]

Re-interpretation of the Opposition. While opposition might make a group of people question what they are doing or saying, in 1 Thess. 2.15 the opposition of the Jews to the churches in Judaea is interpreted

---

1. Jewett's exordium includes 1.1-5 and his *narratio* contains the following sections: congregational imitation (1.6-10); clarification of apostolic example (2.1-12); clarification of Judaean example (2.13-16); Paul's desire for apostolic visit; and *transitus* in benedictory style (3.11-13). The section about the Jews in 1 Thess. 2.14-16 is found within that on the clarification of the Judaean example immediately after the reiteration of thanksgiving in v. 13. The *narratio* is followed by the *probatio* (4.1-5.22) and *peroratio* (5.23-28).

2. *Rh. Al.* 3.1426a.20-29; see also Chapter 5 above.

through Paul's hyperbolic list of the sins of the Jews. Piled one upon the other, it makes the Jews appear to be a great evil.[1] This device legitimizes resistance to all opposition from those who (like the Jews) cause 'the righteous' to suffer. In the case at hand the opponents are the *symphyletai*.

The Formation of a Solid Identity. In this section we examine the implied eschatological categories of 'us' and 'them' in this letter which lead to identity formation. In some other letters Paul has in mind the tripartite language of Jews, Gentiles, and the church of God when he uses the term 'us' (1 Cor. 10.32). However, in 1 Thessalonians he is writing from the perspective of God or from that of the parousia. He has only two categories: the implicit 'us' and 'them' of 2.14-16 and the explicit 'sons of light' and implicit 'sons of darkness' of 5.5-8. In the former case his readers are lined up on the same side as the more eminent models of the righteous who have always suffered (the Lord and the prophets). The ones to be imitated are Paul, the Lord and other persecuted churches. As Castelli puts it,

> In becoming imitators of other's sufferings, their experience is structurally linked to that of all these other persecuted ones. Their sufferings become a way of establishing identity within the group and in the face of 'outsiders', a way for Paul both to praise them and to claim them.[2]

On the other side are the Jews who have always persecuted the righteous and the *symphyletai*. A comparison of the function of hyperbole as polarization between our passage and others will be discussed more fully in Chapter 9.

The explicit 'sons of light' and implicit 'sons of darkness' of 5.5-8 emphasize the parousia where there will be only those who live with the Lord (4.17) and those who are destroyed (5.3). At least one purpose behind this type of polarization is to ensure that doubters are led to a clearer conviction as to which side they are on. In addition, promises of eternal reward and the assurance that divine revenge will befall one's persecutors are sure to lend the righteous much support in remaining steadfast and to brace them for whatever suffering they may yet have to endure.

---

1. *Rh. Al.* 3.1426a.20-29.
2. See now also the recent work by E.A. Castelli, *Imitating Paul: A Discourse of Power* (Louisville, KY: Westminster Press/John Knox, 1991), p. 94.

Denunciation. To place one's opponent completely on the wrong side, an orator frequently amplified or exaggerated the negative results of the opponent's actions and, if possible, repeated a previously held negative judgment. Paul too mentions the negative results of the Jews' actions in hyperbolic fashion: they displease God. That the Jews displease God is a standard accusation in Jewish literature, and that they oppose all humanity was a common view in the Gentile world.[1]

Therefore, it would be reasonable for Paul to use these conventional judgments[2] and to set his statement beside them in order to strengthen his own case, especially since his readers were Gentiles (1.9).

Giving Space to the Opponent on one's own Terms. The author of *Rhetoric to Alexander* advocated that an orator needed to judge the overall effectiveness of either breaking up what he wants to say into parts or saying it all at once. One needed to weigh in each case which would be more effective.[3] It appears that Paul's list castigates the Jews both all at once and in a series of accusations. The overall effect was more intense than if he had either simply stated that the Thessalonians should not be swayed by their opponents or sprinkled accusations throughout the letter.

If Paul's opponents (those who hindered him, v. 15) had arguments against his missionary practice in Thessalonica, he omitted them. It was a standard response to charges to minimize an opponent's views while maximizing one's own points.[4] Paul went beyond that. He omitted the arguments of his Jewish opponents, thereby exposing his readers only to the views presented in vv. 14-16.

Arousing Emotions. Quintilian thought that appeals to emotion were necessary in designing a case against an opponent.[5] As we have seen, it was the duty of the orator to elicit the judge's good will and to divert it from one's opponents.[6] The accuser was to arouse the emotions of

1. See Tacitus, *Hist.* 5.5.
2. See *Rh. Al.* 3.1426a.20-29; see also Chapter 6 above.
3. See *Rh. Al.* 3.1425b.5-10; see Chapter 5 above.
4. See *Rh. Al.* 3.1425b.5-10.
5. *Inst.* 2.17.26-27. See also *On Invention* 1.15.22.
6. See (*captatio benevloentiae*) in *To Gaius Herennius* 1.4.6-1.7.11; *On Invention* 1.15.20–1.18.26. See also Quintilian, *Inst.* 2.17.26-27; 6.1.9.

the judge while the defender had to soften them.[1] It was appropriate for the accuser to employ language that would exaggerate as was expedient.[2] He had to decide what points deserved to 'excite envy, goodwill, dislike or pity' and 'should dwell on those points by which he himself would be most moved were he trying the case'.[3] Paul too stirs the emotions of the readers against their opponents by recounting an exaggerated list of the sins of the Jews who oppose God's plan and the final judgment against them.

Identification with the Writer. Earlier we noted that a favourite method of amplification was to advance a series of statements leading to a climax.[4] This movement primes the listeners for what is to follow: their assent is wanted. In Paul's case his hyperbolic statements march along in quick succession, and their movement prepares the way for his last assertion, the view he wants his readers to hold regarding the current opposition by the Jews and others.

Summary

I have argued that the movement of the phrases of 1 Thess. 2.14-16 leads naturally to the climax in v. 16; the structure of the passage within the plan of the letter is made up of two sets of triads, and the function of polemical hyperbole within the passage is to strengthen the identity of the Thessalonians against their opponents.

We turn now to an investigation of Paul's use of polemical hyperbole in other letters.

1. *Inst.* 6.1.9.
2. *Inst.* 4.1.15.
3. *Inst.* 6.1.9-11.
4. *Inst.* 8.4.27; see Chapter 5 above.

Chapter 8

OTHER INSTANCES OF
POLEMICAL HYPERBOLE IN PAUL'S LETTERS

We have been looking at 1 Thess. 2.14-16 within the context of the letter itself. The argument put forward is that Paul used polemical hyperbole for several reasons: to counter attacks from his opponents whom he deemed to be on the side of error, to convince his readers to be on the side of truth, and to bolster his readers against future attacks from the *symphyletai* who lived in their environment.

Paul's judgment against the Jews who disobey God is equally a judgment against those who persecute the Thessalonians. Paul used hyperbole when describing the sins of the Jews partly because they opposed his work among the Gentiles and he was likely angry about that, and partly because their opposition provided a comparison with those who were bothering the Thessalonians. By amplifying their sins and finally the judgment against them, he polarized the world into the opponents of the church, and the saints. At the same time, his association of common experiences of the church at Thessalonica with those of Judaea automatically elevated the status of the former.

I have suggested that the issues scholars have raised concerning the problem passage can be resolved if we take into account Paul's tendency to engage in polemical hyperbole when he perceived a threat to his converts. But this hypothesis needs to be tested in other places in the letters of Paul. Did Paul use polemical hyperbole in other instances of threatening circumstances?

We shall judge a passage that denigrates people to be polemical hyperbole if it is so by Paul's own standard; that is, if by his own explicit or implicit admission, either in another place or within the same letter, the statements in the passage exceed what he thought at other times, times perhaps less emotionally charged.

To use this standard is completely reasonable, given what is known about the social-historical context of polemic in the world approximately contemporary with Paul. The social context included making conventional denigrating comments[1] about one's opponents. What this kind of exchange indicated was that the opponents were serious rivals. As Seneca puts it, 'People collide only when they are travelling the same path'.[2]

Some examples of conventional denigration include the tendency to call one's opponent a 'hypocrite', a 'charlatan', 'blind' or 'demonic'.[3] Certain vices, such as being lovers of money and glory, were often attributed to opponents. Usually these conventions were not taken as accurate descriptions of the person. Charges were simply applied universally: calling someone a charlatan was an effective way of denigrating any leader.

Sometimes, however, the comment had some basis in reality but was exaggerated. We read in Philo, for example, that his Gentile opponents in Alexandria were 'ready enough with fawning words, but causing universal disaster with their loose and unbridled lips'.[4] Whether or not they were actually 'fawning' is impossible to prove, but the statement about 'universal disaster' is an exaggeration of the harm caused by their speeches.

Competing Hellenistic philosophers tended to brand each other with the same conventional denigrations of their teaching, behaviour and person:

> Their teaching was self-contradictory, or trivial, or it led to bad morals. Their behaviour could be criticized in several ways. Either they preached but did not practice (in which case they were hypocrites), or they lived as they taught and their corrupt lives showed how bad their doctrine was (like the Epicureans). Certain standard categories of vice were automatically attributed to any opponent. They were all lovers of pleasure, lovers of money, and lovers of glory.[5]

It seems to me that these conventions for vilifying persons have the chief concern of the moral philosophers as their content, that is, how one ought to live. What is being said by means of the convention is that a certain rival is in error and is not to be followed and criticisms

1. Johnson, 'Anti-Jewish Slander', pp. 432-33.
2. Seneca, *Ep.* 103.5.
3. Johnson, 'Anti-Jewish Slander', p. 440.
4. Philo, *Leg. Gai.* 25.162 cited in Johnson, 'Anti-Jewish Slander', p. 435.
5. Johnson, 'Anti-Jewish Slander', p. 432.

(true or false) were chosen which would hurt the image of a rival.

Johnson lists some conventions used in Jewish circles against Jewish leaders which he calls slander. The list includes hypocrisy, having a demon, being blind, blaspheming, walking in darkness, being deceitful and so forth.[1] Derogatory polemic generally is typical and conventional. In some cases the accusations are trumped up, in others they are exaggerations, and in some they are both. For instance, the standard charge against Epicureans was that their essence was a 'lack of friends, absence of activity, irreligion, sensuality, and indifference'.[2] These charges have some basis because Epicureans did have communities which separated themselves from the rest of society. However, the list amplifies the most negative portrayal of Epicureans and gives no balance to the picture. That polemical conventions against leaders were exaggerations of negative qualities is illustrated well by Dio of Prusa, who had been a rhetorician before he became a philosopher. As a philosopher he vilified rhetoricians as charlatans, flatterers and fast talkers.[3] Only grudgingly did he admit that they sometimes acted for good (Dio of Prusa, *Oration* 35.9-10).

The reader of Paul's letters can identify many passages in which he used extreme language which, on some other occasion, he might modify or even retract. These cases depend on the context, and one can readily find another context in which he takes a more moderate position on the same topic. Circumcision provides a good example. It can mean that one is severed from Christ (Gal. 5.4), or it can be a matter of indifference (Gal. 5.6; 6.15; 1 Cor. 7.19). This depends on the circumstances: if Paul's Gentile converts are *forced* to accept circumcision, they are severed from Christ, who died in vain if their being circumcised is necessary to salvation. However, in a non-coercive context circumcision does not matter. These two statements can go together: circumcision does not matter, therefore it must not be treated as if it does. In such cases Paul's extreme statement is not hyperbolic; it is his position on a central soteriological issue. It may, however, be hyperbolic in reference to any individuals in the community who had already submitted to circumcision. There is no information to suggest that Paul had them excommunicated as severed from Christ. Apparently they were still members of the church. Thus,

1. Johnson, 'Anti-Jewish Slander', pp. 434-41.
2. Johnson, 'Anti-Jewish Slander', p. 431.
3. Johnson, 'Anti-Jewish Slander', p. 430 (cited from *Oration* 23.11).

his harshest statements are not to be judged as hyperbolic in their own context unless there is evidence to suggest that they are exaggerations.

In other cases extreme statements appear to go beyond the ideal that Paul set for himself. For example, it appears that he was persecuted for not preaching circumcision (Gal. 5.11), and he cursed those who did preach circumcision (Gal. 1.8-9). He also wished that the 'troublers' in Galatia would mutilate themselves. We cannot be sure that his persecutors were the same people as the troublers of the Galatians, but it appears that they took the same position. For the sake of the example, let us assume that they were the same people. Although we cannot prove that Paul was angry when he cursed them or when he wished that the troublers would mutilate themselves,[1] the passage is obviously polemical, and we know that people often make inflammatory statements in polemical situations. We also know that it was Paul's ideal that one should pray for rather than curse one's persecutors (Rom. 12.14). But even if later he repented of having cursed his opponents, it does not mean that he was exaggerating when he uttered curses and maledictions. Perhaps he meant them at the time,[2] without any calculation or awareness that he was saying what he might later wish to retract. If we were to require hyperbole to be a *conscious* exaggeration, we would have to say that statements Paul made when enraged cannot be shown to be hyperbole since we cannot read Paul's mind. It is often possible, however, to determine whether Paul is pressing beyond what he would maintain at another time, and, as was noted in Chapter 6, exaggeration is part of natural speech. I shall now seek to show by exegesis and analysis when Paul's language is extreme, and then look for the rhetorical function of such language. If it can be shown *in what way* his language is extreme, or that he sometimes reveals that he holds a more moderate view, we shall be able to appreciate Paul as a debater who in the heat of controversy sometimes exaggerated and said things that go beyond or seemingly contradict what he says in other, non-polemical contexts. We must try to determine when his comments are fierce assertions of a position he

1. Perhaps Paul had in mind Deut. 23.1—where LXX uses *apokekommenos*—which debars the eunuch from the assembly of the Lord. We cannot be sure. At any rate, the statement is extreme.

2. Cursing was a standard way of designating someone an opponent. Everyone from rival philosophers to rival Jews cursed their opponents. Johnson, 'Anti-Jewish Slander', pp. 440-41.

would seriously maintain and when they are exaggerations employing common conventions to denigrate an opponent.

We shall see that it was not only in 1 Thess. 2.14-16 that Paul used exaggeration in his denigration of opponents. As other examples, we shall look at the terms used in the following places: 2 Corinthians 11 ('superlative apostles' in v. 5, 'false apostles/servants of Satan' in v. 13, and 'servants in Christ' in v. 23) as well as the parallel term 'false brethren' in Galatians 2; the charges against the opponents in 2 Cor. 11.20; 'cunning serpent' and 'pure bride' of 2 Cor. 11.2-3; Paul's comparison of his own hardships with those of his opponents in 2 Cor. 11.23-29; and his statements about the behaviour and motives of Gentiles and Jews in Romans 1 and 2. The question is whether Paul's judgment against some of the other leaders whom he encountered in a polemical context is his final and absolute one. If not, then we consider the judgment to involve hyperbole for the purpose of blaming opponents and drawing others to his own view.

The Terms of 2 Corinthians 11

Chapters 10–13 of 2 Corinthians have sometimes been considered part of a letter by Paul in response to a threat to his apostleship. Victor P. Furnish has given a good review of the various positions taken on this point, and for our purposes we need not deal with this problem.[1] Of these chapters, I am particularly interested in chapter 11. Scholars in the late nineteenth century were drawn to it and there has been much recent interest in it. What arouses the interest is the puzzle of Paul's use of three different main terms for the people he is opposing in the space of 18 verses.[2] These terms are:

1. the 'superlative apostles' (v. 5)
2. the 'false apostles/ servants of Satan' (v. 13)
3. the 'servants of Christ' (v. 23).

Students of this chapter notice that these terms conflict with each other. To make matters even more difficult, some terms are preceded

---

1. See V.P. Furnish, *II Corinthians* (AB, 32A; Garden City, NY: Doubleday, 1984), pp. 35-41, 44-54.

2. For a history of the investigations of this problem, see D. Georgi, *The Opponents of Paul in Second Corinthians* (Philadelphia: Fortress Press, 1986), pp. 1-9.

by accusations which do not seem to fit the term which follows them. For example, just after Paul says that some people preach another Jesus, have a different spirit, and accept a different gospel,[1] he calls them 'superlative apostles'. How are the accusations related to the term? For now I shall simply observe this point, reserving discussion of it until later.

To facilitate study of the terms and the scholarly discussion associated with them, I will give an outline of the key ideas in the chapter and will separate each term under discussion so that other scholars' solutions and my own may be observed more readily.

Key Ideas within 2 Corinthians 11
Note: P. = Paul; C. = the Corinthians

A (11.1-6)

v. 1 — P. asks the C. to bear with him in his *foolishness*.

vv. 2-3 — He fears that the C., like Eve, will be led astray by the *deception and cleverness* of the opponents.

v. 4 — The C. bear with others who preach another Jesus, a different spirit, and a different gospel from P's.

vv. 5-6 — P. is not inferior to these *superlative apostles*; if unskilled in speech, he is not in knowledge.

B (11.7-15)

v. 7 — Did P. sin by abasing himself that the C. might be exalted?

vv. 8-11 — P. took no *money*; he burdened no one; by the truth of Christ he will not cease from this *boast*, a boast which shows that he loves them.

v. 12 — By maintaining his claim to work without burdening the C., he challenges the *boast* of the opponents that they work on the same terms as he does.

v. 13-15 — Such people are *false apostles*, deceitful, servants of Satan.

C (11.16-23)

v. 16 — The C. are not to think P. foolish, but even if they do, he asks them to receive him [bear with him] so that he too may *boast* a little.

vv.17-18 — P. says he speaks in folly, that is, in the *confidence* of *boasting*; many *boast* concerning the flesh; P. will also *boast* of the flesh.

v. 19 — The C. bear with fools, being wise themselves.

v. 20 — The C. bear with those who make slaves of them, etc.

---

1. See parallel accusations in Galatians 1.

v. 21	P. was too weak to treat the C. like that. In whatever way one dares to [*boast*] P., as a *fool*, does also.
vv. 22-23a	Are they Hebrews? Israelites? Sons of Abraham? *Servants of Christ?*

D (11.23b-33)

v. 23b	P. (speaking as if out of his mind) is *more so.*
vv. 23-33	P. [boasts] of his labours and hardships.

Although I have separated the sections of the chapter in order to clarify the discordant terms, I must emphasize that these sections are closely linked: the link is the theme of foolishness and boasting, as we shall see below.

In response to the difficulties of discordant terms (superlative apostles in v. 5, false apostles/servants of Satan in v.13, and servants of Christ in v. 23), there are two main ways of approaching the text.

Two Approaches to Reading the Text

The first approach is aptly described by the words of Adolf Deissmann, who observed—as early as 1926—that many people read Paul in a way that is 'far too exacting'.[1] Such reading immediately notes the different terms and that they are discordant. But the main point is that it settles for the solution that when Paul spoke of the 'superlative apostles' he must have been referring to the Jerusalem apostles; when he said 'false apostles' he meant a different group, people he considered to be non-Christian; and when he said 'servants of Christ' he referred to the first group again.

The second approach contends that Paul wrote against his opposition in a more nuanced fashion and accepts the possibility that the terms refer to the same group, taking into account the polemical context of the statements. More explicitly, it may have been possible for Paul to have called his opponents 'superlative' and 'false' and 'servants of Christ' without our charging him (as Barrett would) with 'using language irresponsibly'.[2]

---

1. Deismann stated that Paul does not proceed in a direct line of argument in controversy and that exegetes have 'treated him far too exactingly in this connection'. A. Deismann, *Paul: A Study in Social and Religious History* (trans. W.E. Wilson; New York: George H. Doran Company, 1926), pp. 104-105.

2. C.K. Barrett, 'Paul's Opponents in 2 Corinthians', in *Essays on Paul* (Philadelphia: Westminster Press, 1982), pp. 60-86 (64). Barrett thought that if all

Obviously I am inclined towards the second approach. Discordant terms should not lead us to propose different groups unless there is proof that the terms are unrelated. In the present case I think that the terms refer to one group and that Paul was using polemical hyperbole in v. 13 to denigrate the apostles whose behaviour he opposed in Corinth. His use of 'false apostles' in v. 13 was not his final and absolute judgment of the apostles but a polemical exaggeration (perhaps an early Christian convention[1] to use against opponents) which temporarily denigrates. If this hypothesis is correct, it calls into question an implicit assumption that the meaning of the chapter can be determined on the basis of a prejudgment about what Paul could or could not have said. We shall see that even some of those who do not partition the text have fallen prey to this tendency.

Reading 2 Corinthians 11 too Exactingly

By far most solutions to date[2] designate 'superlative apostles', 'false apostles' and 'apostles of Christ' as referring to two groups. As I have noted above, reference to the 'superlative apostles' in 2 Cor. 11.5 appears just after the list of items against the people causing trouble in Corinth, those preaching another Jesus, another spirit and a different gospel (v. 4). Käsemann called the discordance between verses 4 and 5 a *Sprunghaftigkeit*.[3] Those who give the text an 'exacting' reading

the terms referred to the same group, one would have to question Paul's use of language.

1. Passages which use terms like 'false teacher' (2 Pet. 2.1), 'false prophet' (Mt. 7.15; 24.11, 24; Mk 13.22; Lk. 6.26; 1 Jn 4.1), and 'false witness' (Mt. 26.60; 15.19; 26.59; 1 Cor. 15.15) may reflect standard Christian conventions of polemical exaggeration or perhaps slander. Such a study of early Christian literature after the destruction of the Jerusalem temple and during the institutionalizing tendency of the church is beyond the boundaries of this research project.

2. See Furnish, *II Corinthians*.

3. See Käsemann, 'Die Legitimität des Apostels', *ZNW* 41 (1942), pp. 33-71, cited by C.K. Barrett, 'Paul's Opponents in 2 Corinthians', *NTS* 17 (1971), pp. 233-54 (242-43). For Bultmann, the transition Käsemann proposed involved too much *Sprunghaftigkeit* to be credible. R. Bultmann, *Exegetische Probleme des zweiten Korintherbriefes* (Uppsala: Wretman, 1947), pp. 203-204. Kümmel thought that a solution of partition need be proposed only if one cannot imagine Paul engaging in controversy with the Jerusalem church (cf. Gal. 1.8-9; 2.5-9, 11, 14). Kümmel took into consideration the polemical context of the statements and saw that Paul could rage against his opponents and still consider them to be part of the

want to partition it, believing that the 'superlative apostles' cannot be the same group of people as those who preached a different gospel.

Barrett, on the other hand, saw no deep discordance; that is, he considered the thought continuous. Verse 5 gives the third of three grounds for the appeal of v. 1. According to Barrett, Paul is saying, 'I ask you to put up with me: a) for I am...really concerned about you; b) for you put up with a false apostle who preaches a false Gospel; c) for I am equal to the highest apostles of all'.[1]

Although Barrett was correct in observing that the thought is continuous, he could not equate the 'superlative apostles' of v. 5 with those accused in v. 4. Before examining his reason for rejecting these verses as referring to the same group, it is necessary to summarize his arguments for the position that the 'superlative apostles' refers either to the Jerusalem apostles in general or Peter and company in particular.

Barrett reasoned that 'superlative apostles' could be 'mild irony'[2] toward the Jerusalem apostles[3] on the basis of the parallel in Galatians 2 where Paul used a similar tone in calling them 'pillars'. Further, he noted that in Galatians 2 Paul deals with two groups: the false brethren and the Jerusalem apostles, Peter, James and John.

Christian movement. W.G. Kümmel, *An die Korinther I.II* (HNT, 9; Tübingen: Mohr, 1969), II, p. 210.

1. C.K. Barrett, *A Commentary on the Second Epistle to the Corinthians* (London: A. & C. Black, 1973), p. 278.

2. I would suggest sarcasm. See C.H. Talbert, *Reading Corinthians: A Literary and Theological Commentary on 1 and 2 Corinthians* (New York: Crossroad, 1987), p. 121. Talbert is correct in saying that it is sarcastic because of the exaggerated claims of the opponents.

3. C.K. Barrett, 'Christianity at Corinth' (Manson Memorial Lectures, John Rylands Library, Manchester, no. 3, 1964), pp. 269-97 (296). Käsemann thought that the presence of the term 'superlative apostles' indicates that Paul's opponents could invoke the Jerusalem apostles and that this was an embarrassment to him. 'He intends to reckon relentlessly with the intruders in Corinth, yet he is neither able nor willing to come into conflict with Jerusalem and the primitive apostles... Perhaps we may formulate the matter thus: He defends himself against the primitive apostles, and smites the intruders in Corinth.' Käsemann, 'Die Legitimität des Apostels', p. 48. (p. 30 of the reprint). See also Barrett, 'Paul's Opponents', p. 70; *idem*, *Commentary on Second Corinthians*, p. 287; F.F. Bruce, *1 and 2 Corinthians* (NCB; London: Oliphants, 1971), p. 239; J. Héring, *The Second Epistle of Saint Paul to the Corinthians* (trans. A.W. Heathcote and P.J. Allcock; London: Epworth Press, 1967), pp. 79-80.

Barrett proposed that since the attitude was the same, namely, a vigorous attack upon the false apostles or false brethren and 'an ironical but unaggressive attitude to...the "pillars"',[1] so were the persons concerned: some false people and the Jerusalem apostles. Thus for him either the 'superlative apostles' was an accurate descriptive term for either those of Jerusalem[2] in general or possibly Peter[3] and his supporters in particular, or in both cases the tone was mild irony[4] (cf. 2 Cor. 11.5; 1 Cor. 15.9; Gal. 2.6, 9). If, by the mild irony of 'superlative apostles', Peter was in his mind, Paul refrains from mentioning him by name because of his eminence and Paul's respect for him.

How is one to account for Barrett's refusal to accept vv. 4 and 5 as referring to the same group? Is it not that he implicitly assumes that the Jerusalem apostles *must* not be charged with preaching another Jesus, and so forth? We see more of this implicit principle of

1. Barrett, *Commentary on Second Corinthians*, p. 278.

2. Not everyone thought that Paul was referring to the Jerusalem apostles. See Lütgert, who thought that they could not have been Judaizers because there is no insistence on circumcision. Rather, they were gnostics and charismatics of Jewish origin, libertine in the interpretation and practice of Christian freedom. W. Lütgert, *Freiheitspredigt und Schwärmgeister in Korinth* (Gütersloh: Bertelsmann, 1908), cited in C.K. Barrett, 'Christianity and Corinth', in his *Essays on Paul*, pp. 1-27 (15).

3. Barrett argues that the number of times Peter is mentioned (1 Cor. 1.12; 3.22; 15.5) as distinct from the other apostles in the Corinthian correspondence indicates that Peter had likely visited Corinth at one time and that a group called the 'Cephas group' had emerged. See 'Cephas and Corinth', in *Essays on Paul*, pp. 28-39 (36). The possibility that Peter had visited Corinth at one time is strengthened when it is recalled that from Gal. 2 we learn that Peter had travelled to Antioch. T.W. Manson proposed that there was an organized attempt to instil Palestinian piety and orthodoxy into Gentile churches. See T.W. Manson, 'The Corinthian Correspondence (1)', in M. Black (ed.), *Studies in the Gospels and Epistles* (Manchester: Manchester University Press, 1962), pp. 190-209, cited by C.K. Barrett in 'Cephas and Corinth', p. 35. That Peter was a potential danger for schism in Corinth might be inferred from 1 Cor. 3.22, where his name slips into a section about those who would make comparisons between Apollos and Paul. This suggests that the entire section (1 Cor. 3.3-23) might have Peter primarily in mind (Barrett, 'Cephas and Corinth', p. 32.

4. C.K. Barrett, *A Commentary on the First Epistle to the Corinthians* (BNTC; London: A. & C. Black, 1968), p. 44; 'Cephas and Corinth', in *Essays on Paul*, pp. 28-39 (37-38).

interpretation in Barrett's insistence that the 'superlative apostles' could not be the 'false apostles' of v. 13: 'Paul is unlikely to have made the modest claim that he was not excelled by those whom in the context (verses 13-15) he was to describe as the servants of Satan'.[1] Further, he reasoned that Paul would not have bothered to compare himself with 'false apostles', so they *cannot* be the 'servants of Christ' with whom he compares himself at length in vv. 23-29.[2] For Barrett the only reasonable solution is to propose two groups of opponents: the Jerusalem apostles, whom Paul treats with irony, and another group, whom he treats with 'vigorous antipathy'.[3] The only other possibility, which he seems not to have seriously entertained, is to suggest that 'Paul was lashing out blindly, and using language irresponsibly'.[4]

Although Barrett proposed that Peter was behind the difficulties in Corinth, it is clear that he could not bring himself to have Peter criticized beyond the mildest rebuke and was far from calling him a 'false apostle'. When he recalled Peter's behaviour in Antioch, Barrett said that Peter's heart was in the right place, but that he was easily frightened, influenced and manipulated. Therefore, in Corinth 'more subtle and less scrupulous ecclesiastical politicians found him useful as a figure-head. Hence Paul's embarrassment.'[5] Construing

---

1. Barrett, *Commentary on Second Corinthians*, p. 278. See also Käsemann, 'Die Legitimität des Apostels', p. 46 (p. 27 of the reprint).

2. Filson also thought that because Paul said that they were 'false', he must have considered them to be non-Christians. As he put it, 'Paul did not regard them as Christians. Moreover, he felt that they never had been Christians', F.V. Filson, *St Paul's Conception of Recompense* (Leipzig: Hinrichs, 1931), p. 95. This raises the problem of anachronism: Christianity and Judaism are now two separate religions, but in the first century the boundary was not yet firm. Further, the Christian movement was not monolithic. We shall return to this topic in the next two chapters. For now, let us assume that 'Christian' denotes the spectrum of persons within the early first century who held to faith in Jesus Christ as Messiah and Lord and looked forward to being with him in the day of the Lord.

3. Barrett, 'Cephas and Corinth', p. 37.

4. See Barrett, 'Paul's Opponents in 2 Corinthians', in *Essays on Paul*, p. 64. Héring was also puzzled about Paul's sweeping generalizations: 'the assimilation of false brethren into instruments of Satan adds up to an enormous accusation. It may be asked, therefore, whether the Apostle Paul had not other more precise complaints of a moral nature against them...', Héring, *The Second Epistle to the Corinthians*, p. 81.

5. Barrett, 'Cephas and Corinth', p. 37.

2 Cor. 10.13 as a territorial dispute, Barrett links the verse to the original agreement with Peter (Gal. 2). It was the embarrassment of the opponents using Peter's name that led to Paul's use of gentle irony when referring to the Jerusalem apostles, while reserving his vigorous attack for the 'less scrupulous ecclesiastical politicians'.[1]

More of this tendency to protect Peter is seen in Barrett's interpretation of 2 Corinthians 11, where Paul distinguishes a true apostleship from a false one. He notes Paul's contention that true apostleship has to do with self-sacrifice, such as his not taking money for his work among the Corinthians; but lest we look critically at Peter, Barrett says that Cephas would doubtless have made sacrifices too in circumstances that he thought called for them. This 'doubtless' fact, according to Barrett, marks him out as a true apostle rather than a false one.[2] This interpretation is another indication of Barrett's bias towards keeping Peter from harsh criticism, forcing him to propose two separate groups in 2 Corinthians 11.

Thus, a 'far too exacting' reading implies certain assumptions about what could or could not have been said. At the same time, such a reading takes Paul's denunciations as his final and absolute judgment and extrapolates from them. Barrett is not alone in using an 'exacting reading'. For example, in attempting to describe the characteristics of the opponents in 2 Corinthians 11, scholars' interpretations range from using Paul's own word 'deceitful',[3] to a host of imposed labels such as 'a poor demeanour',[4] 'hypocritical',[5] and to phrases claiming that the superlative apostles 'availed themselves of every means to deceive and pervert the people'[6] and 'in their heart of hearts...were afraid that people would see through them'.[7] Further, Paul's remarks are taken as empirical evidence of his considered opinions about his opponents. Bornkamm understands 2 Corinthians 11 to indicate Paul's

1. Barrett, 'Cephas and Corinth', p. 37.
2. Barrett, *Commentary on Second Corinthians*, p. 285.
3. J.J. Gunther, *St Paul's Opponents and their Background: A Study of Apocalyptic and Jewish Sectarian Teachings* (Leiden: Brill, 1973), p. 63.
4. Munck, *Paul and Salvation*, p. 186.
5. Bultmann, *Second Corinthians*, p. 208.
6. C. Hodge, *An Exposition of the Second Epistle to the Corinthians* (Grand Rapids: Eerdmans, n.d.), p. 263.
7. W. Barclay, *The Letters to the Corinthians* (Edinburgh: Saint Andrews Press, 2nd edn, 1965), p. 278.

separating truth from lies, truth from false belief, and God from
Satan.[1] Barrett proposed that the passage reveals three kinds of
Judaism. Two of them are worthy and have sincere motives: the
Jerusalem apostles and Paul. The third, the 'false apostles', were
envoys of the Jerusalem church who accepted

> a veneer of non-Jewish practice. If they could make a stronger impression
> by adopting a gnostic framework of thought and the ecstatic accompani-
> ments of pagan religion they were willing to do so... They were making
> (so it seemed to Paul) the worst of both worlds, and were neither honest
> Jews nor honest Christians, but ultimately pagan—the servants of Satan,
> pretending to be apostles and servants of righteousness.[2]

These readings do not allow for Paul's writings to have nuance and
flavour, both of which must be appreciated if we are to properly
understand his thought.

A Nuanced Reading
A more nuanced reading allows Paul to have some scope in using
rhetorical devices to make his case, thereby giving his letters a rich
rather than a flat reading. In 2 Corinthians 11 a nuanced reading
allows for the possibility that Paul called his opponents 'apostles of
Satan' and 'superlative apostles' as part of his polemic against them,
while at the same time acknowledging that they were 'apostles of
Christ'. Talbert saw this merit. He argued that the consensus of 'good
Paul' versus 'bad interlopers' is not good exegesis: 'Both the ministry
of Paul and that of the visiting apostles encompassed preaching,
miracle, and suffering service on behalf of Christ. If so, then where
did the difference lie?'[3]

My proposal of a more nuanced reading can make sense of the
conflicting terms 'superlative apostles', 'false apostles' and 'apostles of
Christ' without partitioning the chapter into unnecessary disparate
sections. I shall compare my nuanced reading of 2 Corinthians 11,

---

1.   Bornkamm, *Paul*, p. 172.
2.   Barrett, 'Paul's Opponents in II Corinthians', p. 254. See also his
'*Pseudapostoloi* (2 Cor. 11.13)', in *Essays on Paul*, pp. 87-107.
3.   Talbert, *Reading Corinthians*, p. 130. See now also T. Callan,
*Psychological Perspectives of the Life of Paul: An Application of the Methodology of
Gerd Theissen* (Lampeter, Wales: Edwin Mellen Press, 1990), pp. 32-36. Caution
must be exercised in suggesting psychological interpretations. Callan argues that Paul
was competing with opponents who appear to have credibility.

which can make sense of the passage as it stands, with Barrett's flat reading, which leads to a partition theory to understand the conflicting terms. Two questions must be asked of his reading:

1. Does the text support the position that there were two separate groups being attacked by Paul?
2. If Peter stood behind the opponents, does that justify Barrett's accusation that Paul was using language irresponsibly when he called him a 'false apostle'?

The Unity of the Passage

With respect to Barrett's hypothesis of two separate groups, one has to imagine 2 Corinthians 11 as having two sections, vv. 5-6 and 23-29, referring to the Jerusalem apostles, separated by another section (11.7-13) plus v. 4 (which is completely severed from its real context), referring to the false apostles. The theory of two groups would make sense if the charges of vv. 2-4 and those of vv. 7-12 were reversed. For it is the accusation that the opponents take money for their work (v. 12) which Barrett has associated with the Jerusalem apostles (1 Cor. 9.4-7), and it is reasonable to charge someone who preaches another Jesus (2 Cor. 11.3) with being a 'false apostle' and a 'deceitful workman' (v. 13).

Unfortunately for the partition hypothesis, we simply cannot scramble the verses in this way. If we leave the verses where they are but still maintain that 'superlative' and 'false' apostles were two different groups, we must suppose Paul to have been extremely confused in arguing the case against them. Not only did he fail to let the reader know that he faced two different groups, he also mixed up his accusations, charging the superlative apostles with preaching another Jesus and the servants of Satan with falsely claiming to work on the same terms as he.

Since the charges are not reversed, and since Barrett argued successfully that Paul might have in mind Peter or the Jerusalem apostles, why not admit that Paul could, in anger, call them 'false apostles'? This solution explains the passage while maintaining its unity.

My view is that the charges and the terminology of the chapter actually fit together. In their boast that they work on the same basis as Paul, the opponents are false. They impose themselves on the

Corinthians who in turn submit.[1] The accusation in v. 20 that the opponents prey upon the Corinthians and make slaves of them is understandable if it refers to taking money from them (vv. 7-12). In effect, to require payment is to preach a different Jesus from the one Paul preaches and it is also to accept a different gospel and have a different spirit (v. 4) from Paul's. This financial support of the opponents[2] who claim to work on the same terms as Paul can logically constitute the deception of both vv. 2-3 and v. 13[3] and forms the background of the charge of 'false apostles/servants of Satan' and the sarcastic (through exaggeration) term 'superlative apostles'.

The sarcasm of the latter term is not all that surprising because, as Bultmann noted, ch. 11 is completely set in a context of 'foolishness' beginning with v. 1 and ending in 12.13.[4] To compare himself with the opponents who commend themselves is, according to Paul, foolishness. Nonetheless, he engages in it.

1.   It seems that they claim to work on the same basis as Paul. They accepted or claimed the right to be supported by the Corinthians. While Paul had been with them, he had received money from Macedonia and apparently this led to his being misunderstood. The Corinthians wondered if he loved them less, or if he had been using money from the Jerusalem collection to line his own pockets. See Furnish, *II Corinthians*, p. 38.

2.   If Paul was criticized as inferior by some who were financially supported by the Corinthians, he took advantage of his supporting himself in order to prove his love for his church. But this stance also led to misunderstandings with the Corinthians. Holmberg has noted 'the close connection between financial relations and authority relations. An unclear, unbalanced and eventually doubtful financial relation inevitably causes any authority relation between the parties to deteriorate. And because authority is so often expressed by a financial obligation, the absence of any financial obligation where this could be expected affects adversely even an authority or power relation built on quite another basis.' B. Holmberg, *Paul and Power: The Structure of Authority in the Primitive Church as Reflected in the Pauline Epistles* (Philadelphia: Fortress Press, 1978), p. 93. Paul's refusal to accept financial support from the Corinthians led to an unfavourable interpretation of the situation. They thought that perhaps they were not as respected and loved as other churches (2 Cor. 11.11; 12.13, 15), that perhaps they had not as yet been given the full share of spiritual gifts (2 Cor. 12.13a), or that perhaps Paul is inferior to those apostles who do not hesitate to accept support (2 Cor. 11.5-13, 20; 12.11-13). See Holmberg, *Paul and Power*, p. 92.

3.   It is also likely that the charge of deception was lodged against Paul by his opponents (2 Cor. 12.16-18).

4.   Now see Furnish, *II Corinthians*, p. 47.

The opponents boast of their qualifications. Herein lies the reason for Paul's term 'superlative apostles' (11.5 and 12.11), which does not reflect his true view. Paul says that he meets every qualification that they have: in the case of the last term (being a servant of Christ) he boasts of superior status, which is then proved by his boast of labours and hardships. The Corinthians have forced him to take up this boast in not commending him to these 'superlative apostles' (12.11). Just as the serpent deluded Eve through its cleverness, they have deluded the Corinthians through their self-commendations (10.12). Thus, 'superlative apostles' is indeed a term of sarcasm.[1]

In vv. 22-23 there is a series of four questions, the last of which is 'Are they "servants of Christ"?' Paul responds, 'I am a better one'. Thrall[2] has noted the grammatical linkage between the four designations in 11.22. To the objection that in vv. 19-20 Paul is describing a different group from those described in vv. 21-23, Thrall notes that the *tis* (anyone) of v. 21 has the same reference as the *tis* of v. 20, clearly the opponents in Corinth.[3] The themes of foolishness and boasting recur in this section and support Thrall's view of its unity. When it is observed that these two themes pervade ch. 11 and were already present in 10.12-18, it is reasonable to treat the chapter as a unity.

Scott E. McClelland also saw that the chapter should be treated as a unity.[4] Nevertheless, he still thought that Paul could have used either the negative terms ('false apostles', 'servants of Satan') or the positive ones ('superlative apostles', 'servants of Christ') only of his opponents. He settled for the negative terms. How did he explain the positive ones? He claimed that when Paul said 'servants of Christ' he was merely repeating the self-description of the opponents and not giving his true view. After all, had he not called them 'false apostles' in 11.13? The latter was Paul's *serious* view.[5] McClelland realized that

1.   See Talbert, *Reading Corinthians*, p. 121: 'The designation of them as superlative is sarcastic because of their exaggerated claims for themselves'.

2.   M.E. Thrall, 'Super-Apostles, Servants of Christ, and Servants of Satan', *JSNT* 6 (1980), pp. 42-57.

3.   Thrall, 'Super-Apostles', p. 51.

4.   S.E. McClelland, '"Super-Apostles, Servants of Christ, Servants of Satan": A Response', *JSNT* 14 (1982), pp. 82-87.

5.   See also C. Forbes, '"Unaccustomed as I Am": St Paul the Public Speaker in Corinth', *Buried History* 19 (1983), pp. 11-16 (14).

the positive terms assume that the opponents are Christian. In his judgment that such positive comments must have been self-designations and not Paul's own view, he reveals his bias about what Paul could have said: Paul *could not* have impugned Christians with the denunciation 'false apostles'.

According to McClelland, Paul did not believe his opponents to be 'legitimate representatives of any branch of the Church at large'.[1] If they had any connection with Jerusalem it might have been of the type of infiltration by 'false (non-)Christian brethren',[2] as in Galatia. He proposes that the Corinthian opponents may have been 'ethnic and religious Jews who masqueraded as Christian leaders in an attempt to impede the gospel, especially the gospel as delivered by Paul'.[3]

This is all questionable. McClelland's last point, that the opponents were Jews who were masquerading as Christians, is difficult to entertain seriously. In the first place, it appears that Paul was accused of lacking any special relationship with Christ (10.7), of being inferior with regard to religious knowledge (11.6), of being an inept public speaker (10.10-11; 11.6), of not being able to carry out the threats he made in his letters,[4] and of conducting himself according to worldly standards.[5] These accusations are not likely to have been made by non-Christian Jews. Why would they have been concerned about these matters, which did not impinge upon the Jewish community in any way?

If the opponents had been Jews, we might have expected them to make accusations regarding Paul's activities among the Gentiles which called the Jewish law into question. But these issues are nowhere in sight. Further, we have Paul's own willingness, however grudging, to

---

1. McClelland, 'Super-Apostles', p. 85.
2. McClelland, 'Super-Apostles', p. 86.
3. McClelland, 'Super-Apostles', p. 86.
4. See D.W. Oostendorp, *Another Jesus: A Gospel of Jewish-Christian Superiority in II Corinthians* (Kampen: Kok, 1967), pp. 7-16. Oostendorp proposes that there was one front and that Paul had failed to punish the wrongdoers as he said he would in 2 Cor. 13.1-4. The opponents, on the other hand, were able to assert their authority when punishment was required (v. 20) and they also expected to be supported. Francis Watson holds a similar view and thinks that Paul was accused of being a 'false apostle' because of his inability to punish the wrongdoers. See F. Watson, '2 Cor. X–XIII and Paul's Painful Letter to the Corinthians', *JTS* 35 (1984), pp. 324-46 (344).
5. See Furnish, *II Corinthians*, p. 50.

be compared with the opponents in 11.22; and as Thrall has pointed out, there is sufficient grammatical linkage to conclude that if Paul accepted the first three terms (Hebrews, Israelites and descendants of Abraham), there is no reason to suppose that he did not accept the fourth, that they were 'servants of Christ'.[1]

Additionally there is the matter of the placement of Paul's real view, which McClelland finds in 2 Cor. 11.13-15.[2] It would be strange for Paul to have placed his true view in the middle of the polemic. Should it not be placed at the beginning or at the end? According to Aristotle (*Rh.* 3.19.1), one ought to recapitulate the 'serious view' at the end of a piece so that the audience gets the point. Forbes, too, did not see this difficulty when he proposed that v. 13 was Paul's serious view. I suspect that the reason he did not see it is the same as McClelland's: if Paul called someone a 'false apostle' it is assumed that this must have been his final and absolute view.

Was Paul Using Language Irresponsibly?

Assuming that 2 Corinthians 11 is a unity, we need to address the claim that Paul used language 'irresponsibly' in calling Peter a false apostle. Barrett suggested that in this chapter Paul argued that true apostleship had to do with self-sacrifice and that, even with Paul himself as the standard against which true apostleship was to be measured, Peter undoubtedly passed the test with flying colours. In fact, however, the text goes in the opposite direction.

In 1 Cor. 9.4-7 Paul states that Peter got paid for his work; thus if Peter claimed to be working on the same terms as Paul (2 Cor. 11.7-12), Peter could logically have been accused of being a 'false apostle'.

Thrall has recently shown that the tradition of Jesus' calling Peter something equivalent to a servant of Satan as well as an apostle (Mt. 16.16-23/Mk 8.33/Lk. 22.31-32) may have been known to Paul.[3] If Jesus could do it, why not Paul? The harshness of the words is not unusual in religious polemic. Since in other contexts Jesus is reported to have thought otherwise of Peter (cf., for example, the deliverance of the keys to the kingdom in Mt. 16.18-19), then his statement that Peter was in league with Satan was hyperbolic and was

---

1. Thrall, 'Super-Apostles', pp. 50-51.
2. McClelland, 'Super-Apostles', p. 86.
3. Thrall, 'Super-Apostles', p. 55.

not the final assessment of him in the tradition. At the least, the tradition asserts that in questioning the necessity for him to suffer and die Peter was not supportive of Jesus.

According to Thrall, Paul recalled this tradition when the opponents praised Peter and presented themselves as having his support. Thus, Paul saw his opponents as playing Peter's dual role as servant of Satan and of Christ and used the term 'servant of Satan' as a warning such as that reflected in Lk. 22.31. Nevertheless, like Peter, the opponents were also servants of Christ.[1] It should not go unnoticed that in Gal. 2.11 Paul says that 'Peter stood condemned'. I think that this judgment is not so very far from that of 2 Cor. 11.13.

If Peter could be called a 'false apostle' without being considered outside the Christian movement, then we need to consider the possibility that the opponents were not Peter himself and his co-workers but others who enjoyed the support of Peter or the Jerusalem apostles. Again, Paul's calling the opponents 'false apostles' does not necessarily mean that he considered them to be outside the Christian movement. Rather, it can mean that they were false on some point: in this case, the claim that they worked on the same terms as Paul.

To sum up, we have seen that the term 'false apostles' alone will not reveal Paul's meaning. He may have meant that the opponents falsely claim to be apostles or that they are apostles who are false on some point. If the chapter is understood as of one piece and as referring to one group, he may have been indicating a group of Christian apostles whom he considered false in regard to their claiming to work on the same basis as he did, because they required payment for their ministry. This seems to be the most likely interpretation, since he recoils from his statement that he is a better apostle than they are.

I have argued that Peter could be called both a 'false apostle' and a 'servant of Christ'. Even if the opponents were *not* Peter, James or John, Paul accepts them as Christians. Since 'false apostles' is not his

---

1.   McClelland, 'Super-Apostles', p. 52. Thrall cites O. Betz as noting a parallel from the Dead Sea Scrolls by which members of a group might be denounced without being ultimately rejected, thus allowing for the possibility that the 'false apostles' are not a separate group from the 'superlative apostles': the psalmist of Qumran thought that members of the community could become Belial's mouthpiece while not being abandoned by God. See O. Betz, 'Felsenmann und Felsen-gemeinde', *ZNW* 48 (1957), pp. 49-77. The relevant passages in the Dead Sea Scrolls are from 1QS8; 1QH 6.91-31, esp. v. 22.

final and absolute judgment, this term is hyperbolic and is used in polemic to be, as Bultmann said, 'a sharp attempt to open the eyes of the Corinthians'.[1] When he is in situations of serious opposition, Paul lashes out in a way that appears to contradict what he says elsewhere. As I have noted, some propose that if Paul used contradictory terms to refer to the same group, he was using language irresponsibly. On the contrary, the apparent contradictions make sense if we consider Paul's use of polemical hyperbole. Situations like the one in Corinth call forth his most intense polemic. His extreme outbursts are followed or preceded by more moderate, sometimes contradictory statements. The extreme remarks rally his church against the opponents and to his side.

When we take full account of the context of polemics and the purpose of the letter, there is no *Sprunghaftigkeit*, the unity of the chapter is maintained, and the meaning of the chapter is clear: the terms 'superlative apostles' and 'false apostles' are both polemical hyperbole, and their force is also sarcastic. Barrett's flat reading is clearly not productive. Paul's nuanced writing requires of the reader an equally nuanced reading.

Before considering the polemical hyperbole in 2 Cor. 11.21-29, let us examine the term 'false brethren' from Galatians 2, which is parallel to 'false apostles' and refers to Christians as well, as we shall see below.

'False Brethren' in Galatians 2.4

The meaning of the term 'false brethren' cannot be defined precisely. It could mean 'people who are pretending to be brethren' or 'brethren who have gone false on this point'. The term itself cannot illuminate Paul's meaning, and thus other evidence must be brought to bear upon it.

The term 'false brethren' occurs in Galatians 2 where, at the meeting in Jerusalem with Peter, James and John, some were present who opposed Paul's handling of the entrance of Gentiles into the Christian movement. Paul implies that their motives were full of deceit when he says that they came in 'secretly' and 'to spy out our freedom...that they might bring us into bondage'; however, there is

---

1.   Bultmann, *Exegetische Probleme*, p. 25.

nothing in Galatians which indicates that Paul considered them non-Christian.[1] They were present in Jerusalem and had access to a meeting of the highest ranking officials. There is no evidence that the 'pillars' threw these 'deceitful ones' out of the meeting. Further, it is noteworthy that the meeting was with 'those who were of repute, the pillars' (Gal. 2.2, 6, 9). It was not a public meeting of Christians which false Christians might infiltrate. Thus, the 'false brethren' were known to the 'pillars'. That Paul made accusations against them for opposing his own view that Gentiles need not be circumcised is no proof that he did not consider them to be Christians. Neither is the implication that they were deceitful, because this seems to be the standard rhetoric of polemic.[2] (The Corinthians had said the same of Paul [2 Cor. 12.16].) The use of 'false' in Galatians 2 and 2 Corinthians 11 is not sufficient to prove that Paul thought his opponents were not within the Christian movement.

If all we had were the Galatians text, we might be inclined to take the meaning of 'false brethren' as 'brethren falsely so-called'. However, on the basis of other letters it is reasonable to think that Paul meant 'brethren gone wrong on some point'. E. Earle Ellis has noted that in the letters of Paul 'brethren' denotes Christians in general and also itinerant missionaries.[3] The term *philoi* was standard in speaking of those within a philosophical movement, and Paul uses the term 'brethren' in addressing other Christians (e.g., 1 Thess. 5.1; Gal. 4.12; 1 Cor. 12.1; 2 Cor. 8.1; Rom. 7.1). The term also appears in the four Gospels as a designation of Jesus' disciples (Mt. 5.22-24, 47; Mk 3.33-35; Lk. 22.32; Jn 20.17). Paul portrayed Christian relationships as determined by God's call and not human virtues (Rom. 1.1, 5; 1 Cor. 1.1-2; 2 Cor. 1.1; Gal. 1.1; 1 Thess. 1.4-5). Thus, Paul's use of the term 'brethren' in Gal. 2.4 may imply his recognition of their essential call by God but their being false on some point (likely the belief that Gentiles needed to be circumcised).

Even stronger support comes to us from Romans, where Paul asked the church to pray that his 'service for Jerusalem may be acceptable to

---

1. See now G. Lüdemann, *Opposition to Paul in Jewish Christianity* (trans. M.E. Boring; Minneapolis: Fortress Press, 1989), pp. 99-101.

2. See Johnson, 'Anti-Jewish Slander'.

3. Further, in Qumran and the rabbinic literature, the term sometimes designates a religious order. See E.E. Ellis, 'Paul and his Co-Workers', *NTS* 17 (1970–71), pp. 437-52 (445-48 and esp. 451).

the saints' (Rom. 15.31). This shows his continued awareness that not everyone in Jerusalem approved of his mission. There is no reason to think that the people whom he previously called 'false brethren' (Gal. 2.4) had changed their ways. On the contrary, in his worry about how he would be received there is a hint that they had not done so. If 'false brethren' in Galatians are 'saints' in Romans, which seems probable, 'false' means 'in error on a given point'. They were still 'brethren'.

In contrast to his letter to the church at Rome, in Gal. 2.11-12 Paul tries to distinguish the false brethren from Peter. He shows that Peter held a mediating position (he shook hands with Paul) until at Antioch he received the message from James. Then Peter withdrew from fellowship with the Gentiles and Paul called his behaviour hypocrisy (*hypokrisei*). Paul's statement that Peter would 'compel' (Gal. 2.14) rhetorically equates him with the false brethren (2.3-4; cf. 6.12). Further, Peter's behaviour implied that he held the same or similar views regarding 'compelling' the Gentiles to be circumcised as did the 'false brethren' of Galatians 2. Even though Paul said that Peter 'stood *condemned*' (Gal. 2.11), he did not cut Peter off from the community or propose that such action be taken. Rather, he confronted him with his hypocrisy. Thus, if at times Paul can rhetorically equate Peter and the false brethren as holding the same views but at other times grant Peter a mediating position and accept him as within the camp of Christianity,[1] then it is reasonable to conclude that the 'false brethren' were also within the Christian movement.

What Galatians has in common with 2 Corinthians 11 is the type of polemical language found in both,[2] not the number of groups that Paul was addressing, although it is worth noting that the position of the false brethren was likely nearer that of James[3] than is usually realized.

---

1. Paul refers to Peter in a more neutral way in his first letter to the Corinthians (1 Cor. 1.12; 3.2; 9.5; 15.5).
2. See the parallel charges of Gal. 1.6-9 and 2 Cor. 11.4. These similarities indicate Paul's polemical style.
3. See A.F. Segal, *Rebecca's Children: Judaism and Christianity in the Roman World* (Cambridge, MA: Harvard University Press, 1986), pp. 112-13. Segal notes the serious and ongoing disagreement and opposition between Paul and the Jerusalem leaders. See also Francis Watson, who thought that Paul exaggerated the extent to which his understanding of the Gentile mission was accepted at Jerusalem. Watson, *Paul, Judaism, and the Gentiles*, p. 55.

In fact, it may well be that in the allegory of Sarah and Hagar Paul impugns the Jerusalem church with the terms 'flesh' and 'bondage' (Gal. 4.21-31). There may be an association of the sons of slavery, the Jerusalem church and the false brethren who were trying to bring the Gentiles into bondage. Paul does not specifically refer to the Jerusalem church, but neither is he careful to exclude it. Who else can be meant by 'the Jerusalem below'? This question will be discussed further in Chapter 9.

With a more nuanced reading of Galatians 2, 'false brethren' can be understood as polemical hyperbole because the persons accused seem to hold similar views to some of the Jerusalem apostles and are therefore Christian. Further, Paul could not have them removed as he could the man who was living with his father's wife in the congregation at Corinth (cf. *airein* 'to remove' in 1 Cor. 5.2), or at least he does not attempt to do so. In addition, at more reflective moments Paul could admit that he was taking up a collection for them which he hoped would be received (Rom. 15.31).

A more sharply perceptive approach to terms like 'false brethren' and 'false apostles' yields information about Paul's response to opposition to certain people within the Christian movement and moves away from the assumption that the terms indicate empirical evidence about non-Christian groups unless stronger evidence on other grounds can be obtained. My work on the 'false brethren' of Gal. 2.4 and the 'false apostles' of 2 Cor. 11.13 indicates that we must use caution before assuming that Paul at calmer moments actually believed all that his words against the Jewish people in 1 Thess. 2.14-16 implied. We return now to 2 Corinthians 11 and examine Paul's polemic against the behaviour of his opponents. Does he use hyperbole here as well?

Charges Against the Opponents in 2 Corinthians 11.20

An examination of Paul's charges against his opponents reveals that what looks like a long list of points is in reality a single one.

The charges against his opponents in v. 20 are as follows:

1. they make slaves of the Corinthians;
2. they prey upon them (devour or exploit them) and take advantage of them or trap them;
3. they act haughtily;
4. they strike the Corinthians in the face.

Let us take these points one by one. For the most part the charges are synonymous: the opponents make slaves of the Corinthians, are haughty, exploit them, and strike them. In a word, they are high-handed. But how so? How do the opponents make slaves of the Corinthians? How do they prey upon them and take advantage of them? How do they act haughtily? What do they say?

The four items in 11.20 are all based on only two pieces of data: the opponents took money and someone got struck in the face. The other statements seem to be amplifications.

The list is a series ('making slaves of them, preying on them, putting on airs, and slapping them in the face') which begins with the most unlikely occurrences. No one can suppose that Paul actually meant that some missionaries were making actual slaves of the Corinthians. The word *katadouloi* (enslaves) expresses the same metaphorical charge as that against the 'false brethren' of Gal. 2.4; but in the context of 2 Cor. 11.20 it does not seem to be related to circumcision. Rather, behind *katadouloi* lie synonymous terms: *katesthiei*, which is best translated 'exploit'; *lambanei*, 'taking advantage of'; and *epairetai*, 'raises up in opposition', or 'acts haughtily'. These lesser charges are similar and may refer to the pressure from Paul's opponents for financial support. Since Paul disapproved of such coercion, he may well have considered it an attempt to 'enslave' the Corinthians. The result of the metaphor is to exaggerate the significance of the relatively minor items. Further, we know from 1 Cor. 9.4-7 that at calmer moments Paul acknowledged that an apostle deserved to be paid, although in Corinth he did not operate on that basis.

The statement that someone was slapped, *ei tis eis prosōpon humas derei*, is the most concrete of the charges. Of course, we cannot be certain that such an incident occurred. As far as I know there is no idiom in the ancient world comparable to the modern 'slap in the face'. Plutarch in *Moralia* 713c uses *epi korres rapizon* in the sense of 'rejecting contemptuously', but the metaphorical use does not seem to be common. It was customary for a slave to be slapped. To slap a free man, on the other hand, would be thought to be a great indignity. Therefore the phrase *ei tis eis prosōpon humas derei* in 2 Cor. 11.20 can be taken as figurative or perhaps as referring to an actual humiliating slap.

The list certainly creates the impression that many charges have been laid, but upon closer examination they turn out to be synonymous in meaning. The list amplifies the negative behaviour of the opponents. Perhaps someone did receive a slap in the face. Paul's amplification of that 'fact' might be to charge the opponents with 'putting on airs' and eventually with 'making slaves' of the Corinthians.

At the very least, I suggest that the repetition of similar phrases makes the opponents seem more evil than each charge would by itself, and serves to intensify the emotional level of the passage. Thus the passage is not dissimilar to Paul's rhetoric against the Jews in 1 Thess. 2.14-16, where his charges are sweeping in content and his accumulation of denigrating assertions seems designed to make an impact on the readers, as though he had said a great deal. The almost identical charges in 2 Cor. 11.4 are a parallel in that the accusations (that the opponents preach another Jesus, a different gospel, and have a different spirit) appear to be synonymous since these are simply stated with no further development.

Let us turn now to the allegory of the serpent and the pure bride in 2 Cor. 11.3. If in this passage the opponents are made to appear more evil than at other times and if the Corinthians are made to appear better than Paul knew them to be, then we have another example of polemical hyperbole.

The Cunning Serpent and the Pure Bride in 2 Corinthians 11.3

The tone for the chapter is set out in 11.1, 'I wish that you would bear with me in a little foolishness. Do bear with me.'[1] Paul begins v. 2 with an allegory of the 'pure bride' who represents the Corinthians and of the 'cunning serpent' which represents the opponents.

We know that it was standard rhetorical form to compare a lesser thing with a greater thing in order for the lesser thing to appear greater. One could discredit an opponent in a number of ways: by exaggerating the discreditable qualities of that person, by increasing the power of a word employed to describe a person, by comparing the lesser to the greater, by accumulating words or sentences identical in meaning, or by making the thought rise to a climax.[2] Examples were

1. Compare Bultmann, *Exegetische Probleme*, p. 27.
2. Quintilian, *Inst.* 8.4.27. See Chapter 6.

frequently used, sometimes fables, sometimes enthymemes.[1] While Paul's allegory is not one of these, it functions in the same way.

The story from Genesis was probably well known to Paul's readers, who would recognize the serpent as the villain of the piece. The implicit identification of the villain with the opponents makes them appear to be more evil than they would be otherwise and leads the readers to accept Paul's polemic against his rivals, thus severing their dependency on the rivals and encouraging their return to him as father.[2]

In the same fashion, for Paul to compare the Corinthian church to a 'pure bride' (11.2) makes the Corinthians appear pure and innocent, perhaps more so than they really are. He fears that they will be 'led astray', 'ruined', 'corrupted' or 'seduced'. The analogy exaggerates their innocence and places sole responsibility for the situation upon the shoulders of his opponents.

In a polarized contrast there is no middle ground. Paul's tendency to use such a contrast will be taken up in the next chapter. For now, it is enough to note that he makes no mention of either the possible good intentions of the opponents or any party of opposition to his rivals among the Corinthians. Obviously, however, there must have been a middle ground in the controversy or he would not have heard about the difficulties. Further, 10.11 and 13.2-3 suggest that those who have been swayed are only a select group.

We know that Paul does not always consider the Corinthians to be 'pure' and innocent. In fact, 2 Cor. 11.19-21 and 12.20-21 offer another view. The verb in 11.20, *anechesthai*, means 'to endure, to bear with, to put up with'. The fault is that of the Corinthians! They bear with all sorts of insults. They are not innocent victims of deception, but fools. Paul does not call them fools directly, but makes the charge by implication. If they put up with fools, they are foolish themselves. While in 11.3 the focus is on the opponents and their deception, in vv. 19-21 it is on the Corinthians and their foolishness. These are two sides of the same coin.

---

1. Quintilian, *Inst.* 5.14.24-29. An enthymeme draws its conclusions from incompatibles such as 'Can money be a good thing when it is possible to put it to a bad use?'

2. A relationship based upon cooperation between loving father and children is appealed to by Paul rather than the model of superior to subordinate. See Holmberg, *Paul and Power*, pp. 77-79.

The development of the chapter proceeds with an assertion by Paul that he speaks as a fool, a charge against the opponents as 'fools', and a sarcastic statement about the Corinthians being wise. All of this increases the intensity of the polemic so as to drive home the point. Paul does not really think he is a fool (11.16), nor does he think the Corinthians are wise. Although he had just referred to them as a 'pure' bride, he now quickly comes to the point: he is a fool (*aphrona*), the opponents are fools (*aphronōn*), but the Corinthians are wise (*phronimoi*), especially in the way they endure fools. In other words, he is a fool, the opponents are more so, but the greatest of fools are the Corinthians! For Paul to compare the Corinthians with a 'pure bride' is hyperbole, because it clearly exaggerates the situation at hand. Verses 19-20 are more nuanced. This modification of the image of the 'pure bride' suggests that the function of the latter was to polarize the Corinthians away from the opponents, the 'cunning serpent'.

In addition to polarization, the use of the language of betrothal in 2 Cor. 11.2 and that of paternalism in 12.14-15 shames the readers and leads them to respond to Paul as someone who loves them, who is willing to undergo all sorts of hardships on their behalf, and who, in contrast to his opponents, has their welfare at heart.[1] It is in terms of this continuous relationship that Paul's polemic needs to be seen. Indeed, shaming the reader was a standard method of rebuke for the purpose of inducing repentance.[2] Although in 2 Cor. 10.1-12 we learn that Paul's letters were often viewed as harsh (and certainly 11.19-21 is not mild language), his language of betrothal and paternalism indicates a more subtle method of rebuke.

Paul's rhetoric in 2 Corinthians 11 has the effect of revealing to the Corinthians their gullibility in being swayed by boasted

---

1. Further, it indicates Paul's authority over them. In Gal. 4.19 Paul uses the term 'little children': 'My little children, with whom I am again in travail until Christ is formed in you!' By this statement Paul appeals to his congregation to submit to his authority as God's apostle rather than to his opponents (Gal. 5.8; 2 Cor. 11.13-15). By submitting, they show their growing maturity. Holmberg has pointed out that when Paul speaks of his 'parenthood' he reminds the church not only that Paul has given them life, but that a continuing educational relationship exists between them, a relationship consisting of three elements: teaching, imitation and correction. Holmberg, *Paul and Power*, pp. 77-78.

2. Stowers, *Letter-Writing*, pp. 128, 133-34.

qualifications and demands. His applying the language of betrothal to the Corinthians in 11.2 stands in contrast to his lashing out at them in 11.13-15. Thus the Corinthians and Paul are set up as standing up to the opponents who want to deceive, thereby effectively lowering the status of the latter while raising their own. In serving his larger task, Paul must prove his own equality with the opponents and his superior right to claim the allegiance of the Corinthians. The opponents, however, may continue in another field, one in which Paul has not already laboured (10.13-18).

Paul: A Better Apostle than his Opponents in 2 Corinthians 11.23-28

After having said that he would not compare himself with those who were commending themselves (2 Cor. 10.12), Paul admits in 2 Cor. 11.21b that he is about to boast. To boast of one's achievements or to engage in self-praise was considered quite appropriate in situations of countering attacks.[1] Paul begins with a list of synonyms referring to his status as a Jew and ends with the term 'servants of Christ'. With regard to this term he gives himself higher marks than his opponents. The piling up of synonyms leads to it, and although he recoils at having said that he was a better servant of Christ ('I am talking like a madman', v. 23), nevertheless the point surely remained in the minds of the Corinthians.

Verses 23-28 continue with Paul's list of the hardships he has suffered.[2] Modeled perhaps after a literary convention of the time (*peristasis* catalogues),[3] Paul's list is used in 2 Corinthians 11 to argue that he is superior to his opponents. All of the hardships may be true; but the sweeping content, accumulation of items, and his own admission of speaking like a madman lead me to suppose that the list is

---

1. J.T. Fitzgerald, *Cracks in an Earthen Vessel: An Examination of the Catalogues of Hardship in the Corinthian Correspondence* (SBLDS; Atlanta: Scholars Press, 1988), pp. 107-14.

2. Compare Paul's other hardship lists in the Corinthian correspondence, for example, 1 Cor. 4.9-13; 2 Cor. 4.8-9; 6.4b-5, 8-10; 12.10.

3. See R. Hodgson, 'Paul the Apostle and First Century Tribulation Lists', *ZNW* 74 (1983), pp. 59-80. Hodgson has shown that these lists stem from a widespread literary convention of the first century. He finds such lists in Josephus and the mythological labours of Heracles and not simply from Stoic writings and Jewish apocalyptic as had been proposed earlier by R. Bultmann and W. Schrage.

constructed to make his sufferings in vv. 23-28 bulk as large as possible. The list amplifies his point that he is a better servant of Christ.

Fitzgerald has argued that the hardships which Paul recounts are like those difficulties that a sage endured and through which character was revealed. By using a list of trials endured with God's help, Paul asserts that he suffered more than his opponents and is therefore superior and the one the Corinthians should heed. From 'greater labours, far more imprisonments, countless beatings' to 'often near death', Paul has asserted his superior ability to endure and transcend hardships, each hardship exceeding the previous one, and the whole list magnifying the greatness of his qualifications as an apostle.[1]

I am not suggesting that Paul did not suffer all of these things. Indeed, he certainly has a theology of suffering which is demonstrated with great rhetorical force in Rom. 8.16c-17: 'we are children of God and if children, then heirs, heirs of God and fellow heirs with Christ, provided we suffer with him in order that we may also be glorified with him.' What we should notice in 2 Cor. 11.23-29 is the effort made to amplify his comparative experience of each item. He says *perissoterōs* ('far greater'), *huperballontōs* ('surpassing', cf. RSV's 'countless'), *perissoterōs* ('to a much greater degree') and *pollakis* ('often' or 'repeatedly'). Although the last in the list seems weaker than the rest, the fact that it goes with death gives it considerable force. How often was Paul near death? Even in prison he wrote letters and had visitors. The repetition of *perissoteros* together with the strong word *hyperballontōs* increases the rhetorical force.

A look at the nouns accompanying these words brings to mind Quintilian's advice that an orator could enhance a speech by increasing the power of words: 'labours...imprisonments...beatings...deaths'. For Paul to have said that he had far greater labours and even far more imprisonments is likely amplification. Did he actually compare sufferings with the other apostles? He says that he received 'countless beatings'. Perhaps his beatings did surpass those of the other apostles. In any case, he seems to give actual account of them: five times by the Jews (forty lashes less one) and three times by the Romans (rods). Even if he was beaten more than his opponents, hyperbole is present when the *hyperballontōs* is added to the other items in vv. 23-28.

---

1. The list functions in part to show Paul's composure just as the *peristasis* catalogues indicated the serenity of the sage. See Fitzgerald, *Earthen Vessel*, p. 166.

While he is counting, he seems to get carried away (2 Cor. 11.23-29[1]). His catalogue indicates the following:

1. five times the forty lashes less one from the Jews
2. three times beaten with rods
3. once stoned
4. three times shipwrecked
5. a night and a day adrift at sea
6. on frequent journeys
7. in danger from rivers
8. danger from robbers
9. danger from his own people
10. danger from Gentiles
11. danger in the city
12. danger in the wilderness
13. danger at sea
14. danger from false brethren
15. in toil and hardship
16. through many a sleepless night
17. in hunger and thirst
18. often without food
19. in cold and exposure
20. anxious daily for all the churches[2]

Perhaps the enumerated hardships are credible,[3] but Paul manages to list every sort of danger and suffering imaginable: from the lack of basic needs for physical survival (hunger, thirst, exposure, cold and sleepless nights) to assaults from all people (Romans, robbers, Jews, Gentiles, false brethren), from every city and from the natural world (seas, wilderness).

Picture the social-historical reality of Paul's missionary circumstances:

1. Paul was an itinerant preacher who often stayed at the homes of some of his converts[4] (1 Cor. 16.19; Phlm. 22; Rom. 16.23).

---

1. See a parallel passage in 1 Cor. 4.13 and K.A. Plank, *Paul and the Irony of Affliction* (Atlanta: Scholars Press, 1987), p. 85.
2. Fitzgerald, *Earthen Vessel*.
3. Sanders, *Paul, the Law, and the Jewish People*, p. 190.
4. A.J. Malherbe, *Social Aspects of Early Christianity* (Philadelphia: Fortress Press, 2nd edn, 1983), pp. 92-112.

2. Women made up a good portion of his converts. Sometimes they held meetings of the churches in their homes. Paul received hospitality and possibly money from many of them and their families (1 Cor. 16.19; Rom. 16.1-3, 6-7, 13).

3. He received support from some of his churches (Phil. 4.15-18) and from individuals (Rom. 16.2).

4. He worked with his hands as he went from place to place. Possibly he was a tentmaker.[1] This must have given him access to some income (1 Thess. 2.9; 1 Cor. 4.12).

5. Paul was from a social class above many of his converts and would thus have skills which quite probably enabled him to cope reasonably well with his missionary plans, plans which were worked out systematically and allowed for the coming and going of those who worked with him (1 Cor. 16.5-7, 10, 12, 17). Paul's skills would also have enabled him to work out the details of his travel and sojourns in cities so that he had access to people for his preaching and could spend his time profitably as a missionary. Although his work with his hands was a source of shame for him, it is also likely that it afforded him an opportunity to preach. It was not a distraction.[2]

This social-historical reality suggests that Paul not only suffered; in fact, he often 'abounded in plenty' (Phil. 4.12). I am not suggesting that he did not sometimes have sleepless nights or that he was not ever cold or hungry, but the piling up of sufferings, the quick succession of short phrases and the repetitions have the effect of making the sufferings seem greater than a straightforward statement would. Only in the Corinthian correspondence does Paul mention his hunger, thirst, sleeplessness, exposure and so forth. One would expect that he might mention such deprivations more often had they been as severe as he suggests in this passage. He might have written his own letters had he really been impoverished, and he might have stopped sending assistants on trips.

That Paul sometimes suffered and received punishment is not in question.[3] My point is that in 2 Cor. 11.23-27 he amplifies his

---

1. R.F. Hock, *The Social Context of Paul's Ministry: Tentmaking and Apostleship* (Philadelphia: Fortress Press, 1980), pp. 20-25.

2. Hock, *The Social Context of Paul's Ministry*, pp. 26-68.

3. Gal. 6.17 reflects the punishment Paul received for his stance against circumcision of Gentiles: 'I bear on my body the marks of Jesus'. In 1 Thess. 2.2 we learn that he did suffer and was insulted at Philippi. Rom. 8.35-38 lists a number

experiences through emphasizing their frequency and severity. While he used other hardship lists in the Corinthian correspondence (2 Cor. 6.4b-5; 12.10), the catalogue in 2 Cor. 11.23-28 is both more extensive and repetitive as we shall see below. The list of difficulties in Phil. 4.12 (an antithetical list) is more nuanced. There he says that he knows 'how to be abased' and 'how to abound', 'how to face plenty and hunger' and so on.

One must notice that in 2 Cor. 11.23-27 Paul repeats himself several times. For him to say both 'hungry' and 'without food' is at least amplification: the second expression is more extreme than the first and the repetition of the same idea makes the point more prominent. When he says he goes hungry (abases himself for the sake of his churches, 11.7) he implies that he and he alone goes hungry whereas his opponents have impure motives and take money. He attenuates the situation of his opponents by exclusion: he does not say whether they ever go hungry. He only mentions them in ways that denigrate them.

Four times Paul refers to troubles at sea. These repetitions are mostly synonymous (see numbers 4, 5, 7 and 13 in the catalogue above) and are interspersed within the list, making the point over and over. He mentions his being shipwrecked but also his being adrift at sea, in danger from rivers, and in danger at sea. Further, he intersperses his specific sufferings (possibly the enumerated ones) with vague generalizations: toil and hardship, labours and so on.

Every group of people threatens Paul: Romans, robbers, the Jews, the Gentiles and the false brethren. It appears that he sees himself as the sole agent of righteousness. A more balanced, unpolemical assessment of his own physical welfare and that of the other apostles would probably show that he was not the only one who gave up things for the gospel (Mt. 10 and parallels must reflect social reality to some degree). Quite possibly he suffered more than did many others. The point in 2 Corinthians 11, however, is to polarize the situation, to cast himself in a good light and the others in a completely bad one with no redeeming features. At the same time it must be acknowledged that the self-praise is not an end in itself. Paul is able to endure the hardships because of God's sustaining power. Paul says that his real boast is in his weakness, implying God's power in him.

of sufferings, but they are general and Paul does not claim that he had experienced some of them: 'Who shall separate us from the love of Christ? Shall tribulation, or distress, or persecution, or famine, or nakedness, or peril, or sword?'

Peristasis lists were standard in philosophical and rhetorical circles. Seneca, upbraiding Lucilius for his complaints about the philosophic life, says that life is really a battle.

> For this reason those who are tossed about at sea, who proceed uphill and downhill over toilsome crags and heights, who go on campaigns that bring the greatest danger, are heroes and front-rank fighters; but persons who live in rotten luxury and ease while others toil, are mere turtle-doves—safe only because men despise them. (Seneca, *Ep.* 96.5)

Seneca's list of troubles pales when compared with Paul's. In a recent study of 2 Corinthians 10–12 Charles Talbert notices the rhetorical function of these chapters. They are cast 'in the form of a reputable philosopher's response to disreputable sophists. At virtually every point the positions of the participants are described by Paul with conventional means.'[1] But the crucial point for us is Talbert's conclusion that we must not interpret Paul's rhetoric as descriptive of his opponents' actual motives and of his final assessment of their characters.[2] Talbert suggests that one can determine the theological issues only in a general way: Paul thinks that his opponents are self-promoting.[3]

Too often scholars have failed to consider the rhetorical function of Paul's words. For example, they have been puzzled by the duplication of sufferings that he describes. In trying to understand why in 2 Cor. 11.27 he notes first his frequent hunger and then his lack of food, some have suggested that in the latter case he means that he frequently fasted.[4] But we have no knowledge of this fact from his letters. Another example is how the entire list of sufferings is handled. Often commentators describe Paul in graphic language. He is said to be 'conscious of his powers of endurance',[5] 'ailing, ill treated, weakened

---

1.   Talbert, *Reading Corinthians*, pp. 121-30. See now L.T. Johnson, *The Writings of the New Testament: An Interpretation* (Philadelphia: Fortress Press, 1986), p. 294.

2.   'Both the ministry of Paul and that of the visiting apostles encompassed preaching, miracle, and suffering service on behalf of Christ. If so, then where did the difference lie?' Talbert, *Reading Corinthians*, p. 130.

3.   Talbert, *Reading Corinthians*, p. 130.

4.   H.L. Goudge, *The Second Epistle to the Corinthians* (London: Methuen, 1927), p. 109.

5.   W.H.C. Frend, *The Rise of Christianity* (Philadelphia: Fortress Press, 1984), p. 97.

by hunger and perhaps by fever'.[1] Further, he had 'an unparalleled experience of adventures with gangsters and fanatics, disasters and difficulties on land and sea'.[2] Finally, one scholar, who knew that the conditions for travel had improved a great deal in the first century and yet wanted to believe Paul, hardship for hardship, ended up taking the words of Seneca literally—despite the fact that Seneca thought that by hyperbole we come to the truth![3]

> It is true that in his time the roads and the sea were safer than they had ever been, but they were still dangerous... 'Think', said Seneca, 'any day a robber might cut your throat'.[4]

A solemn, flat reading of Paul is unfortunate, since it passes over the flavour and nuance of his rhetoric, and thus it misses his argumentative ploys and devices. In 2 Corinthians 11 he is, at the very least, amplifying: he lists only hardships and opponents, no good times and friends; he repeats the same hardship more than once; he does not give any account of difficulties faced by the other apostles. Did they always sail in fair weather? Did they have ample funds? When they travelled by land, did thieves stay clear of the roads and inns?

Does Paul's incomplete account of his situation amount to hyperbole? One might define exaggeration rigidly, thus requiring one or more points in Paul's catalogue to be in error: actually other apostles were arrested more often than he, or actually he was flogged only four times rather than five. However, the nature of the evidence does not allow this sort of exaggeration to be proved.

Throughout the list the amplification is so extreme as to be misleading. While Paul does not say explicitly that other missionaries did not experience difficulties, the effect of 2 Cor. 11.23-28 is to depict himself as always unfortunate and labouring under unique difficulties. The implied 'always' and 'unique' are not true. Like Paul, Barnabas had to work for a living, at least some of the time (1 Cor. 9.6); the Judaean Christians would also have faced some difficulties in their travels and even in their churches in Judaea (1 Thess. 2.14). We

1. Deissmann, *Paul*, p. 63.
2. R.P.C. Hanson, *II Corinthians* (London: SCM Press, 1954), p. 85.
3. See Seneca, cited by Erasmus, *On Copia of Words and Ideas* (trans. D.B. King and H.D. Rix; Milwaukee: Marquette University Press, 1963), p. 35.
4. Barclay, *Letters*, p. 254.

must assume that the other travelling apostles experienced difficulties on the road and at sea. We can believe every phrase in Paul's list and still see that the overall effect is exaggerated.

In my estimation, 2 Corinthians 11 shows that Paul used hyperbole to advance the case that he had suffered more than his opponents and was therefore a better apostle. Let us proceed to Romans 1 and 2 and observe the polemical hyperbole in Paul's accusations of the Gentiles and Jews.

Romans 1 and 2

If my hypothesis is correct—that in polemic Paul tended to use hyperbole—a more nuanced reading of Romans 1 and 2 would prevent scholars from taking his hyperbolic statements as his final position. Rather, such passages, presenting a polemic against Gentile and Jewish behaviour would be understood as rhetoric to denigrate certain people (in this case, first the Gentiles and then the Jews) in order to make his main point, that the whole world is under the power of sin.

In discussing these passages, scholars often assume that Paul is describing actual empirical evidence of Gentile moral degeneration and Jewish behaviour. Gentile behaviour is described as 'degraded conduct'[1] and Jewish behaviour as the 'discrepancy between his [the Jew's] claim and his God-dishonouring conduct'.[2] Paul's words in Rom. 2.17-24 are taken to be indicative of the observable inability of Jews to obey the law.[3]

---

1. J.A. Fitzmeyer, *Pauline Theology: A Brief Sketch* (Englewood Cliffs, NJ: Prentice-Hall, 1967), p. 54. Similarly H.N. Ridderbos, *Paul: An Outline of his Theology* (trans. J.R. De Witt; Grand Rapids: Eerdmans, 1975), p. 135. Bultmann thought that in Rom. 1 Paul was attempting to 'expose the guilt of the heathen'. R. Bultmann, *Theology of the New Testament* (trans. K. Grobel; New York: Charles Scribner's Sons, 1951), I, p. 229. According to Ridderbos, Rom. 1.18-32 refers to the 'coarse and unvarnished egoism, and "animosity and hatred of one man toward another" which "manifests itself among the gentiles"'. Ridderbos, *Paul*, p. 295. See also R. Martin, *Reconciliation: A Study of Paul's Theology* (Atlanta: John Knox, 1981), p. 48.

2. Bornkamm, *Paul*, p. 6. J. Christiaan Beker says that the Jew's boasting in God and in the law is 'empirically contradicted by his immoral behaviour and by the public transgression of the law (2.23-24)'. Beker, *Paul the Apostle*, p. 82.

3. Bultmann, *Theology*, p. 263. See also C.E.B. Cranfield, *A Critical and*

But are these conclusions just? In the same section of Romans, Paul argues that some Gentiles observe the law even without knowing it and indicates that they may be 'excused' at the judgment, and proposes that all people are equally under sin. One of these statements is hyperbolic. In another passage (Phil. 3.6) he says that he himself had been righteous by the law. This may be compared with his claim that no one is righteous by the law. One of these statements is exaggerated. In Paul's view, at least in Rom. 2.13-16, some Gentiles were decent. His extreme statements lead, of course, to the conclusion that every mouth is to be stopped and the whole world held accountable for their sins (Rom. 3.19).

The hyperbolic characterization of both Jews and Gentiles was to lead to Paul's assertions about universal sinfulness (3.9, 20), judgment on the same basis (2.11), and the need for faith in Christ (3.22).

While there is no actual opponent evident (the Roman church was unknown to him personally), Paul uses the rhetoric of polemic and he exaggerates a great deal. Sanders has pointed out that ch. 2 may be a synagogue sermon:

> It is slashing and exaggerated, as many sermons are, but its own natural point is to have its hearers become better Jews on strictly non-Christian Jewish terms, not to lead them to becoming true descendants of Abraham by faith in Christ.[1]

In any case, Paul was not the only Jew in history to use the outsider as a model to accuse his own group. Joseph Yabetz had this to say to his congregation:

> If you open your eyes, you will be envious of them [Christians], for you will see them fulfilling the rational commandments—'doing justice, and loving mercy' (Mic. 6.8)—better than we do...[2]

Likewise, Rabbi Jonathan Eybeschuetz in 1747 rebuked his congregation by reminding them that certain commandments were better

---

Exegetical Commentary on the Epistle to the Romans (Edinburgh: T. & T. Clarke, 6th edn, 1975), I, p. 169. Cranfield has cited Rom. 2.17-24 as proof that no one can obey the law. See also C.K. Barrett, *A Commentary on the Epistle to the Romans* (BNTC; London: A. & C. Black, 1957), p. 56.

1. Sanders, *Paul, the Law, and the Jewish People*, p. 129.

2. J. Yabetz, *Hasdê Adonay*, p. 56, cited in M. Saperstein, 'Christians and Jews—Some Positive Images', in G.W.E. Nickelsburg with G.W. MacRae (eds.), *Christians Among Jews and Gentiles* (Philadelphia: Fortress Press, 1986), p. 244.

observed by the Christians than by the Jews:

> honoring of father and mother and [the prohibitions against] robbery and
> fraud, and many like them.[1]

And lastly:

> Look at the Gentiles among whom we live. We learn from them styles of
> clothing and haughtiness, but we do not learn from them silence during
> prayer. We are like them in eating their cheeses and their wine, but we are
> not like them we [sic] regard to justice, righteousness and honesty. We
> are like them in shaving our beard or modelling it in their style, but we are
> not like them in their refraining from cursing or swearing in God's
> Name...[2]

Marc Saperstein has urged that the use of the outsider as a model for
one's own group has 'a long history as a powerful weapon in the
arsenal of the rhetoric of self-criticism'.[3] Aside from the examples of
Lk. 10.25-37 (the 'good Samaritan') and Mal. 1.11-12, he cites the
Christian admiration of Jewish piety, education, purity of motive, and
willingness to suffer for the faith. For example, the virulently anti-
Jewish preacher Chrysostom conceded that Jews take their worship
attendance seriously. He identified worship as an area in which his
own listeners frequently fall short:

> You Christians should be ashamed and embarrassed at the Jews who
> observe the Sabbath with such devotion and refrain from all commerce
> beginning with the evening of the Sabbath. When they see the sun
> hurrying to set in the west on Friday they call a halt to their business
> affairs and interrupt their selling.[4]

Paul, like others of his time and later, used the outsider as a model of
religious piety in order to accuse his own group. In Romans 2 Paul
uses the Gentiles as models of those who obey the law. Did Paul think
that Jews could not obey the law? In answer, we are fortunate to have
the following statements by Paul to another Jew, Peter. In Gal. 2.15
Paul says,

---

    1.   J. Eybeschuetz, *Ya'arôt Debas* (Jerusalem: Lewin-Epstein, 1965), §99a,
cited in Saperstein, 'Christians and Jews', p. 245.
    2.   S. Morteira, *Gib'at Sha'ul* (Warsaw, 1902), 'Debarim', §129a, cited in
Saperstein, 'Christians and Jews', p. 245.
    3.   Saperstein, 'Christians and Jews', p. 237.
    4.   Saperstein, 'Christians and Jews', p. 238.

> We ourselves, who are Jews by birth and not Gentile sinners, yet who
> know that a person is not justified by works of the law but by faith in
> Jesus Christ, even we have believed in Christ Jesus, in order to be
> justified by faith in Christ, and not by works of the law, because by
> works of the law shall no one be justified.

Clearly, the problem with the law was neither that it was impossible
to fulfil nor that Jews could not fulfil it. In fact, the distinction
between Jews and 'Gentile sinners' reveals that Paul thought that his
life under the law was superior to the life of Gentiles before
conversion.[1] Nonetheless, righteousness is now by faith in Christ and
not by the law, and every Jew (and Gentile) must now acknowledge
this. It is not a question of inability to fulfil the law, rather a new
righteousness, one by faith in Christ.[2] Paul's statements in Phil. 3.6-9
about his former life in Judaism support this conclusion. He fulfilled
the law, but is now under a better righteousness. That his sweeping
generalizations about the Jews in Rom. 2.17-24 were not his position
at other times shows that they are hyperbolic.

The accusations that Paul makes against the Jews are also
hyperbolic. However, for him to say that a certain Jew had stolen
from a temple would not be hyperbole. There was actually one Jewish
person in Rome, described by Josephus in *Ant.* 18.81-84,[3] who, with
three confederates, misappropriated the funds entrusted to him by a
woman of high rank for the temple. But while Paul may have known
of this one example, there is no evidence to support the claim that
Jews in general were stealing articles from idol-temples.[4] Thus, for
him to set up the argument in rhetorical questions, which make it
appear that all Jews rob temples, commit adultery and steal, is
hyperbole.[5]

1.   See Sanders, *Paul, the Law, and the Jewish People*, p. 151.
2.   Sanders, *Paul, the Law, and the Jewish People*, pp. 39-45.
3.   See Watson, *Paul, Judaism and the Gentiles*, p. 114.
4.   Cranfield, *Commentary on Romans*, pp. 169-70.
5.   See Quintilian, *Inst.* 7.3.22. Quintilian uses the example of theft of private
money from temples as a familiar example to instruct orators of the courts how to
respond to such accusations on the part of one's opponents. This indicates that such
accusations frequently were found in the courts of Rome. However, these charges
are not said to be laid against Jews as such. More likely, charges of this nature were
commonplace against opponents. Käsemann ('Die Legitimität des Apostels', pp. 33-
71) takes Paul's accusations as his complete view because there are similar passages
in Epictetus (2.19.19; 3.7.17), the Dead Sea Scrolls (CD 4.15), and Philo (*Conf.*

Why did Paul need to use hyperbole against the Gentiles and the Jews in Romans 1 and 2? It was not enough to show that all people fall short of their *intentions*. He made his utterances about the degraded state of the world serve his larger purpose: to show God's universal mercy in sending Christ. The section on the depravity of the Gentile is standard Jewish polemic against them;[1] the section on Jewish sins and the statements that Gentiles who do not have the law fulfil its requirements even better than the Jews is designed to convict Jews of their sinfulness.

Summary

An exacting reading of Paul's letters might lead us to propose a piecemeal approach for explaining contradictions in the text, to conclude that Paul was using language irresponsibly, or to decide that part of a letter is an interpolation. A less exacting but more nuanced reading recognizes Paul's skills as a debater and writer, and offers a fruitful approach to explain Paul's exaggerated language and its func-tion in the argument of large sections. It maintains the unity of the text and, rather than taking Paul's polemical statements as his final and absolute judgment, it leads interpreters to an awareness of his ability to use language creatively in response to real and diverse situations.

A more nuanced reading of the text not only enables us to appreciate Paul as a debater and polemicist, but also prevents us from taking his hyperbole so exactingly as to derive the motives and attributes of his opponents from it. Further, a recognition of his use of hyperbole can protect us from falling under the influence of his

Ling. 163). However, none of these documents refers to actual individual cases. They are more likely to be commonplace charges against opponents. For example, in CD 4.15 the unrighteous of Israel shall fall into the nets of Satan, which are fornication, riches and profanation of the temple; in Philo a soul which lacks good sense finds an easy path to sin as a murderer, temple robber, or adulterer, but these passages, like Rom. 2.17-24, can hardly be descriptive of characteristics of Jews in general even if some Jews stole or committed adultery. Rather, they are rhetoric designed to lead the righteous into the right paths. That outsiders are described in exaggerated terms of wickedness is only to be expected. The passages in Epictetus are general exhortations of Stoics to be scrupulous in actions so as to avoid criticism from others.

1.   See now S. Westerholm, *Israel's Law and the Church's Faith: Paul and his Recent Interpreters* (Grand Rapids: Eerdmans, 1988), p. 157.

rhetoric and from seeing his opponents only as completely in the wrong.

Such a nuanced approach is helpful in interpeting 1 Thess. 2.14-16 because Paul's statements there can be seen for what they truly are: polemical hyperbole in the light of difficult circumstances which draw out his pastoral concern for his church, a concern which led him to consign his opponents to damnation.

We have seen that Paul uses polemical hyperbole against Jews and also against Christians. Biblical scholarship has focused mostly upon the former. I know of no study that has attempted to compare the level of rhetorical intensity of Paul's polemic directed at each of these groups. Such a study is obviously necessary and will be provided in Chapter 9. There we will examine two related issues: (1) Paul's level of rhetorical intensity against the Jews compared with that against his Christian brethren, and (2) his level of rhetorical intensity against the Jews referred to in Romans 2 and 9–11 compared with that against the Jews referred to in 1 Thess. 2.14-16. This two-sided examination will help us discern what the polemical hyperbole in the problem passage tells us about Paul's attitudes towards the Jewish people early in his career.

Chapter 9

LEVELS OF RHETORICAL INTENSITY IN PAUL'S POLEMICS

I have placed 1 Thess. 2.14-16 within the context of other instances of Paul's use of polemical hyperbole. In Chapter 8 we saw that the use of exaggerated language occurred during crises which mushroomed from his churches, such as the compelling of Gentiles to be circumcised (Galatians) and the paying of leaders who were perceived as and may have claimed to be more qualified than Paul (2 Cor. 11). These crises indicate the competition which existed within the early Christian movement. Romans 1 and 2 is perhaps not addressed to a crisis situation, yet Paul uses polemical hyperbole to argue for the equal footing of Jews and Gentiles[1] under Christ. He likely did not have actual opponents in the latter case (he had never been to the Roman church), but used a type of polemic first against Gentiles and then against Jews as part of his argument.

Now I shall attempt to observe the levels of intensity of polemic within the passages which have been designated as instances of polemical hyperbole in Paul's letters. It is necessary at the outset to set forth some criteria for determining intensity. To my knowledge there are no established criteria for such a determination and thus I shall suggest what they might be.

When polemical hyperbole is used, a logical outcome is a distancing from one's opponents resulting in polarization. In 1 Thess. 2.14-16 distancing occurs by denigrating the Jews through making their sinful actions loom large and by positively associating Paul's church with the eminent figures of the Lord Jesus, the prophets and the Jerusalem church through the theme of suffering. If we can determine what other methods Paul uses to gain distance from his opponents for himself and his congregations, we shall have a way to compare

---

1. Sanders, *Paul, the Law, and the Jewish People*, pp. 123-35.

passages in order to determine the levels of intensity. Thus, in each passage one might (1) observe Paul's extreme language, (2) identify other polemical elements, and (3) pay attention to how much of the letter is devoted to polemic.

In Chapters 5 through 7 we discussed how to locate and identify extreme language generally, and in some of Paul's letters specifically. It can be shown that bipolar categories can support extreme language in such a way as to intensify the level of polemical rhetoric. First we must identify the bipolar categories which exist in the polemical passages we have studied in Chapter 8. Then we will be able to determine levels of intensity by comparing the passages according to (1) quantity of bipolar categories employed and (2) their use in the context. We turn now to the identification of bipolar categories.

Bipolar Categories

In Chapter 6 we saw how the use of 'sons of light' and 'sons of darkness' in 1 Thess. 5.5 implied the formation of a solid identity of Paul and his church at Thessalonica and a distance between them and the receivers of wrath (5.9). There is the sense of 'us' and 'them'. We shall observe that sometimes Paul uses the emphatic personal pronoun (i.e., *hēmeis* 'we'[1]) to draw his readers more closely to his side and to distance himself and them from his opponents. I am most interested in the use of *hēmeis* for the latter purpose, but we need to observe that Paul used this pronoun even outside of polemic to nurture the church by showing solidarity with its members. The emphatic 'we' draws the circle more tightly around the insider group and implicitly contrasts those who are external to the core group.

The Pronominal Bipolar Terms 'us'/'them'
1. Pronominal 'us'/'them' outside of Polemic
Sometimes by the emphatic first person plural pronoun Paul means 'we who have faith in Christ', sometimes he means himself and his co-workers, and sometimes he means to gather the readers together with

---

1.   See discussions of *hēmeis* in Milligan, *Thessalonians*, pp. 131-32. Milligan indicates that sometimes *hēmeis* can be used to mean 'I' and that it can also mean 'we' in a close sense. He attributes the use in 1 Thessalonians to a joint-authorship with Silvanus and Timothy; see also Rigaux, *Thessaloniciens*, pp. 77-80. I find it is used to develop a close identity with the church.

himself and his co-workers. In this last use, the term has an encompassing function. Although the book of Romans has few emphatic first person plural pronouns, we shall look at one of them.

In Romans 3–7 Paul does not want his church to cling to the law as a necessary prerequisite to life in Christ. In Rom. 5.20 he is explaining that through the law sin abounded but grace abounded even more. He asks, 'Shall we continue in sin so grace may abound?' (6.1). This is an extreme proposal. He retreats from it by saying, 'By no means! How can we who died to sin still live in it?' Clearly Paul is not trying to convince himself not to live in sin. He had in mind the church and the possibility that it could be deceived by persons misinterpreting his message (cf. 3.8). These first two uses of 'we', although not emphatic, create a sense of solidarity with the congregation and, in this case, a congregation he had not visited. Three verses later he asserts, 'We were buried therefore with him by baptism into death, so that as Christ was raised from the dead by the glory of the Father, *we* too might walk in newness of life' (6.4). Here the emphatic first person plural gathers together Paul, the saints at Rome and the risen Christ. Another example of the encompassing function of the emphatic first person plural is in 1 Cor. 12.13, where Paul uses it to gain solidarity between Paul, Jews, Gentiles, slave and free. All have the same Spirit. The emphatic 'we' where 'you' would suffice has the effect of creating and intensifying emotional solidarity between Paul and his churches. In these cases there does not seem to be an opposing party, and while 'we' implies a 'they', the referent is general, vague and shadowy.

2. *Pronominal 'us'/'them' within Polemic*

Association with Someone of Prominence. Sometimes Paul uses the emphatic first person plural within polemic to indicate to the reader that someone of prominence agrees with him, a persuasive technique which has the effect of making Paul's case stronger and drawing readers to his side. In Antioch controversy arose over Jews eating with Gentiles. At first Peter ate with them, but when certain men came from James who questioned the practice, he removed himself. In Paul's account of the incident in his letter to the Galatians he relates a conversation held with Peter:

> If you, though a Jew, live like a Gentile and not like a Jew, how can you compel the Gentiles to live like Jews [to be circumcised]? We ourselves

[*hēmeis*], who are Jews by birth and not Gentile sinners, yet who know that a man is not justified by works of the law but through faith in Christ Jesus, even we [*hēmeis*] have believed in Christ Jesus, in order to be justified by faith in Christ, and not by works of the law... (Gal. 2.14-16).

Paul emphasizes 'We Jews' or 'we, you and I, Peter', trying to put Peter into his own camp. Thus, the repetitive use of *hēmeis* here serves to intensify the polemic because it puts Peter, a prominent figure, on his side.

Drawing Boundaries. In the heat of his polemic in 2 Corinthians 10–13 Paul uses *hēmeis* twice, but they clearly refer to himself and his co-workers and are not encompassing terms. The *hēmeis* stands over against an implied 'them' against whom he rages. In 10.7 Paul asserts that 'If anyone is confident that he is Christ's, let him remind himself that as he is Christ's, so are *we*'. Here Paul has claimed equality with his opponents under Christ. However, in the next three uses of *hēmeis* he distances himself from his opponents. In 10.13 he says, 'But *we* will not boast beyond limit, but will keep to the limits God has apportioned us...' What is implied is that 'they' have not kept to the limit. In 11.12 Paul says that some people boast that they work on the same basis as *we* do, but he denies it and, as will be seen below, engages in name-calling (v. 13) which distances the *we* even further from his opponents. And in 11.21 after saying that his opponents have made slaves of the Corinthians, Paul asserts, '*we* were too weak for that'. The implication is that the opponents were high handed. Paul's use of emphatic *hēmeis* in 2 Corinthians 10–13 does not encompass himself and the church. Even the emphatic 'we' in 13.4, 6, 7 and 9 refers to Paul and his co-workers as distinct from 'you' Corinthians.

How is this usage to be explained? The absence of assertions of 'us' in this conflict might indicate Paul's lack of confidence in the relationship between himself and the church, the intensity of the personal animosity between Paul and his opponents, or a combination of these possibilities.

Dropping out the Middle. In polemic, hyperbole can be used to build up one side of an issue and to put down the other. If both extremes are presented it follows that no middle ground is acknowledged. In its bipolar form the extremes have the effect of appealing to the listeners or readers to take one side or the other.

On many occasions Paul, in polemic, makes use of the emphatic first person plural to refer to those on his side, thereby separating them from the opponents and leaving no room for any middle positions. A reader is forced into one position or the other. A detailed study of these uses would take us beyond the limits of this work, but a few examples will make the point clear.

Paul's use of 'us' language occurs usually after the most heated polemic against his opponents, who are classed as 'them'. For example, in the letter to the Galatians Paul argues against their submitting to circumcision, often using the second person and moving back and forth between 'you' and 'us' with sometimes an emphatic 'I, Paul'. In Gal. 4.26 it is the Jerusalem above that is 'our' mother; the 'our' emphasizes that the Galatians are on the right side and implies that the heavenly Jerusalem is not 'their' (the opponents') mother. From 'our' mother Paul moves to '*you* are children of the promise according to Isaac' and back to '*we* are not of the slave but of the free woman'. This use of pronouns groups the Galatians, Paul and his co-workers together. Then the pronouns change from 'us' to 'you' again. 'For freedom Christ has set *us* free; stand [*you* stand] fast therefore' (Gal. 5.1). From a place of solidarity with those who are resisting circumcision[1] Paul can exhort the Galatians, 'Now *I*, Paul, say to *you* that if *you* receive circumcision, Christ will be of no advantage to *you*'. However, he quickly returns to the first person plural: 'For through the Spirit, by faith, *we* wait for the hope of righteousness' (v. 5). The movement returns to 'you' in v. 7: '*You* were running well. Who hindered *you* from obeying the truth?'. Then in v. 12 it is 'I', 'you' and 'them' (implied by 'the ones unsettling you'): '*I* wish those who unsettle *you* would mutilate *themselves*'. The next 12 verses are 'I, Paul' exhorting 'you' Galatians with a return to 'we' in v. 25, which again has an encompassing effect: 'If *we* live by the Spirit, let *us* also walk by the Spirit'. What is implied is that 'they' (those who are compelling the Galatians to be circumcised) do *not* 'walk by the Spirit'.

Whereas at the beginning of Galatians 6 there was more than one position—Paul's, the opponents', and a variety of responses by the Galatians which required Paul's intervention by letter—at the end of

---

1. W. Hendriksen, *A Commentary on Galatians* (London: The Banner of Truth Trust, 1969), p. 197. See also G.S. Duncan, *The Epistle of Paul to the Galatians* (London: Hodder & Stoughton, 1948), p. 156.

the chapter there are only two: those who walk by the Spirit and those who walk according to the Flesh. The use of bipolar categories has the effect of excluding any middle position, thereby intensifying the conflict.

Conceptual Bipolar Categories 'us'/'them' within Polemic
Within polemic, in addition to the actual pronominal bipolar categories 'us'/'them', many times there is what can only be described as a conceptual category 'us'/'them'. The insiders comprise an implicit 'us' group, which is opposed by an implicit outsider group 'them'. These groups are constructed by the association of respective common positive and negative experiences and by the use of bipolar terms which drop out any middle positions.

Common Experiences. In 1 Thess. 2.14-16 there is a conceptual 'us' and 'them'. The Thessalonians and the rest of the suffering righteous (the Lord Jesus, the prophets, 'us' and the Jerusalem church) are the insider group, whereas those who persecute (the *symphyletai* and the Jews) are the outsider group.

The temporary success of Paul's opponents and consequent suffering experienced by him and others are interpreted from Paul's point of view as proof that the righteous, like Christ, often suffer.[1] Ultimately, those who persecute are fighting a losing battle.[2] That Paul is frequently persecuted for the gospel indicates that he is on God's side. He takes Christ as the model (Rom. 8.17; 2 Cor. 1.5; 4.10; 11.23-27; Phil. 3.10). Others, who advocate circumcision, simply want to escape persecution. They 'glory in the flesh' while Paul glories 'in the cross of our Lord Jesus Christ' (Gal. 6.14-16). This combining of groups into two main categories—those who suffer and

---

1.   Indications of suffering abound: 1 Thess. 1.3, 6; 2.14-16; 3.4; 1 Cor. 3.16-17; 4.12; 15.9; 2 Cor. 1.5-8; 2.4; 4.8, 9, 17; 6.4; 7.4-5; 8.2, 13; 11.23-25; 12.10, 12; Gal. 1.13, 23; 3.4; 4.29; 5.7, 10, 11; 6.12; Phil. 1.13, 17, 29; 2.17; 3.4, 6, 8, 10; 4.14; Rom. 2.7; 3.8; 5.3, 4; 8.17-18; 8.25, 35; 12.12, 14; 15.4, 5, 31. Some of these have to do with the 'woes' at the end of the age. Some have to do with Paul's suffering but others refer to congregations which are troubled as well. The sufferings have positive results for the churches. They produce endurance and courage (Phil. 1.14) and they reflect the suffering of Christ (1 Thess. 1.6). On the other hand, for those who cause the suffering the results are negative (1 Thess. 2.16).

2.   Frend points out that 'the persecutors were faced with the hopeless task of fighting against God' (p. 150); similarly Okeke, 'I Thessalonians 2.13-16', p. 134.

those who cause suffering—leads to forcing everyone into one of two positions. The establishing of common experiences of insiders serves to divide the various positions in a conflict into insider and outsider groups—what I call a conceptual bipolar category.

Dropping out the Middle: Themes of Persecution and Suffering. As in other places, so too in speaking of suffering Paul excludes some middle positions. In 1 Thess. 2.14-16 there are six main players: (1) the Jews, (2) the Gentile persecutors, (3) Paul, (4) the Thessalonians, (5) the Judaean churches and (6) the Lord and the prophets. The first extreme position is made up of an equation of those who oppose the church (1 and 2). This group is then placed over against Paul (3), who has aligned himself with the Lord and the prophets (6). There is a third group: the church at Thessalonica and the churches of Judaea (4 and 5). Through the theme of suffering, he combines 3, 4, 5 and 6. Presumably not every Jew persecuted the church and not every Christian suffered. The themes of suffering and persecution lend themselves to bipolar conceptual categories of 'us'/'them'.

Dropping out the Middle by means of Bipolar Terms. Many bipolar terms appear in Paul's letters:

1 Thessalonians:	'sons of light/sons of darkness' (5.5).
2 Corinthians:	'pure virgin Eve/the deceitful serpent' (11.3); 'servants of Christ/servants of Satan' (11.23, 15).
Galatians:	'children of the free woman/children of the slave' (4.31); 'spirit/flesh' (5.13–6.13); 'sons/slave' (4.1-5); 'children of the promise/children of the flesh' (4.23, 28).
Philippians:	'like-minded/ otherwise minded' (3.15).
Romans:	'slaves of obedience and righteousness/slaves of sin' (6.16-18), 'vessels of mercy/vessels of wrath' (9.22-23).

These terms are useful in building conceptual 'us'/'them' categories. The terms are exaggerations used to create solidarity and distance through the dropping out of any middle positions and the pressing of all players into two opposing groups. In Galatians Paul polarizes the various players in the conflict into two extreme positions (flesh/spirit; slave/free) by impugning the middle players with the same charges (evil motives or actions) he uses against the players at the extreme of the negative pole. The players are as follows: (1) Paul, (2) Gentiles in Galatia, (3) mediating 'pillars', (4) 'false brethren' in Jerusalem, whose position Paul equates with (5) troublers of the Galatians (5.12) and with (6) potential persecutors of the troublers (6.12). In the fiercest part there are three main players: Paul, the Galatians and Christian opponents (hounded by potential persecutors). Polarization moves several players to the extreme position: Peter, distinguished from 'false brethren' in the account of the meeting in Jerusalem, is more or less equated with troublers in Paul's denunciation (Gal. 2.14: Peter 'compels'; cf. the false brethren 'compel' in Gal. 2.3; the troublers 'compel' in Gal. 6.12). This virtually eliminates the mediating position (3) and allows Paul to lump 3, 4 and 5 together. He then appeals to the Galatians to join his side, which results in further polarization (with the potential persecutors in a remote third position). By attributing the same negative action or intention ('to compel', *anankadzein*) to the players in the mediating position as to those in the extreme position, Paul eliminates the former one. In addition to actions, the maligning of motives denigrates Paul's opponents, so that their motives range from wanting to spy out the freedom of the churches (2.4) and wanting to enslave them (5.1) to wanting to escape persecution (6.12).

We have already discussed the discrediting of the character of the Jews in 1 Thess. 2.15 in Chapters 6 and 7. By using hyperbole to besmirch the actions of the Jews, Paul denigrates them.

Although Paul asserts the negative terms in antithesis to the positive terms as if they were absolutes, in the last chapter we saw that the terms 'false brethren' (Gal. 2.4), 'false apostles' and implicitly 'servants of Satan' (2 Cor. 11.14-15) were attributed to people Paul knew to be Christian. The point to be noted is that the attribution is made in order to have bipolar conceptual terms of 'false brethren/true brethren', 'false apostles/true apostles', and 'apostles of Satan/apostles of Christ'. Distance is created between Paul and his opponents, and the latter are pushed into an extreme position, the sharing of Satan's realm. The result is the dropping out of any middle positions, thereby enabling Paul to push for solidarity with the reader in the positive position. Once he begins using bipolar language, he does not have middle positions. His anthropological and theological language did not allow for them. There are no middle positions in his terminology, although in some cases there were in social reality, as we shall see in the case of Peter (Gal. 2) below.

In the conflict in Galatians the bipolar terms 'flesh/spirit' and 'slave/free' indicate that groups of people are polarized into diametrically opposed categories with no provision for an intermediate possibility. The positions are simply asserted. It is obvious that the terms 'flesh' and 'slave' are negative (see also 1 Cor. 3.1-2; Rom. 6–7) while the 'spirit' and 'free' are positive.

That Paul knew that the categories were not absolutes is clear when we recognize that the term 'being in the flesh' does not refer only to those outside Christ. It can mean that one is not in Christ (Rom. 5.19-21; 8.4-8), but not in every context. For example, in 1 Cor. 3.1-4, it is evident that those whom Paul is upbraiding as being 'in the flesh' are Christians. It is clear that the old in the Corinthians had not passed away (2 Cor. 5.17). Paul realized that they were still 'babes'. What is more, they were 'still in the flesh'. As such they were not expelled from the church but received 'milk' from Paul. That is, he still considered them in the Christian movement.

The allegory of Sarah and Hagar in Gal. 4.21-31 is helpful to our discussion. In this passage who is represented by the terms 'flesh' and 'slavery' is not explicit. All who are of the 'flesh' persecute the children of the promise (the Galatians and Paul). By so saying, Paul implies that in holding this position the false brethren, and possibly other parts of the Jerusalem church, who 'compel' belong to the 'flesh' (see below). Even Peter is tainted by being drawn into the category of those of the 'flesh' (2.12-14; 4.29). The exclusion of mediating positions allows Paul to reprimand his opponents who are Christian by charging them with being in the 'flesh'.

The phrases 'son of a slave'/'son of a free woman' (4.31) and the 'Jerusalem below'/'Jerusalem above' (4.24-26) function in a similar way. The negative term puts everybody else in the wrong covenant, and Paul and his colleagues in the right one, with an appeal to the Galatians to join him and his co-workers. Just who is meant by 'the Jerusalem below' is ambiguous. Does Paul include Christians who follow the law? That is, does he include his opponents from the Jerusalem church? It appears so. By employing extreme positions he has forced his Christian opponents into a position against God.

As we have seen, the conflict in Galatia called forth a letter where there is rather a lot of explicit and implicit pushing of opponents into an extreme position ('flesh') usually occupied by outsiders. However, it is not in every case that three groups are forced into two positions; in some cases (2 Cor. 11) there may be only two groups. But however many groups there are to start with, in polemic there are two diametrically opposed adversaries—Paul and the opponents—plus the onlookers, who are urged to join him/God.

We have seen that sometimes the negative extremes of Paul's bipolar categories (false apostles, servants of Satan, those in the flesh) were his attempt to besmirch and distance his opponents. His use of extreme positive terms appears sometimes to glorify his churches and to guide them into his own camp. His calling the church at Corinth a 'pure bride' is an example noted in the last chapter.

In their being dominated by his opponents (2 Cor. 11.20), Paul did not consider the Corinthians pure or innocent. The term 'pure bride' glorifies the church. This term may have shamed some people or it may have caused them to regard in a new way, a polarized way, the people in Corinth who opposed Paul and to whom they had given support. If the church accepted his designation of them as 'pure bride', they also had to accept that those whom they had supported were 'deceitful serpents'. By disagreeing with the latter term, they were calling into question their own purity. For anyone who accepted these polarized terms, a great distance was created between them and Paul's opponents.

Paul's calling the church at Thessalonica the 'sons of light' may be another example of an exaggerated positive term. Did he really think that they were the sons of light? That he wanted them to be 'blameless' is clear from 3.13 and also 5.23. However, it is doubtful that he thought that all the Thessalonians were already 'blameless' and lived as 'sons of light'; otherwise he would not have had to give direction about sexual morality (4.3-8). By using the positive term 'sons of light' and exhortation, he was subtly urging the Thessalonians to remain on the 'blameless' side. 1 Thess. 4.6 and 4.8 lead one to think that Paul must have known about people who were not following his directives and needed to be warned. Recently it has been suggested that the Thessalonian Christians had behaved as a fertility cult and Paul responded by seeking to eliminate such elements from worship.[1] Whatever the situation to which Paul was responding in

1. H. Ulonska, 'Christen und Heiden: Die paulinische Paränese in I Thess 4, 3-8', *TZ* 43 (1987), pp. 210-18.

1 Thess. 4.1-8, the warning in 4.6-8 was stern and suggests that all was not as befitted the 'sons of light'. Further, almost half the letter is devoted to paraenetic material, and the presence of the many imperatives[1] he uses indicates more than formalistic moralizing.[2] While Paul tells the church that he is certain that it will escape the wrath to come, the extent of his exhorting lets us know that he was not so certain after all.[3]

To sum up, Paul uses bipolar terms and the conceptual bipolar categories of 'us'/'them' in order to intensify a conflict. An important part of determining the levels of intensity between the letters is the number of such bipolar terms. We turn now to the fourth in the series of ways in which Paul uses bipolar conceptual categories within polemic in order to polarize opponents from his churches.

Dropping out the Middle through an Eschatological Framework. The players in Paul's religious polemic are divided into two conceptual categories typical within an eschatological framework: 'those on the side of God' and 'those on the side of Satan'.

The association of the church with the eminent righteous and with God in 1 Thess. 2.14-16 has the effect of creating solidarity on one side of the conflict, while presentation of the opponents as against God and therefore implicitly in league with Satan produces solidarity on the other side.

In Gal. 5.8 Paul says that the path the church is taking is not from God. The implication is that those who compel the Galatians to be circumcised and those Galatians who follow this persuasion are on the side of Satan. Verse 8 is an appeal to the Galatians to turn from it. Placing the conflict in terms of supernatural powers is less explicit in this example than the one in 1 Thessalonians. When Gal. 1.8-10 is taken into account, it is at least as severe: anyone (even an angel) who

---

1.   See 1 Thess. 4.18; 5.13; four in 5.14; two in 5.15; all the verbs in 5.16-22.

2.   See Malherbe, *Paul and the Thessalonians*, pp. 61-109; *idem*, 'Exhortation in First Thessalonians', *NovT* 25 (1983), pp. 238-56. Also R.F. Collins, 'This Is the Will of God: Your Sanctification (I Thess. 4.3)', *Laval* 39 (1983), pp. 27-53.

3.   See also D.W. Palmer, 'Thanksgiving, Self-Defense, and Exhortation in I Thessalonians 1–3', *Colloquium* 14 (1981), pp. 23-31. Palmer correctly notes that Paul praises and exhorts the Thessalonians on the same issues: faith, love, deeds. See also H. Räisänen, *Paul and the Law* (Tübingen: Mohr, 2nd edn, 1987), p. 115 n. 108.

preaches a gospel which differs from Paul's is to be accursed.

Although the total number of positions in Paul's correspondence to the Corinthians is unclear, there are at least three: Paul, the Corinthians and the opponents. We remember that Paul knew the opponents to be Christian although he had serious disagreements with them. In trying to persuade the Corinthians to side with him, he pressed the opponents into the extreme position of being on the side of Satan and appealed to the Corinthians to join him. In this case, too, the conflict was polarized in terms of a conceptual 'us' (on the side of God) and 'them' (on the side of Satan) as seen in 2 Cor. 11.13-15, 23.

The Threat of Judgment and Punishment. It is generally agreed that Paul fully expected that the saved would be with Christ and those who opposed God would receive punishment. When he reassured his congregations that his opponents would be judged and receive their due (Gal. 5.10; 1 Thess. 2.16), his implicit or explicit association of his opponents with the realm of Satan forced them into an extreme opposing position. The level of rhetorical intensity is high.

Paul's judgment against his opponents in 2 Corinthians 11 was put this way: 'Their end will correspond to their deeds' (2 Cor. 11.15). This statement reveals that at some stratum he acknowledged the possibility of his opponents' changing their position on the disagreement and corroborates his view in 1 Cor. 3.12-15 and in Rom. 2.13-16 that ultimate judgment would be on the basis of works. A parallel example to 2 Cor. 11.15 is in Gal. 5.10 (the one who is troubling the Galatians will bear his judgment). When in 1 Thess. 2.16 Paul says that God's wrath has come upon the Jews *eis telos*, the intensity is greater: there is no room for a change of behaviour on the part of the Jews. The judgment is final and has already come upon them, whereas in 2 Cor. 11.13 Paul calls his opponents 'servants of Satan' only at the fiercest stage of the polemic, and allows for a change in behaviour before the end of the age.

There appears to be consistency with regard to the tactics used in religious polemic for persuading an audience to support one of two positions. In Paul's letters such language includes the use of bipolar terms, accusations of evil actions and motives, the belief that the situation involves opposing supernatural powers, the threat of judgment and punishment, and the interpretation of opposition as persecution with its consequent suffering. These tactics make up the negative side of the bipolar categorization.

In summary, when Paul is in polemical situations, he amplifies his own side of the argument by hyperbole that makes use of at least three bipolar categories: explicit pronominal 'us'/'them' terms, conceptual (implicit) bipolar categories of 'us'/'them', and explicit bipolar terms.

The first and the third bipolar categories are straightforward and require no further explanation. The conceptual (implicit) bipolar categories of 'us'/'them' are supported by descriptions of present behaviours and motives, a framework of supernatural warfare, and the looming of the future judgment in mutually exclusive terms.

The bipolar categories polarize the situation, underline Paul's authority, and place his congregation solidly on his side. It is the number, combination and context of these tactics which must be examined in determining the levels of intensity of passages. The following table indicates the extent to which Paul uses these tactics in polemical situations. In the rest of the chapter we shall discuss each passage in terms of three foci (the quantity of bipolar categories, their combinations, and an analysis of their context) and compare passages against the Jews with those against Christian brethren. We shall observe that the harshest language is reserved for insiders.

The Harshest Language is Reserved for the Insiders

The main point to be observed from Table 1 is that there are similarities in the aspects of Paul's polemic against the Jews and against his competitors within the Christian movement. The polemic against the former is not more severe than that against the latter. A look at the elements within polemic which contribute to its intensity supports this conclusion. While there are only two verses employed in the polemic against the Jews in 1 Thessalonians, there are approximately 29 in 2 Corinthians 11 and approximately 16 in Galatians 2 against his Christian opponents. We shall see below that the polemic against Gentiles and Jews in Romans 1 and 2 is part of a larger argument which Paul is constructing rather than polemic against actual opponents, and therefore I shall not count verses for these passages.

The fact that there are fewer verses of polemic in 1 Thess. 2.14-16 does not prove that Paul's vitriolic statements against the Jews were less harsh than his strictures against his Christian competitors. It is

	Implicit Bipolar	Explicit Bipolar	Suffering	Punishment/ Judgment	Evil Acts	Evil Motives	Satan
1 Thessalonians 2.14-16	**	–	*	*	*		–
2 Corinthians 11	*	***	*	*	*	*	*
Galatians 2–5	*	*****		*	*	*	–
Romans 1–2	*	–	–	*	*	*	–
Romans 9–11	–	***			–		–

Note: An asterisk indicates each time that a particular element occurs within the passage being investigated.

Table 1. *Levels of Rhetorical Intensity*

true, however, that in 1 Thessalonians Paul devotes more verses to
the discussion of sexual matters and the problem of deaths in the
community than he does to the denunciation of the Jews. Perhaps the
amount of space counts for something. It may show the severity of the
polemic, the seriousness of the threat, or both. We cannot be certain.
It certainly indicates that in Thessalonica there were other problems
which needed attention. It is not enough to consider quantity of
polemic alone; qualitative factors must be examined as well.

Qualitative factors can be dealt with by comparing Paul's levels of
rhetorical intensity against Christians, Jews and outsiders.

Intensity against Christians and against Jews

'Vessels of Wrath', 'False Apostles', and 'False Brethren'. How does
the explicit bipolar term 'vessels of wrath' (Rom. 9.22-23) compare
in intensity with the 'false apostles' (2 Cor. 11.13-15) or 'false
brethren' (Gal. 2.4)? Out of context, these terms all sound severe.
'False brethren' and 'false apostles' are explicit negative phrases used
to characterize fellow Christians. One might call this explicit naming
of only one side of the bipolar category 'name-calling'. It *assumes* the
bipolar opposites 'true brethren' and 'true apostle'. The similar
meaning of the negative terms suggests that they function as
equivalents.

'Vessels of wrath' is the negative bipolar term given to the
unbelieving Jews in Rom. 9.22. Its positive bipolar term 'vessels of
mercy' (v. 23) refers to the Gentiles. Thus, the meaning of 'vessels of
wrath' must be in relation to 'vessels of mercy'.

'Vessels of wrath' is not accompanied by a list of evil actions or
motives as are the terms 'false bethren' or 'false apostles', as we shall
see below. In fact, there is no mention of evil actions of the Jews in all
of Romans 9–11. The closest that Paul comes to describing an evil
action is nearly a chapter later than 9.22-23: they do not believe (10.3;
11.7). In response, God gave them 'a spirit of stupor' (11.8) and so
on, but their unbelief is shown to be part of God's plan such that Paul
says, 'through their trespass salvation has come to the Gentiles, so as
to make Israel jealous' (11.11). Further, Paul fully expects the Jews to
be included in the final salvation: 'Now if their trespass means riches
for the world, and if their failure means riches for the Gentiles, how
much more will their full inclusion mean!' (11.12, 26).

In Rom. 9.22 Paul says that the 'vessels of wrath' are made for destruction. The word 'destruction' can be misleading. The discussion in Romans 9 is not about the destiny of the Jewish people, but about the will of the creator in giving preference to certain people in the past and in the present. The role of Jews and Gentiles in God's plan is shown to be similar to the will of a potter who decides which pot will be saved and which destroyed. The term 'destruction' in this context has nothing to do with eternal destruction. The focus is on the will of the potter to save the ones which are usually not considered worthy of saving. In this case, the Gentiles are given an unexpected prominent role in God's salvation. That by 'destruction' Paul is not referring to the eternal destiny of the Jews is clear from Rom. 11.26, where he says that Israel will be saved.

To be called 'vessels of wrath' is unflattering but, as seen above, Paul does not amplify his term with charges of judgment, evil acts and evil motives, nor does he attribute Jewish unbelief to the work of Satan. In this instance it is the positive work of God. Paul's phrases are used in an attempt to explain the rejection of the gospel by many Jews. Paul is not defending his gospel against specific opponents. Indeed, he credits the Jews with the 'sonship, the glory, the covenants, the giving of the law' (Rom. 9.4-5). Thus, for him to call the Jews 'vessels of wrath' in Rom. 9.22-23 is less harsh than either to call his Christian opponents 'false apostles' and 'false brethren' or to imply that they were 'servants of Satan'.

One can also compare the intensity of the bipolar terms which accompany the main terms. 'Vessels of wrath' is supported by a negative term and *one* bipolar term. The explicit negative term is 'enemies of God' (11.28), whose meaning here is quite different from that of Phil. 3.18, where Paul has in mind either actual Jewish opponents or Gentiles. The context in Romans clarifies the meaning: 'As regards the gospel they are enemies of God *for your sake* [my emphasis]; but as regards election they are beloved for the sake of their forefathers'. Paul emphasizes that the Jews are enemies for the sake of the Gentiles. Earlier in the letter he says that the Gentiles were 'enemies' before they were reconciled with Christ (Rom. 5.10). In other words, the statement about the Jews as enemies *for their sake* is a warning against the Gentiles becoming too proud of their status with God.

The second bipolar term is found in Rom. 9.8: 'Children of the flesh'/'children of the promise' is equivalent to Paul's imagery of 'vessels of wrath'/'vessels of mercy'. The phrase 'children of the flesh' in this case is not as negative as it is in Galatians where those of the flesh are said to persecute those of the spirit. In Romans 'children of the flesh' simply means the physical people who have descended from Abraham including the believing Gentiles (Rom. 9.8). The Jewish people are not blamed. In fact, they are praised (9.4-5). The focus in Rom. 9.8-18 is on *God's choice* of people for election: the believing Gentiles as well as believing Jews.

In contrast to the less intense bipolar term 'vessels of wrath' of Rom. 9.22-23 supported by two other bipolar terms, the bipolar term 'false brethren' in Galatians is supported by *five* additional forceful bipolar terms (see Table 1 above): 'children of the free woman/ children of the slave' (4.31); 'spirit/flesh' (5.13-6.13); 'sons/slave' (4.1-5); 'children of the promise/children of the flesh' (4.23,28); and the explicit 'us/them' (Gal. 4.26–5.25). In 2 Corinthians the term 'false apostles' is surrounded by *three* additional bipolar terms (see Table 1 above): 'pure virgin Eve/the deceitful serpent' (11.3); 'servants of Christ/servants of Satan' (11.15, 23); and the explicit 'us/them' (2 Cor. 10.7–11.21). In view of the number of bipolar terms alone, 'vessels of wrath' is less intense than 'false apostles' or 'false brethren'.

In addition to bipolar terms, the terms 'false brethren' and 'false apostles' are accompanied by mention of evil actions. We recall from Chapter 8 that the 'false brethren' held the same attitude as those of the flesh who 'compelled' the Gentiles to be circumcised so that they would not be persecuted (Gal. 4.29; 6.12). Further, they 'slipped in to spy out' the freedom of the Gentiles in order to bring them into bondage. The term 'false apostles' is also accompanied by charges of evil actions and motives. As we have seen above (Chapter 8), the opponents seem to take money for their work (2 Cor. 11.7-15, 20).

From Table 1 we see that the 'false brethren' and 'false apostles' are threatened with judgment according to their deeds. This threat in Gal. 5.10 and 2 Cor. 11.15, as was pointed out above, seems to be in line with what Paul thought at other times (Rom. 2.6-11). However, in 2 Cor. 11.13-15 the threat is heightened by an accusation of an alignment of the opponents with Satan. Similarly, in Galatians, Paul curses his opponents (1.9; cf. 3.10). These threats, curses and alignments with Satan are not found in Romans 9–11. Therefore, the bipolar terms implicating the Jews in Romans 9–11 are less severe than those against Christian brethren in Galatians 2–5 and 2 Corinthians 11.

With regard to suffering, Gal. 2.10 and 2 Cor. 11.20 imply that the church suffers from those who 'trouble' them and 'prey upon' them. Romans 9–11 does not stress the suffering of the church. The forceful bipolar terms and the suffering mentioned indicate that the situation in Galatia and Corinth was serious and accounts for the more intense rhetoric of Galatians and 2 Corinthians 11. Within their context, 'vessels of wrath' is clearly not as intense as 'false brethren' or 'false apostles'.

Implicit Bipolar Terms in 1 Thessalonians 2.14-16 compared to Explicit Terms in Galatians 2–5 and 2 Corinthians 11. Is what Paul says about the Jews in 1 Thess. 2.14-16 more intense than what he says about his non-Christian opponents in Galatians and 2 Corinthians? On the basis of the above arguments regarding the many bipolar terms which the polemic in Galatians and 2 Corinthians gathers around itself, I judge the polemic in the problem passage to be less intense. The passage does have an implicit bipolar 'us/them' simply by Paul's citing the suffering that the *symphyletai* and the Jews caused and by his drawing together the Thessalonian church, the Judaean church, the Lord Jesus, the prophets and 'us' as those righteous people who suffer. Further, there is an implicit 'those who are saved' and 'those who are damned' in v. 16.[1] The Gentiles (and presumably Paul, the prophets, the Judaean churches and the Thessalonian church) are the saved and the Jews are the damned. However, these terms are not explicit. Further, the passage does not abound with explicit polemical bipolar terms as do the passages in Galatians 2–5 and 2 Corinthians 11 (Table 1).

In the latter part of 1 Thessalonians we do find the positive bipolar term 'sons of light' (5.5). The negative term 'sons of darkness' is only implicit. Thus, the emphasis is on the positive term, and while Paul may have regarded the Jews and the *symphyletai* as 'sons of darkness', he did not take pains to point it out explicitly. This contrasts with his emphasizing the negative bipolar term in Gal. 2.4 and 2 Cor. 11.13-15. Since the term occurs late in 1 Thessalonians, it is not included in Table 1. Even if I were to include it, the polemic in 2 Corinthians 11

---

1. Okeke, 'I Thessalonians 2.13-16', p. 132.

and Galatians 2–5 is still more intense because it contains more bipolar terms, more threats, curses and alignments with Satan.

Even though the passage in 1 Thess. 2.16 may appear at first to be more severe than Paul's judgments in Gal. 5.10 and 2 Cor. 11.15, on closer examination it turns out to be less severe. In 2 Cor. 11.15 Paul relegates his opponents to the enclave of Satan and *then* says that their end will correspond to their deeds, implying that their end will be Satan's if they continue in their ways. Similarly, Paul's cursing his opponents in Gal. 1.9 cancels the apparently milder statement about judgment in 5.10. Aligning his opponents with Satan and cursing them would seem to be at least as severe as saying that by some current disaster God's wrath had come upon the Jews. Even his adding *eis telos* does not alter the matter. Everyone knew that there were still Jews around. If he wished that there were none around, it was understandable given whatever harassment they were giving him about his work. But then, he also wished that his Christian opponents in Galatia would castrate themselves!

The Sins of both the Jews and Paul's Christian Opponents. In 1 Thess. 2.15 Paul says that the Jews 'killed the Lord Jesus and the prophets and persecuted us'. This charge is strong. We have seen that by association Paul implied that some of the Christians in the Jerusalem church had been killed. Thus, the charge of the Jews 'killing' some people appears more severe than either the charges in 2 Cor. 11.20 that his Christian opponents 'prey upon' and 'make slaves of' the church or those in Galatians 2–5 that the Christians' opponents 'compel' the church to be circumcised.

We must remember that Paul in 1 Thess. 2.15 was likely drawing upon a long Jewish tradition which was critical of its *insiders*: they always killed their prophets (at least one or two). Paul could amplify this tradition by adding the death of Jesus to it, thus adding fuel to the charges and succeeding in making the Jews appear incorrigible. On the other hand, he could not say that his Christian opponents had killed anybody. The history of the Christian movement was not yet old enough for him to lay this charge against his opponents, let alone amplify it.

Paul's charges do, however, have bite. He impugned the opponents in Corinth with charges of being 'false apostles', of preaching a different Jesus, and of being in league with Satan (2 Cor. 11.13-15), and those in Galatia with being 'false brethren' who were preaching a different gospel and surreptitiously trying to bring the Galatians into slavery by compelling them to be circumcised (Gal. 2.4). These charges refer to events in the present or in the recent past.

In 1 Thess. 2.14-16 the charges of 'killing' are directed to events which took place in the more distant past. What we learn about the current circumstances in Thessalonica is that the Jews are hindering Paul from preaching to the Gentiles. They are not killing anybody. Surely Paul would have mentioned it, if they had.

The situation in Galatia and Corinth was a recent occurrence, perhaps preventing Paul from using a history of iniquity against his opponents. Besides, they apparently had recommendations from Jerusalem. The denigration of Peter and the statement about the intruders being servants of Satan may reflect Paul's knowledge of the earlier tradition about Jesus calling Peter 'Satan'.[1] Paul's labelling his Christian opponents 'servants of Satan' and implying that the Jerusalem church and Peter were associated with the realm of the 'flesh' is at least as severe as his using a traditional charge against the Jews to incriminate them in the present.

Jews: Romans 2, 9–11 and 1 Thessalonians 2.14-16. Romans 2 is not a polemic against actual Jews as such but part of a larger argument which Paul constructs in Romans 1–3. Nevertheless, one can observe that there is the implicit bipolar term 'us/them' in which the members are alternately Gentiles or Jews. There are no explicit bipolar terms and suffering is not mentioned, while the evil actions and motives of Jews are. While robbing and adultery are mentioned, killing of the religious elite is not. The passage therefore appears less intense than that in 1 Thess. 2.14-16 and more intense than the passages about the Jews in Romans 9–11.

Is the level of polemic in the problem passage more intense in what it says about the Jews than in Romans 9–11? From the evidence considered above, it seems clear that the intensity of Paul's list of charges against the Jews in the former passage, which results in the implicit bipolar conceptual category 'us/them', is greater than his statements about the Jews in Romans 9–11. However, the context is important. We need to recall that the judgment of Paul against the

---

1. So Thrall, 'Super-Apostles', p. 55.

Jews in 1 Thess. 2.16 is connected to the situation of the Thessalonians. They were suffering at the hands of their compatriots, who may have included some Jews. At any rate, Paul says that Jews were harassing him. The situation in Romans 9–11 is different. There the Jews are not opponents, and so any polemic against them is less intense.

Intensity against True Outsiders

We have seen that Paul's polemic is most intense in the heat of conflict within the *ekklēsia* in Christ. While he threatens the members with punishment and judgment, he does not seem to concern himself with the question of what will happen to actual outsiders, those who do not intend to obey the God of Israel.

Aside from the implicit condemnation of Gentiles in 1 Cor. 6.9-11 and 2 Cor. 6.14-7.1, Paul does not seem to spend time judging those outside the Christian messianic movement. He does condemn the Gentile world in Romans 1, but his judgment is part of a larger argument designed to lead to a particular theological conclusion, and therefore one cannot say that it is a final soteriological conclusion. While 1 Thess. 1.10 and 5.9 mention the 'wrath to come', these passages are more for the admonishment of insiders than judgment of outsiders. It is noteworthy that those who jailed Paul are never judged. His view in 1 Cor. 5.12-13 that he had nothing to do with judging those who were outside the Christian movement seems to be consistent with his actions for the most part.

It may be that Phil. 3.18-19 is an exception to Paul's focus on insiders for chastisement, but this is not certain. If the passage does refer to outsiders, then it would be an exception to the rule that the most severe language is used for insiders. Apparently Paul did think that people in general would be accused on the day of judgment (Rom. 2.13-16). Nonetheless, he did not express a clear plan with regard to the final salvation of the Gentiles as a group. Perhaps he thought that God would find a way to save them all (Rom. 11.32). If Phil. 3.18-19 is an exception, then it seems to me to be an exception that proves the rule: Paul's vituperation is usually directed against opposition, either within the Christian movement (Galatians; 2 Cor. 11) or within Judaism (those who hindered him, i.e., 1 Thess. 2.16).

Summary

By comparing the levels of intensity in Paul's polemic against the Jews and against the 'false brethren', we see that the polemic against his kinsmen by race was not more severe than that against his 'Christian' competitors.

Levels of intensity can be determined by comparing the quantity of Paul's castigations and their quality. The level of intensity of his vituperation increases when he is facing opposition from within the *ekklēsia* in Christ. As regards Judaism proper, his polemic decreased from the time he wrote 1 Thessalonians to the writing of Romans. In the former the Jews are perceived as opponents (whether in Thessalonica or elsewhere), while in Romans 9–11 they are not.

A study of the levels of rhetorical intensity goes a long way towards understanding passages where extreme language is used, the social historical context of such passages, the early Christian movement, Paul's relationship to Judaism, and his life as an apostle.

We can return now to 1 Thess. 2.14-16 to discuss four issues: (1) how the passage sheds light upon Paul's relationship with the Jewish people early in his career and stands in contrast to Romans 9–11; (2) what the focus of conflict was between Paul and the Jews; (3) how rigid the boundary was between them; and (4) what the polemical hyperbole tells us about Paul the apostle himself.

Chapter 10

THE CONTEXT OF 1 THESSALONIANS 2.14-16 IN PAUL'S CAREER

I began this study with the observation that Paul's letters reveal two different views about the Jewish people: the wrath of God has come upon them completely (so 1 Thess. 2.14-16) and their estrangement from God is only temporary (so Rom. 9–11). We saw that Paul's statements in the problem passage must be understood in their own right. As such they can yield knowledge as to his relationship to the Jewish people during that early period in his career (c. 51 CE).

In the preceding chapter we saw that Paul's statements against the Jews (1 Thess. 2.14-16) are less intense than those in other places against Christian opponents (2 Cor. 11 or Gal. 2–5). Since in the latter passages I do not propose that Paul was displaying an anti-Christian attitude, it is better not to conclude that in 1 Thess. 2.14-16 he held an anti-Jewish one.[1] In other words, this study has shown that Paul's condemnations of the Jews were not meant as his final and absolute judgment against them any more than his harsh criticisms of his Christian brethren were. Further, the sharp assertions against the Jews in the problem passage must not be seen within the modern context of polemic between two religions but within the ancient context: they indicate a lively argument within Judaism. In the next section we will focus on the fluidity of boundaries between the Christian movement and Judaism at this nascent stage of Paul's work with Gentiles.

---

1. J. Hurd, 'Paul ahead of his Time', pp. 33-36. See also U. Schnell, 'Der erste Thessalonicherbrief', pp. 207-24.

The Early Christian Movement and Judaism:
No Rigid Separation

It has been emphasized that Judaism and Christianity were not separate religions in the first century.[1] This point is often forgotten when scholars are assessing Paul's polemic against the Jews in 1 Thessalonians. That Paul still considered himself to be part of Judaism is evident in that he was punished by the synagogue. If he had thought of himself as having left Judaism, he could have stopped frequenting the synagogue.

From the side of Judaism, the fact of his punishment does not constitute a separation. There is no evidence from before 200 CE that a ban existed as a means of cutting someone off from the Jewish community on a permanent basis.[2]

Before 70 CE Judaism was pluralistic. There was not much impetus for uniformity and even if uniformity had been desired, it could not have been implemented. It only became a possibility after 70 CE with the ascendancy of the Pharisees.[3] Thus, the hostile statements in 1 Thess. 2.14-16 hardly constitute evidence of a separation from Judaism. Rather, they indicate an ongoing relationship—in this case conflict—between Jews.[4] As we have seen, in the early first century,

---

1.   There was a wide variety within Judaism in the first century. See M. Simon, *Verus Israel: A Study of the Relations between Christians and Jews in the Roman Empire, 135–425* (trans. H. McKeating; New York: Oxford University Press, 1986), for an excellent review of the literature, especially of the diaspora. For a review of Palestinian Judaism, see Sanders, *Paul and the Palestinian Judaism*. John Gager identified a number of voices in the conversation about Judaism: '...the voice of Christians who saw no need to repudiate Judaism even while embracing Christianity as well as the voices of the Gentiles who saw in Judaism a religion for all humanity', *The Origins of Anti-Semitism*, p. 269. See also the important early work of C.G. Montefiore, *Judaism and St Paul: Two Essays* (London: Max Goshen, 1914). Montefiore used the term 'the Judaisms of his [Paul's] age' (p. 13).

2.   S.T. Katz, 'Issues in the Separation of Judaism and Christianity after 70 CE: A Reconsideration', *JBL* 103 (1984), pp. 43-76 (49 and 74).

3.   Katz, 'Separation of Judaism and Christianity', p. 51.

4.   G. Simmel, *Conflict* (trans. K.H. Wolff; Glencoe, IL: Free Press, 1955), pp. 67-68, cited by R.L. Wilken, *John Chrysostom and the Jews: Rhetoric and Reality in the Late 4th Century* (Berkeley: University of California Press, 1983), p. 69. A.E. Segal, *Paul the Convert, the Apostolate and Apostasy of Saul the Pharisee* (New Haven: Yale University Press, 1990), p. 284.

there was conflict not between two separate religions, but between Paul and other Jewish Christians on the one hand, and *some* Jewish people on the other.

Assuming no rigid separation between Paul's churches and the Jews per se, what does the statement that '[the Jews] hinder us from preaching to the Gentiles that they might be saved' (1 Thess. 2.16a) reveal about the conflict? There seem to be two possibilities: competition or confrontation.

Competition

Nothing in our passage excludes the picture in Acts that the reason for the conflict between Paul and the Jews at this early stage in his career with Gentiles had to do with competition. According to Acts 17.5, the Jews were jealous (*zēlōsantes*) of his success in gaining converts (a large number of worshipping Greeks and a significant number of notable women) and hence were competing with him.

What other evidence is there (aside from Acts and possibly our passage) to support the claim that Judaism was a competitor with Christianity in the early decades of the Christian movement? Although Marcel Simon has shown that Judaism was a 'real, active, and often successful competitor with Christianity'[1] during the years 135–425 CE,[2] there is little evidence for his contention that proselytizing by Jews was 'worldwide in its scope' before 135 CE.[3] In fact, the only piece of support he has is Mt. 23.15, which is hardly clear evidence of

---

1. Simon, *Verus Israel*, p. 385. See also Wilken's assessment of the early Christian literature which shows that 'Christians and Jews continued to have contact with each other well into the fifth century, and that Christians devoted a good part of their exegetical, theological, and catechetical endeavors to dealing with questions raised by the continuing presence of Jews'. R.L. Wilken, *Judaism and the Early Christian Mind: A Study of Cyril of Alexandria's Exegesis and Theology* (New Haven: Yale University Press, 1971), p. 36. See also M. Whittaker, *Jews and Christians: Graeco-Roman Views* (Cambridge: Cambridge University Press, 1984), p. 15.

2. The political catastrophes in Palestine in 70 and 135 did not put an end to Jewish expansion, but the appeal of the synagogue for Christians goes on at least into the fourth century. See Simon, *Verus Israel*, pp. 270-305.

3. Simon, *Verus Israel*, pp. 283, 391. Some scholars maintain that Jews in the first century were actively engaged in competing for Gentiles who were casually associated with the synagogue (so Acts) or for Gentiles in general. P. Borgen, 'The Early Church and the Hellenistic Synagogue', *ST* 37 (1983), pp. 55-78 (58-61).

widespread missionary activity. There are now more doubts about Simon's view.[1] There is, however, significant evidence of such activity by the fourth century. Yet there was competition from the Jews in the sense that Judaism was one option for Gentiles in the Graeco-Roman world. Further, that Judaism proved to hold an attraction or at least an interest for Gentiles[2] is enough evidence for us legitimately to consider this group as competition for Paul, although not as serious or active a competitor as his Christian brethren from Jerusalem, as this study has indicated. To overemphasize competition from Jews is to create an imbalance which skews the historical picture.[3]

If 1 Thess. 2.14-16 indicates competition by Jews for Gentiles, then Paul's letters reflect a three-way relationship with competition on two levels: (1) competition for Gentiles by both Jews and Paul and his co-workers (1 Thessalonians), and (2) competition between the Christian missionaries from Jerusalem and Paul and his co-workers (Galatians, Corinthians). Luke, in writing his history some 30 or 40 years after Paul,[4] had already virtually amalgamated the Christian missionaries from Jerusalem with Paul and his co-workers, and then emphasized the competition between this melded entity and the Jews. He portrays the churches in Jerusalem and those of Paul as being in harmony and the Jews as their jealous competitors (Acts 17.5). An example of how Acts has amalgamated the Christian movements can be seen in Luke's treatment of Peter and Paul. They are in complete

---

1. M. Goodman, 'Proselytising in Rabbinic Judaism', *JJS* 40 (1989), pp. 175-85.

2. See the continuing discussion of the extent of the association of Jews and Gentiles of the first century in the work of R.S. MacLennan and A.T. Kraabel, 'The God-Fearers: A Literary and Theological Invention', *BARev* 12 (1986), pp. 46-53. See also A.T. Kraabel, 'The Roman Diaspora: Six Questionable Assumptions', *JJS* 33 (1982), pp. 445-64; *idem*, 'Greeks, Jews, and Lutherans in the Middle Half of Acts', in Nickelsburg with MacRae (eds.), *Christians Among Jews and Gentiles*, pp. 147-57. Also, J.G. Gager, 'Jews, Gentiles, and Synagogues in the Book of Acts', in Nickelsburg with MacRae (eds.), *Christians Among Jews and Gentiles*, p. 99; J. Reynolds and R. Tannenbaum, *Jews and God-Fearers at Aphrodisias* (Cambridge: Cambridge Philological Society, 1987), pp. 85-92; L. Feldman, 'The Omnipresence of the God-Fearers', *BARev* 12 (1986), pp. 58-63.

3. See for example Segal's recent work which omits a comparison between Paul's opposition from Jews as such and that from Jewish Christians. Segal, *Paul the Convert*.

4. Kümmel, *Introduction to the New Testament*, pp. 105-106.

agreement as to food laws and circumcision (Acts 10–11; 15; 21.17-27), topics which we know from Paul's letters were issues which stirred up controversy. The competition between the early Christian movement and the Jews is described as the result of the latter's jealousy and their inciting people against the early Christian movement (Acts 13.45, 50; 14.2, 5, 19; 17.13; 21.27; 23.12; etc.). This was the beginning of the rigidifying of the movements mentioned above into two main groups: Christians and Jews. In describing these movements in the early part of the first century sometimes scholars have done the same. But this is to ignore the fact that the boundary between the early Christian movement and Judaism was still quite fluid. Further, it ignores Luke's tendency to attribute Jewish opposition to the social factor of competition for converts of high status while portraying their allies against the Christian movement as persons of the lower class.[1] As I have indicated, most of the competition for Gentiles took place within the Christian movement although Gentiles continued to be attracted to Judaism.

While Judaism was an option for Gentiles and in that sense constituted competition for Paul, if we look closer we find that confrontation as a result of Paul's false practice of Judaism (not requiring the Gentiles as part of the people of God to be circumcised) was a more likely reason for the hostility between Paul and the Jews.

Confrontation

Okeke[2] was partly correct when he pointed to the eschatological context for an explanation of the two spheres of salvation and damnation which Paul articulates in 1 Thess. 2.14-16. This investigation points to an additional reason: confrontation. The passage reflects the situation of a double confrontation: Paul's being hindered from preaching to the Gentiles and the Thessalonians' being troubled by their compatriots.

With regard to the former, the passage reflects early Jewish opposition to his work with Gentiles, and corroborates what he wrote in other letters, namely, that as a leader of a Jewish movement he was subject to and accepted punishment from Jews for not circumcising Gentiles.[3]

---

1. Malherbe, *Paul and the Thessalonians*, p. 17.
2. Okeke, 'I Thessalonians 2.13-16', p. 132.
3. See Sanders, *Paul, the Law, and the Jewish People*, pp. 190-92.

With regard to the second confrontation, the Thessalonians' being troubled by their compatriots, let us observe the following. If by 'hindering us from speaking to the Gentiles that they may be saved' (1 Thess. 2.16) Paul means that Jews (at Thessalonica or elsewhere) were confronting him because he did not require circumcision for Gentiles as an entrance requirement into a movement that considered itself Jewish, then we have a triangular relationship in which the Jews confront Paul and his co-workers while maintaining relatively good relations with the Christian missionaries from Jerusalem.

The language of hyperbole in 1 Thess. 2.14-16 helped to portray the world in diametrically opposed terms and thus it showed the Thessalonians that they were on the right side. Paul's polemical hyperbole about the sins of the Jews and God's judgment against them provides the Thessalonians with an example against which they can understand their own experiences of persecution by Gentiles. In this paradigm the Jews were portrayed negatively as opposing God's purposes. The judgment in v. 16c was an implicit warning to opponents outside or inside the church.

When Paul says that the Jews hindered him from preaching to the Gentiles that they might be saved, he reveals that opposition from Jews was a reality in his life, one which called forth the articulation of a negative role for them: opposition to God. They are roundly condemned for hindering his work as a missionary but not for rejecting the gospel. The difficulty seems centred upon Paul and his work among the Gentiles. It is likely that a Jewish Paul was being punished or harassed for admitting Gentiles into a religious movement seen to be Jewish without demanding circumcision.

In Paul's correspondence with the Galatians and the Corinthians the Jews are not his real concern; they are peripheral.[1] And by the time Romans was written the Jews are not the opponents of Paul. The context is different: Paul has almost fulfilled his mission (Rom. 15.18-20) and has begun to think about the role of the Jews in God's plan (Romans 9–11). He knew that he might face more confrontation when he arrived in Jerusalem with the offering—confrontation from Jews per se and possibly also from some Jewish Christians (15.31). Thus the theme of suffering still plays a significant role in the letter, but the

---

1. R. Penna, 'L'évolution de l'attitude de Paul envers les juifs', in A. Vanhoye (ed.), *L'apôtre Paul, personnalité, style et conception du ministère* (Leuven: Leuven University Press, 1986), pp. 401, 408.

letter itself does not indicate actual competition or confrontation in the present.

Paul, in Romans, considers the unbelieving Jews to be disobedient (*apeithountōn*), but his tone has changed from 1 Thessalonians. The Jews are vessels of wrath (Rom. 9.22), disobedient (11.30), even enemies of sorts (11.28), but they do not oppose God. Rather, they are used by God for special purposes, namely, the reconciliation of the world (11.15). In Rom. 11.31-32 he mentions the disobedience of the Jewish people positively, as being under the control of God and responsible for the mercy shown to Gentiles. Paul finds a positive role for them: their destiny is under the control of God. He leaves the problem of the unbelieving Jews to God (11.26): 'The Deliverer will come from Zion, and will banish ungodliness from Jacob'. As Penna puts it, 'In the beginning they constitute an antithesis; at the end, they are a mystery'.[1]

Penna is correct in proposing that Paul's attitude had changed from 1 Thessalonians to Romans. Certainly the situations are completely different. When thinking about God's plan, Paul takes a different approach; there the Jewish people have a primary place in God's plan: every time 'the Jews' are placed alongside 'the Greeks' it is the Jews who have the first position.[2] In the end Paul seems to have thought out a role for himself, albeit indirect, which would bring about the inclusion of the Jewish people in God's plan.

The positive and negative portrayal of the Jewish people is somewhat parallel to the negative and positive views Paul expressed with regard to the topic of the law.[3] In arguing hotly against his Galatian converts following the law (Gal. 3.19), Paul said that the law was given through angels and not directly by God. Later, in Gal. 3.22-24, the law is positively connected to sin so that the presence of sin carries out God's will. In Rom. 5.20-21 Paul begins with a positive connection between the law and God's will. By Rom. 7.14-25, in the process of arguing against the law, he has broken the positive connection between the law, sin and God's will. Rather, the law is used by an independent force which is opposed to God's will (Rom. 7.13). Nevertheless, by the time he wrote Rom. 9.4-5 Paul cited the law as one of the glories of Israel, and in Rom. 11.32 he implied that the law

1. Penna, 'L'évolution de l'attitude de Paul', p. 419.
2. Penna, 'L'évolution de l'attitude de Paul', p. 420.
3. See Sanders, *Paul, the Law, and the Jewish People*, pp. 70-91.

was positively under the control of God.

The positive and negative portrayals of both the law and the Jewish people indicate that their role in God's plan in Christ was thought out by Paul on a day-to-day, crisis-by-crisis basis. In that process confrontation and competition play a role in how he speaks about the law. The letter to the Galatians reveals a situation of competition (5.1) and confrontation (5.11) with Christian missionaries from Jerusalem. Paul is *arguing* for the freedom of the Gentiles against those who insist that if the Gentiles want to consider themselves the people of God they must submit to circumcision. Under threat Paul gives the law a negative role: all who rely on works of the law are under a curse. Further, all who submit to the law (receive circumcision) are severed from Christ.

By Romans 9, however, Paul is *explaining* the role of the Jewish law in God's plan in history rather than confronting real opponents, as he was in Galatians. We learn that not only did his thought about the law develop over the years,[1] but also that as a result of opposition Paul was driven to hyperbole about the origin of the law (Gal. 3.19) and its association with death (2 Cor. 3.6; Rom. 7), in order to make his view of religious practice persuasive. Räisänen[2] recognized that Paul, writing in a conflict setting, did not do justice to the form of piety he had given up. It appears that when Paul found himself in a polemical situation, he often resorted to hyperbolic statements which he softened or revoked at other times.

The task in trying to sort out Paul's relationship to the Jews requires knowing where in the Pauline corpus to begin. We need to determine Paul's thoughts about his mission (that he understood himself to be called to preach to the Gentiles): that can best be learned from Romans, when much of his work was behind him. Apparently, at the early part of his career he did not set out to preach to Jews.[3]

---

1. For a more thorough treatment of the topic of the development of the law in Paul's thought, see H. Räisänen, 'Paul's Conversion and the Development of His View of the Law', *NTS* 33 (1987), pp. 404-19.

2. Räisänen, *Paul and the Law*, pp. xxvi-xxvii.

3. *Contra* the book of Acts (e.g., 17.1; 18.4, etc.) and Watson, *Paul, Judaism, and the Gentiles*, p. 177.

We also learn much from 1 Thessalonians:

1. Jews did not generally persecute Gentile churches.
2. Jews hindered Paul's work in some way.
3. Confrontation with Jews over his work with Gentiles likely occurred early in his career, although it is likely that actual punishment did not occur until later.
4. Paul responded to opposition from some Jews by using hyperbole and in so doing braced his church in their sufferings.
5. By using polemical hyperbole Paul could cast his Jewish opponents completely on the wrong side, the side opposing God and salvation.

From this study of Paul's career, we have learned that Paul could hold both positive and negative views of the Jewish people, just as he could of his Christian competitors.

Summary

The problem passage is best understood within the context of opposition encountered during a Jewish missionary's career as apostle to the Gentiles, a career which involved bringing the Gentiles into the people of God without requiring their circumcision. The opposition comes not from outside Paul's religious framework but from within it.

There were in the first century 'several Judaisms, all more or less fluid and growing'.[1] In this study we have noted the Judaism that was hindering Paul, the Jewish Christians in Jerusalem, and Paul himself. These groups were all actively engaged with each other, having at least some elements in common (Jewish scriptures, tradition and aspects of Jewish thought, e.g., 'sons of Abraham').

We must also acknowledge the differences between Paul and his Jewish brethren. Sanders has pointed out that the church was not the synagogue, baptism was not circumcision, the eucharist was not the Passover meal.[2] Further, it is somewhat correct to say that Paul 'converted': not to another God, but he nevertheless 'turned to the Lord' and he thought that other Jews needed to do the same (2 Cor. 3). Yet we must not overemphasize the difference between Paul the

---

1. Montefiore, *Judaism and St Paul*, p. 3.
2. Sanders, *Paul, the Law, and the Jewish People*, pp. 207-10.

Jewish apostle who allowed Gentiles into the Christian movement without circumcising them and other Jews, particularly Jews like those to whom Philo alludes who gave circumcision a philosophical interpretation and gave up its literal requirement.[1] Further, the church was more like a synagogue than the stoa or a pagan temple. There was as yet no rigid separation between Paul's movement and Judaism. Rather, the main opposition from Jews seems to come from a different interpretation of the status and role of the Gentiles within Judaism at the end of the age. The persecution/punishment of Paul is to be taken as evidence that he still stood within Judaism.

Opposition to Paul, however, has been overemphasized. In order to balance the historical picture, we must take the competition from Christian brethren into consideration. When that happens we see that conflict in and of itself does not indicate severed relationships between groups. On the contrary, it indicates lively relations, relations that change with circumstances. Furthermore, the variations of Paul's statements within a letter, or from letter to letter, do not indicate an inconsistent or muddled mind, but a human being whose rhetoric reflects his passionate involvement with his churches and God's work.

In the conclusion that follows, I shall summarize the importance of the research method employed in this study. There I shall emphasize (1) the significance of the placing of Paul's writings—whether 1 Thessalonians, Romans or his other letters—in the context of the rhetorical, social and historical milieu of his day, and (2) the necessity of the study of his rhetorical polemic for a valid social-historical picture of the early Christian movement, of Paul's relationship to Judaism, of his thought, and of his person. Further, I shall suggest several directions for future research.

---

1.   Philo, *Migr.* 89-93, specifically 92.

CONCLUSION

'When I use a word', Humpty Dumpty said, in rather a scornful tone,
'it means just what I choose it to mean—neither more nor less'.
'The question is', said Alice, 'whether you can make words mean so
many different things'.
'The question is', said Humpty Dumpty, 'which is to be master—that's
all'.[1]

The goal of understanding Paul's charges against the Jews in
1 Thess. 2.14-16 cannot be reached on the basis of word studies,
syntax and structural analyses alone. Further, a comparison of his
language in this passage with his remarks about the Jews in Romans
does not assist us, because such a study tends to impose theological
harmonization upon the material or to deny the authenticity of the
verses in 1 Thessalonians on the basis of incongruity.

I have proposed a new approach, one which focuses upon the letter
itself, tries to place the letter and the passage in context, and
recognizes Paul's ability to write in a nuanced and forceful manner
which derived not only from his being immersed in Jewish tradition
but also from his familiarity with the wider rhetorical world of his
day.

Attention to the historical situation enabled us to perceive Paul's
statements as exaggerations of the historical reality behind them.
Study of Paul's rhetoric helped us to analyze the polarizing function
of hyperbole in the context of polemical situations. I did not attempt
to draw conclusions about literary dependency, but assumed that
general patterns of rhetoric would have been known by many people
at the time simply by being part of the same milieu.

Once it was established that some phrases were exaggerations, then
the general flow and structure of the language in the passage were
examined. A triadic pattern was seen to dominate the passage, and its

---

1. L. Carroll, *Alice in Wonderland* (ed. D.J. Gray; New York: W.W. Norton,
1971), p. 163.

general flow seemed to lead to an accumulation and climax of the sins of the Jews before breaking the flow with the judgment that God's wrath had come upon them completely.

The suffering of the Judaean churches was exaggerated by Paul, but the association of the suffering of the Thessalonians with that of the Judaean churches served to build solidarity between Paul and his church at Thessalonica, a church which likely was surprised at experiencing persecution from local citizens (cf. 1 Pet. 4.12). At the same time, the hyperbole polarized the righteous—the Lord, the prophets, Paul, possibly the other apostles, and the Thessalonians—against all the opponents of God's plan, namely, the Jews and the local citizens who caused suffering. By piling up the sins of the Jews in a series of exaggerated charges which are disrupted with the judgment that God's wrath has come upon them, Paul implies a pronouncement against all the opponents of the church, including those who are causing the Thessalonians to suffer.

Had we focused only upon 1 Thess. 2.14-16 and perhaps the passages in Romans, we would have learned that Paul used polemical hyperbole when in conflict with some Jews; but the historical picture would have been skewed. It would have presented Paul as more vituperative in his relationship with Judaism than is apparent when his polemical hyperbole against his fellow Christians is examined also. Our study of the polemical hyperbole that Paul employs against his fellow Christians reveals that the bipolar categories and the recitation of evil motives and actions were not less in their case but perhaps even more scathing than those he uses against the Jews. That Paul could make vitriolic denunciations of his fellow Christians leads us to be cautious about hastily judging his charges against the Jews as indicating anti-Judaism.

Paul's statements in 1 Thess. 2.14-16 are, to be sure, an unfortunate set of accusations. Seen in the context of denunciations against others, however, they reflect not his final and absolute view but his way of dealing with conflict.

Therefore, although later writers used Paul's vituperation against the Jews to fan the flame of anti-Judaism, such charges cannot be laid at the feet of Paul. Nevertheless, he dealt a major blow to Judaism by admitting Gentiles without circumcision and calling the new creation the 'sons of Abraham'. Extreme language in the letters of Paul needs to be studied carefully. We learn that words can indeed mean different things. In the case of 1 Thess. 2.14-16 opposition to Paul's work can place Jews against God, whereas in Romans Jews in their opposition are interpreted as positive instruments of God. By further studying Paul's extreme language, we will learn more about the man, his churches, his competitors and his times.

To study Paul's extreme language is to direct our attention to that aspect of his words which seeks, as Humpty Dumpty said, 'to be master'—that is, to argue a case, to brace a church, to be part of God's plan and, when necessary, to compete with insider opponents so as to be God's best apostle.

The use of rhetorical studies for future research in Paul's letters appears to be a fruitful one indeed. Each of his letters could be examined thoroughly for its exaggerated language. Such examinations would yield information about their context, the early Christian church, and the apostle himself. Further, the present study did not focus upon the letter to the Philippians because of the great number of partition hypotheses and the difficulty of determining who the opponents are in that letter. A study of Paul's polemic and exaggerated language in Philippians does, however, need to be done.

The study of polemical hyperbole which has been undertaken here may lead to a more productive approach to the intense language so much a part of Paul's letters.

BIBLIOGRAPHY

Primary Sources

The Apocrypha and Pseudepigrapha of the Old Testament (ed. and trans. R.H. Charles; repr.; Oxford: Clarendon Press, 1979 [1913]), II.

Aristotle, *The Art of Rhetoric* (trans. J.H. Freese; LCL; Cambridge, MA: Harvard University Press, 1967).

[Aristotle], *Rhetoric to Alexander* (trans. H. Rackham; LCL; Cambridge, MA: Harvard University Press, 1967).

Cicero, *To Gaius Herennius on the Theory of Public Speaking* (trans. H. Caplan; LCL; Cambridge, MA: Harvard University Press, 1964).

—*On Invention* (trans. H.M. Hubbell; LCL; Cambridge, MA: Harvard University Press, 1960).

—*For Ligarius* (trans. N.H. Watts; LCL; Cambridge, MA: Harvard University Press, 1964).

—*On the Making of an Orator* (trans. E.W. Sutton and H. Rackham; LCL; Cambridge, MA: Harvard University Press, 1959–60).

—*Philippics* (trans. E.W. Sutton and H. Rackham; LCL; Cambridge, MA: Harvard University Press, 1950–60).

The Dead Sea Scrolls in English (ed. and trans. G. Vermes; Harmondsworth: Penguin Books, 3rd edn, 1987).

Erasmus, Desiderius, *On Copia of Words and Ideas* (trans. D.B. King and H.D. Rix; Milwaukee: Marquette University Press, 1963).

The Greek New Testament (ed. K. Aland, M. Black, C.M. Martini, B.M. Metzger and A. Wikgren, United Bible Societies, 3rd edn, 1983).

Josephus (trans. H.StJ. Thackeray; LCL; Cambridge, MA: Harvard University Press, 1926–65), I, II, IX, X.

Lucian (trans. A.M. Harmon; LCL; Cambridge, MA: Harvard University Press, 1961), I.

New Oxford Annotated Bible with Apocrypha. RSV (ed. H.G. May and B.M. Metzger; New York: Oxford University Press, 1977).

The New Testament in the Original Greek (ed. B.F. Westcott and F.J.A. Hort; Chicago: F.H. Revell, 1902).

Philo (trans. F.H. Colson and G.H. Whitaker; LCL; Cambridge, MA: Harvard University Press, 1958–61), IV, VII, Supp. I.

Quintilian, *The Institutio Oratoria* (trans. H.E. Butler; LCL; Cambridge, MA: Harvard University Press, 1966).

Seneca, *The Epistles of Seneca* (trans. R.M. Gummere; LCL; Cambridge, MA: Harvard University Press, 1962), III.

Tacitus, *The Histories* (trans. C.H. Moore; LCL; Cambridge, MA: Harvard University Press, 1968).

Virgil, *Aeneid* (trans. H.R. Fairclough; LCL; Cambridge, MA: Harvard University Press, 1974).

Secondary Sources

Bammel, E., 'Judenverfolgung und Naherwartung', *ZTK* 56 (1959), pp. 294-315.

Barclay, W., *The Letters to the Corinthians* (Edinburgh: Saint Andrew Press, 2nd edn, 1965).

Barrett, C.K., 'Cephas and Corinth', in his *Essays on Paul* (Philadelphia: Westminster Press, 1982), ch. 2.

—'Christianity and Corinth', in his *Essays on Paul*, ch. 1.

—'Christianity at Corinth' (Manson Memorial Lectures, John Rylands Library, Manchester, no. 3, 1964), pp. 269-97.

—*A Commentary on the Epistle to the Romans* (BNTC; London: A. & C. Black, 1957).

—*A Commentary on the First Epistle to the Corinthians* (BNTC; London: A. & C. Black, 1968).

—*A Commentary on the Second Epistle to the Corinthians* (BNTC; London: A. & C. Black, 1973).

—'Paul's Opponents in 2 Corinthians', in his *Essays on Paul*, ch. 7.

—'Paul's Opponents in II Corinthians', *NTS* 17 (1971), pp. 233-54.

—'*Pseudapostoloi* (2 Cor. 11.13)', in his *Essays on Paul*, ch. 5.

Baur, F.C., *Paul the Apostle of Jesus Christ: His Life and Work, his Epistles, and his Doctrine* (ed. E. Zeller, trans. A. Menzies; London: Williams, 2nd edn, 1875–76).

Beck, N.A., *Mature Christianity: The Recognition and Repudiation of the Anti-Jewish Polemic in the New Testament* (London: Associated University Presses, 1985).

Beker, J.C., *Paul the Apostle: The Triumph of God in Life and Thought* (Philadelphia: Fortress Press, 1980).

Best, E., *A Commentary on the First and Second Epistles to the Thessalonians* (London: A. & C. Black, 1972).

—*II Corinthians* (Interpretation: A Bible Commentary; Atlanta: John Knox, 1987).

Betz, H.D., *Galatians: A Commentary on Paul's Letter to the Churches in Galatia* (Hermeneia; Philadelphia: Fortress Press, 1979).

Betz, O., 'Felsenmann und Felsengemeinde', *ZNW* 48 (1957), pp. 49-77.

Bicknell, E.J., *First and Second Epistles to the Thessalonians* (London: Methuen, 1932).

Borgen, P., 'The Early Church and the Hellenistic Synagogue', *ST* 37 (1983), pp. 55-78.

Bornkamm, G., *Early Christian Experience* (London: SCM Press, 1969).

—*Paul* (trans. D.M.G. Stalker; New York: Harper & Row, 1971).

Brandon, S.G.F., *The Fall of Jerusalem and the Christian Church* (London: SPCK, 2nd edn, 1957).

Broer, I., '"Der Ganze Zorn ist schon über sie gekommen" Bemerkungen zur Interpolationshypothese und zur Interpretation von 1 Thess 2,14-16', in Collins (ed.), *The Thessalonian Correspondence*, pp. 137-59.

Brown, R., *The Gospel according to John* (AB, 29A; Garden City, NY: Doubleday, 1970), II.

Bruce, F.F., *1 and 2 Corinthians* (NCB; London: Oliphants, 1971).

Bultmann, R., *Exegetische Probleme des zweiten Korintherbriefs* (Uppsala: Wretman, 1947).

—*The Second Letter to the Corinthians* (ed. E. Dinkler, trans. R.A. Harrisville. Minneapolis: Augsburg, 1985).

—*Theology of the New Testament* (2 vols.; trans. K. Grobel; New York: Charles Scribner's Sons, 1951).

Burke, K., *A Rhetoric of Motives* (Berkeley: University of California Press, 1969).

Burton, E.D.W., *Syntax of the Moods and Tenses in New Testament Greek* (Chicago: Chicago University Press, 3rd edn, 1898).

Callan, T., *Psychological Perspectives on the Life of Paul: An Application of the Methodology of Gerd Theissen* (Lampeter, Wales: Edwin Mellen Press, 1990).

Castelli, E.A., *Imitating Paul: A Discourse of Power* (Louisville, KY: Westminster Press/John Knox, 1991).

Carmody, T.R., 'The Relationship of Eschatology to the Use of Exclusion in Qumran and New Testament Literature' (PhD dissertation, The Catholic University of America, 1986).

Carroll, L., *Alice in Wonderland* (ed. D.J. Gray; New York: W.W. Norton, 1971).

Catchpole, D.R., 'The Problem of the Historicity of the Sanhedrin Trial', in E. Bammel (ed.), *The Trial of Jesus* (SBT, II/13; London: Allenson, 1970), pp. 47-65.

Cohen, S., *Josephus in Galilee and Rome: His Vita and Development as a Historian* (Leiden: Brill, 1979).

Collins, R.F., 'A propos the Integrity of I Thes', *ETL* 55 (1979), pp. 67-106.

—'This is the Will of God: Your Sanctification (I Thess. 4.3)', *Laval* 39 (1983), pp. 27-53.

Collins, R.F. (ed.), *The Thessalonian Correspondence* (Leuven: University Press, 1990).

Cranfield, C.E.B., *A Critical and Exegetical Commentary on the Epistle to the Romans* (2 vols.; Edinburgh: T. & T. Clark, 6th edn, 1975–79).

—'A Study of 1 Thessalonians 2', *IBS* 1 (1979), pp. 215-26.

Crouch, J.E., *The Origin and Intention of the Colossian Haustafel* (Göttingen: Vandenhoeck & Ruprecht, 1972).

Cummins, S.A., 'Historical Conflict and Soteriological Reflection: An Exegesis of 1 Thessalonians 2.13-16 with Particular Reference to 1 Thessalonians and Romans 9-11' (MA thesis, McGill University, Montreal, 1988).

Daube, D., *The Sudden in the Scriptures* (Leiden: Brill, 1964).

Deissmann, A., *Paul: A Study in Social and Religious History* (trans. W.E. Wilson; New York: George H. Doran, 1926).

Dibelius, M., *An die Thessalonicher I, II* (Tübingen: Mohr, 1937).

Dobschütz, E. von, *Die Thessalonicher-Briefe* (MeyerK, 10/7; Göttingen: Vandenhoeck & Ruprecht, 1909).

Dodd, C.H., *Epistle of Paul to the Romans* (MNTC; New York: Harper & Brothers, 1932).

Donfried, K.P., 'Justification and Last Judgment in Paul', *ZNW* 67 (1976), pp. 90-110.

—'Paul and Judaism: I Thessalonians 2.13-16 as a Test Case', *Int* 38 (1984), pp. 242-53.

Downing, F.G., 'Cynics and Christians', *NTS* 30 (1984), pp. 584-93.

Duncan, G.S., *The Epistle of Paul to the Galatians* (London: Hodder & Stoughton, 1948).

Dunkle, J.R., 'The Greek Tyrant and Roman Political Invective of the Late Republic', *TAPA* 98 (1967), pp. 151-71.

—'Study of the Rhetorical Tyrant in Rome of the First Century BC' (PhD dissertation, University of Pennsylvania, 1965).

Du Toit, A.B., 'Hyperbolical Contrasts: A Neglected Aspect of Paul's Style', in J.H. Petzer and P.J. Hartin (eds.), *A South African Perspective on the New Testament* (Leiden: Brill, 1986), pp. 178-86.

Easton, B.S., *Early Christianity: The Purpose of Acts, and Other Papers* (ed. F.C. Grant; Greenwich, CT: Seabury Press, 1954).

Eckart, K.G., 'Der zweite echte Brief des Apostels Paulus an die Thessalonicher', *ZTK* 63 (1961), pp. 30-64.

Ellis, E.E., 'Paul and his Co-Workers', *NTS* 17 (1970–71), pp. 437-52.

Feldman, L., 'The Omnipresence of the God-Fearers', *BARev* 12 (1986), pp. 58-63.

Filson, F.V., *St Paul's Conception of Recompense* (Leipzig: Hinrichs, 1931).

Findlay, G.G., *The Epistles to the Thessalonians* (Cambridge: Cambridge University Press, 1904).

Fischel, H.A., 'Martyr and Prophet', *JQR* 37 (1946–47), pp. 265-80.

Fitzgerald, J.T., *Cracks in an Earthen Vessel: An Examination of the Catalogues of Hardships in the Corinthian Correspondence* (SBLDS; Atlanta: Scholars Press, 1988).

Fitzmeyer, J.A., *Pauline Theology: A Brief Sketch* (Englewood Cliffs, NJ: Prentice-Hall, 1967).

Forbes, C., '"Unaccustomed as I Am": St Paul the Public Speaker in Corinth', *Buried History* 19 (1983), pp. 11-16.

Forkman, G., *The Limits of the Religious Community* (Lund: Gleerup, 1972).

Frame, J.E., *A Critical and Exegetical Commentary on the First Epistle of St Paul to the Thessalonians* (ICC, 38; Edinburgh: T. & T. Clark, 1912).

Frend, W.H.C., 'Persecutions: Some Links Between Judaism and the Early Church', *JEH* 9 (1958), pp. 141-58.

—*The Rise of Christianity* (Philadelphia: Fortress Press, 1984).

Furnish, V.P., *II Corinthians* (AB, 32A; Garden City, NY: Doubleday, 1984).

Gager, J.G., 'Jews, Gentiles, and Synagogues in the Book of Acts', in G.W.E. Nickelsburg with G.W. MacRae (eds.), *Christians Among Jews and Gentiles* (Philadelphia: Fortress Press, 1986), pp. 91-99.

—*The Origins of Anti-Semitism: Attitudes Toward Judaism in Pagan and Christian Antiquity* (New York: Oxford University Press, 1983).

Gaston, L., *No Stone on Another: Studies in the Significance of the Fall of Jerusalem in the Synoptic Gospels* (Leiden: Brill, 1970).

—*Paul and the Torah* (Vancouver: University of British Columbia Press, 1987).

Georgi, D., *The Opponents of Paul in Second Corinthians* (Philadelphia: Fortress Press, 1986).

Goodman, M., 'Proselytising in Rabbinic Judaism', *JJS* 40 (1989), pp. 175-85.

—*The Ruling Class of Judaea: The Origins of the Jewish Revolt Against Rome, AD 66–70* (Cambridge: Cambridge University Press, 1987).

Goudge, H.L., *The Second Epistle to the Corinthians* (London: Methuen, 1927).

Grayston, K., and G. Herdan, 'The Authorship of the Pastorals in the Light of Statistical Linguistics', *NTS* 6 (1959), pp. 1-15.

Gunther, J.J., *St Paul's Opponents and their Background: A Study of Apocalyptic and Jewish Sectarian Teachings* (Leiden: Brill, 1973).

Hanson, A.T., *The Wrath of the Lamb* (London: SPCK, 1957).

Hanson, R.P.C., *II Corinthians* (London: SCM Press, 1954).

Hare, D.R.A., *The Theme of Persecution of Christians in the Gospel according to St Matthew* (Cambridge: Cambridge University Press, 1967).

Hays, R.B., 'Relations Natural and Unnatural: A Response to John Boswell's Exegesis of Romans 1', *JRE* 14 (1986), pp. 184-215.

Hendriksen, W., *A Commentary on Galatians* (London: The Banner of Truth Trust, 1969).

—*Exposition of I and II Thessalonians* (Grand Rapids: Baker, 1975).

—*New Testament Commentary* (Grand Rapids: Baker, 1955).

Hengel, M., *Acts and the History of Earliest Christianity* (trans. J. Bowden; London: SCM Press, 1979).

—*Between Jesus and Paul: Studies in the Earliest History of Christianity* (Philadelphia: Fortress Press, 1983).

—*Crucifixion* (Philadelphia: Fortress Press, 1977).

Héring, J., *The Second Epistle of Saint Paul to the Corinthians* (trans. A.W. Heathcote and P.J. Allcock; London: Epworth Press, 1967).

Hickling, C.J.A., 'Centre and Periphery in the Thought of Paul', in E.A. Livingstone (ed.), *Studia Biblica 1978. III. Papers on Paul and Other New Testament Authors* (JSNTSup, 3; Sheffield: JSOT Press, 1980), pp. 199-214.

Hock, R.F., *The Social Context of Paul's Ministry: Tentmaking and Apostleship* (Philadelphia: Fortress Press, 1980).

Hodge, C., *An Exposition of the Second Epistle to the Corinthians* (Grand Rapids: Eerdman, n.d.).

Hodgson, R., 'Paul the Apostle and First Century Tribulation Lists', *ZNW* 74 (1983), pp. 59-80.

Holmberg, B., *Paul and Power: The Structure of Authority in the Primitive Church as Reflected in the Pauline Epistles* (Philadelphia: Fortress Press, 1978).

Holtz, T., 'The Judgment on the Jews and the Salvation of All Israel. 1 Thes 2,15-16 and Rom 11,25-26', in Collins (ed.), *The Thessalonian Correspondence*, pp. 284-94.

Holtzmann, H.J., *Praktische Erklärung des I. Thessalonicherbriefes* (Tübingen: Mohr, 1911).

Hübner, H., *Gottes ich und Israel: Zum Schriftgebrauch des Paulus in Römer 9–11* (Göttingen: Vandenhoeck & Ruprecht, 1984).

—*Law in Paul's Thought: Studies in the New Testament and its World* (ET; Edinburgh: T. & T. Clark, 1983).

Hughes, F.W., *Early Christian Rhetoric and 2 Thessalonians* (JSNTSup, 30; Sheffield: JSOT Press, 1989).

—'The Rhetoric of 1 Thessalonians', in Collins (ed.), *The Thessalonian Correspondence*, pp. 94-116.

Hultgren, A.J., *Paul's Gospel and Mission* (Philadelphia: Fortress Press, 1985).

—'Paul's Pre-Christian Persecutions of the Church: Their Purpose, Locale and Nature', *JBL* 75 (1976), pp. 97-111.

Hurd, J.C., 'Paul ahead of his Time: I Thess. 2.13-16', in P. Richardson (ed.) with D. Granskou, *Anti-Judaism in Early Christianity: Paul and the Gospels* (Studies in Christianity and Judaism, 1; Waterloo: Wilfrid Laurier University Press, 1986), pp. 21-36.

Jewett, R., *The Thessalonian Correspondence: Pauline Rhetoric and Millenarian Piety* (Philadelphia: Fortress Press, 1986).

Johanson, B.C., *To all the Brethren: A Text-Linguistic and Rhetorical Approach to I Thessalonians* (Stockholm: Almqvist & Wiksell, 1987).

Johnson, L.T., 'The New Testament's Anti-Jewish Slander and the Conventions of Ancient Polemic', *JBL* 108 (1989), pp. 419-41.

—*The Writings of the New Testament: An Interpretation* (Philadelphia: Fortress Press, 1986).

Judge, E.A., 'Paul's Boasting in relation to Contemporary Professional Practice', *AusBR* 10 (1968), pp. 37-50.

—'St Paul and Classical Society', *JAC* 15 (1972), pp. 19-36.

Juel, D., *I Thessalonians* (Augsburg Commentary on the New Testament; Minneapolis: Augsburg, 1985).

Jülicher, D.A., *Einleitung in das Neue Testament* (Tübingen: Mohr, 1906).

Käsemann, E., *Exegetische Versuche und Besinnungen* (Göttingen: Vandenhoeck & Ruprecht, 1965), I.

—'Die Legitimität des Apostels', *ZNW* 41 (1942), pp. 33-71.

Katz, S.T., 'Issues in the Separation of Judaism and Christianity after 70 CE: A Reconsideration', *JBL* 103 (1984), pp. 43-76.

Kimelman, R., 'Birkat Ha-Minim and the Lack of Evidence for an Anti-Christian Jewish Prayer in Late Antiquity', in E.P. Sanders (ed.), *Jewish and Christian Self-Definition. II. Aspects of Judaism in the Graeco-Roman Period* (Philadelphia: Fortress Press, 1981), pp. 226-44.

Kennedy, G.A., *New Testament Interpretation through Rhetorical Criticism* (Chapel Hill: University of North Carolina Press, 1984).

Knox, J., *Chapters in a Life of Paul* (New York: Abingdon Press, 1950).

Knowling, R.J., *The Testimony of St Paul to Christ* (New York: Charles Scribner's Sons, 1905).

Koester, H., *History and Literature of Early Christianity* (2 vols.; Philadelphia: Fortress Press, 1982.

Kraabel, A.T., 'Greeks, Jews, and Lutherans in the Middle Half of Acts', in G.W.E. Nickelsburg with G.W. MacRae (eds.), *Christians Among Jews and Gentiles* (Philadelphia: Fortress Press, 1986), pp. 147-57.

—'The Roman Diaspora: Six Questionable Assumptions', *JJS* 33 (1982), pp. 445-64.

Kümmel, W.G., *An Die Korinther I.II* (HNT, 9; Tübingen: Mohr, 1969).

—*Introduction to the New Testament* (trans. H.C. Kee; Nashville: Abingdon Press, 1973).

Leon, H.J., *The Jews of Ancient Rome* (Philadelphia: Jewish Publication Society of America, 1960).

Lübking, H.-M., *Paulus und Israel im Römerbrief: Eine Untersuchung zu Römer 9–11* (Bern: Peter Lang, 1986).

Lüdemann, G., *Opposition to Paul in Jewish Christianity* (trans. M.E. Boring; Minneapolis: Fortress Press, 1989).

—*Paulus, der Heidenapostel. I. Studien zur Christologie* (Göttingen: Vandenhoeck & Ruprecht, 1980).

Lünemann, G., *Critical and Exegetical Handbook to the Epistles of St Paul to the Thessalonians* (trans. P.J. Gloag; Edinburgh: T. & T. Clark, 1880).

Luetgert, W., *Freiheitspredigt und Schwarmgeister in Korinth* (Gütersloh: Bertelsmann, 1908).

MacGregor, G.H.C., 'The Concept of the Wrath of God in the New Testament', *NTS* 7 (1960–61), pp. 101-109.

MacLennan, R.S., and A.T. Kraabel, 'The God-Fearers: A Literary and Theological Invention', *BARev* 12 (1986), pp. 46-53.

Malherbe, A.J., *Ancient Epistolary Theorists* (Atlanta: Scholars Press, 1988).

—'Antisthenes and Odysseus and Paul at War', *HTR* 76 (1983), pp. 143-73.

—*The Cynic Epistles* (Missoula, MT: Scholars Press, 1977).

—'Exhortation in First Thessalonians', *NovT* 25 (1983), pp. 238-56.

—'"Gentle as a Nurse" The Cynic Background to 1 Thess. ii', *NovT* 12 (1970), pp. 203-17.

—'*Me Genoito* in the Diatribe and Paul', *HTR* 73 (1980), pp. 231-40.

—*Moral Exhortation: A Greco-Roman Sourcebook* (Philadelphia: Westminster Press, 1986).

—*Paul and the Moral Philosophers* (Minneapolis: Fortress Press, 1989).

—*Paul and the Thessalonians* (Philadelphia: Fortress Press, 1987).

—'Paul: Hellenistic Philosopher or Christian Pastor?', *ATR* 68 (1986), pp. 3-13.

—*Social Aspects of Early Christianity* (Philadelphia: Fortress Press, 2nd edn, 1983).

Manson, T.W., 'The Corinthian Correspondence (1)', in M. Black (ed.), *Studies in the Gospels and Epistles* (Manchester: Manchester University Press, 1962), pp. 190-209.

Marrow, S.B., *Paul: His Letters and his Theology* (New York: Paulist Press, 1986).

Marshall, I.H., *1 & 2 Thessalonians* (Grand Rapids, Michigan: Eerdmans, 1983).

Marshall, P., *Enmity in Corinth: Social Conventions in Paul's Relations with the Corinthians* (Tübingen: Mohr, 1987).

Martin, R., *Reconciliation: A Study of Paul's Theology* (Atlanta: John Knox, 1981).

Marxsen, W., *Introduction to the New Testament: An Approach to its Problems* (trans. G. Buswell; Philadelphia: Fortress Press, 1964).

Masson, C., *Les deux épîtres de Saint Paul aux Thessaloniciens* (Paris: Delachaux & Niestlé, 1957).

Mattern, L., *Das Verständnis des Gerichts bei Paulus* (Zürich: Zwingli Verlag, 1966).

McClelland, S.E., '"Super-Apostles, Servants of Christ, Servants of Satan": A Response', *JSNT* 14 (1982), pp. 82-87.

Milligan, G., *St Paul's Epistles to the Thessalonians* (London: Macmillan, 1908).

Moffatt, J., *The First and Second Epistles of Paul the Apostle to the Thessalonians* (The Expositor's Greek Testament, 4; London: Hodder & Stoughton, 1910).

—*Introduction to the Literature of the New Testament* (Edinburgh: T. & T. Clark, 1927).

Montefiore, C.G., *Judaism and St Paul: Two Essays* (London: Max Goshen, 1914).

Moore, A.L., *1 and 2 Thessalonians* (The Century Bible; Greenwood, SC: Attic, 1969).

Morris, L., *The Epistles of Paul to the Thessalonians* (Grand Rapids: Eerdmans, 1984).

Morton, A.Q., and J. McLeman, *Christianity and the Computer* (London: Hodder & Stoughton, 1964).

Moulton, J.H., *The Grammar of New Testament Greek. I. Prolegomena* (Edinburgh: T. & T. Clark, 2nd edn, 1906).

Munck, J., *Christ and Israel: An Interpretation of Romans 9–11* (Philadelphia: Fortress Press, 1967).

—'Jewish Christianity in Post-Apostolic Times', *NTS* 6 (1960), pp. 103-16.

—*Paul and the Salvation of Mankind* (trans. F. Clarke; London: SCM Press, 1959).

Mussner, F., *Der Galaterbrief* (HTKNT; Freiburg: Herder, 1974).

Neil, W., *The Epistles of Paul to the Thessalonians* (London: Hodder & Stoughton, 1950).

Neirynck, F., 'Paul and the Sayings of Jesus', in A. Vanhoye (ed.), *L'apôtre Paul: Personnalité, style et conception du ministère* (Leuven: Leuven University Press, 1986), pp. 265-321.

Nickelsburg, G.W.E., *Jewish Literature between the Bible and the Midrash* (Philadelphia: Fortress Press, 1981).

Nisbet, R.G.M., 'The *In Pisonem* as an Invective', in Cicero, *In L. Calpurnium Pisonem: Oratio* (Oxford: Clarendon Press, 1961), Appendix 6.

North, H.F., 'The Concept of Sophrosyne in Greek Literary Criticism', *Classical Philology* 43 (1948), pp. 1-7.

Okeke, G.E., 'I Thessalonians 2.13-16: The Fate of the Unbelieving Jews', *NTS* 27 (1980–81), pp. 127-36.

Oostendorp, D.W., *Another Jesus: A Gospel of Jewish-Christian Superiority in II Corinthians* (Kampen: Kok, 1967).

Orchard, J.B., 'Thessalonians and the Synoptic Gospels', *Bib* 19 (1938), pp. 23-42.

Palmer, D.W., 'Thanksgiving, Self-Defense, and Exhortation in I Thessalonians 1–3', *Colloquium* 14 (1981), pp. 23-31.

Parkes, J., *The Conflict of the Church and the Synagogue* (New York: Hermon Press, 1974).

Pearson, B.A., 'I Thessalonians 2.13-16: A Deutero-Pauline Interpolation', *HTR* 64 (1971), pp. 79-94.

Penna, R., 'L'évolution de l'attitude de Paul envers les juifs', in A. Vanhoye (ed.), *L'apôtre Paul: Personnalité, style et conception du ministère* (Leuven: Leuven University Press, 1986), pp. 390-421.

Perelman, C., *The Idea of Justice and the Problem of Argument* (London: Routledge & Kegan Paul, 1963).

Plank, K.A., *Paul and the Irony of Affliction* (Atlanta: Scholars Press, 1987).

Plummer, A., *A Commentary on St Paul's First Epistle to the Thessalonians* (London: Robert Scott, 1918).

Plummer, A., and A. Robertson, *A Critical and Exegetical Commentary on the First Epistle of St Paul to the Corinthians* (ICC, 38; repr.; Edinburgh: T. & T. Clark, 1955 [2nd edn, 1911]).

Räisänen, H., *Paul and the Law* (Tübingen: Mohr, 1983).

—'Paul's Conversion and the Development of his View of the Law', *NTS* 33 (1987), pp. 404-19.

Reynolds, J., and R. Tannenbaum, *Jews and God-Fearers at Aphrodisias* (Cambridge: Cambridge Philological Society, 1987).

Richardson, P., *Israel in the Apostolic Church* (London: Cambridge University Press, 1969).

Ridderbos, H.N., *Paul: An Outline of his Theology* (trans. J.R. De Witt; Grand Rapids: Eerdmans, 1975).

Riddle, D.W., *Paul: Man of Conflict* (Nashville: Cokesbury Press, 1940).

Rigaux, B., *Saint Paul les épitres aux Thessaloniciens* (Paris: Librairie Lecoffre/ Gabalda, 1956).

Ritschl, A., *Rechtfertigung und Versöhnung* (Bonn: Adolph Marcus, 2nd edn, 1882), II.

Robertson, A.T., *A Grammar of the Greek New Testament in the Light of Historical Research* (New York: Hodder & Stoughton, 2nd edn, 1915).

Roetzel, C.J., *Judgement in the Community: A Study of the Relationship between Eschatology and Ecclesiology in Paul* (Leiden: Brill, 1972).

—'Theodidaktoi and Handwork in Philo and I Thessalonians', in A. Vanhoye (ed.), *L'apôtre Paul: Personnalité, style et conception du ministère* (Leuven: Leuven University Press, 1986), pp. 324-31.

Sanders, E.P., *Jesus and Judaism* (London: SCM Press, 1985).

—*Paul and Palestinian Judaism: A Comparison of Patterns of Religion* (Philadelphia: Fortress Press, 1977).

—'Paul on the Law, his Opponents, and the Jewish People in Philippians 3 and 2 Corinthians 11', in *Anti-Judaism in Early Christianity. I. Paul and the Gospels* (Waterloo: Wilfrid Laurier Press, 1986), pp. 75-90.

—*Paul, the Law, and the Jewish People* (Philadelphia: Fortress Press, 1983).

—Review of M. Hengel, *Between Jesus and Paul*, *JTS* 37 (1986), pp. 167-72.

Sanders, J.T., *The Jews in Luke–Acts* (Philadelphia: Fortress Press, 1987).

Saperstein, M., 'Christians and Jews—Some Positive Images', in G.W.E. Nickelsburg with G.W. MacRae (eds.), *Christians among Jews and Gentiles* (Philadelphia: Fortress Press, 1986), pp. 236-46.

Schiffman, L., 'At the Crossroads: Tannaitic Perspectives on the Jewish-Christian Schism', in E.P. Sanders (ed.), *Jewish and Christian Self-Definition* (Philadelphia: Fortress Press, 1981), II, pp. 115-56.

Schippers, R., 'The Pre-Synoptic Tradition in I Thessalonians II 13-16', *NovT* 8 (1966), pp. 223-34.

Schmidt, D., 'I Thess. 2.13-16: Linguistic Evidence for an Interpolation', *JBL* 102 (1983), pp. 269-79.

Schmidt, P.W., *Der erste Thessalonicherbrief neu erklärt* (Berlin: Reimer, 1885).

Schmiedel, P.W., *Die Briefe an die Thessalonicher und an die Korinther* (HKNT, 2; Freiburg: Mohr, 1891).

Schmithals, W., *Paul and the Gnostics* (trans. J.E. Steely; Nashville: Abingdon Press, 1972).

—'Die Thessalonicherbriefe als Briefkomposition', in E. Dinkler (ed.), *Zeit und Geschichte: Dankesgabe an Rudolf Bultmann zum 80. Geburtstag* (Tübingen: Mohr [Paul Siebeck], 1964), pp. 295-315.

Schnelle, U., 'Der erste Thessalonicherbrief und die Entstehung der paulinischen Anthropologie', *NTS* 32 (1986), pp. 207-24.

Schoeps, H.-J., 'Die jüdischen Prophetenmorde', in his *Aus früchristlicher Zeit* (Tübingen: Mohr, 1950), pp. 126-43.

Schrader, C., *Der Apostel Paulus* (Leipzig, 1836), V.

Scroggs, R., 'Paul: *Sophos* and *Pneumatikos*', *NTS* 14 (1967), pp. 33-55.

Segal, A.F., *Paul the Convert: The Apostolate and Apostasy of Saul the Pharisee* (New Haven: Yale University Press, 1990).

—*Rebecca's Children: Judaism and Christianity in the Roman World* (Cambridge, MA: Harvard University Press, 1986).

Shaw, G.B., *Pygmalion*, in *Androcles and the Lion, Overruled, Pygmalion* (London: Constable, 1916).

Simmel, G., *Conflict* (trans. K.H. Wolff; Glencoe, IL: Free Press, 1955).

Simon, M., *Verus Israel: A Study of the Relations between Christians and Jews in the Roman Empire, 135–425* (trans. H. McKeating; New York: Oxford University Press, 1986).

Smith, M., 'The Reason for the Persecution of Paul and the Obscurity of Acts', in E.E. Urbach, R.J. Zwi Werblowsky and C. Wirszubske (eds.), *Studies in Mysticism and Religion* (Jerusalem: Magnes, 1967).

Smyth, H.W., *Greek Grammar* (repr.; Cambridge, MA: Harvard University Press, 1968 [1920]).

Somers, H.H., 'Statistical Methods in Literary Analysis', in J. Leed (ed.), *The Computer and Literary Style* (Kent, OH: Kent State University, 1966).

Spitta, F., 'Der zweite Brief an die Thessalonicher', in *Zur Geschichte und Literatur des Urchristentums* (Göttingen: Vandenhoeck & Ruprecht, 1893), pp. 109-54.

Stauffer, E., *New Testament Theology* (trans. J. Marsh; London: SCM Press, 1955).

Steck, O.H., *Israel und das gewaltsame Geschick der Propheten: Untersuchungen zur Überlieferung des deuteronomistischen Geschichtsbildes im Alten Testament, Spätjudentum und Urchristentum* (Wageningen, Netherlands: H. Veenman & Zonen, 1967).

Stowers, S., *Letter Writing in Greco-Roman Antiquity* (Philadelphia: Westminster Press, 1986).

Talbert, C.H., *Reading Corinthians: A Literary and Theological Commentary on 1 and 2 Corinthians* (New York: Crossroad, 1987).

Thrall, M.E., 'Super-Apostles, Servants of Christ, and Servants of Satan', *JSNT* 6 (1980), pp. 42-57.

Ulonska, H., 'Christen und Heiden: Die paulinische Paränese in I Thess 4,3-8', *TZ* 43 (1987), pp. 210-18.

Vickers, B., *In Defense of Rhetoric* (Oxford: Clarendon Press, 1988).

Watson, F., '2 Cor. X–XIII and Paul's Painful Letter to the Corinthians', *JTS* 35 (1984), pp. 324-46.

—*Paul, Judaism and the Gentiles: A Sociological Approach* (Cambridge: Cambridge University Press, 1986).

Weatherly, J.A., 'The Authenticity of 1 Thessalonians 2.13-16: Additional Evidence', *JSNT* 42 (1991), pp. 79-98.

Welborn, L.L., 'On the Discord in Corinth, 1 Corinthians 1–4 and Ancient Politics', *JBL* 106 (1987), pp. 85-111.

Westerholm, S., *Israel's Law and the Church's Faith: Paul and his Recent Interpreters* (Grand Rapids: Eerdmans, 1988).

—*Jesus and Scribal Authority* (Lund: Gleerup, 1978).

Whiteley, D.E.H., *Thessalonians* (Oxford: Oxford University Press, 1979).

Whittaker, M., *Jews and Christians: Graeco-Roman Views* (Cambridge: Cambridge University Press, 1984).

Wilken, R.L., *John Chrysostom and the Jews: Rhetoric and Reality in the Late 4th Century* (Berkeley: University of California Press, 1983).

—*Judaism and the Early Christian Mind: A Study of Cyril of Alexandria's Exegesis and Theology* (New Haven: Yale University Press, 1971).

Winter, P., *On the Trial of Jesus* (Berlin: de Gruyter, 1961).

Wolff, R., *First and Second Epistles of Paul to the Thessalonians* (Wheaton, IL: Tyndale House Publishers, 1970).

Yadin, Y., 'Pesher Nahum (4Q Pnahum) Reconsidered', *IEJ* 21 (1971), pp. 1-12.

Zahn, T., *Introduction to the New Testament* (trans. M.W. Jacobson, assisted by C.S. Thayer; Edinburgh: T. & T. Clark, 1909), I.

INDEXES

INDEX OF REFERENCES

OLD TESTAMENT

NEW TESTAMENT

CLASSICAL AUTHORS

OTHER ANCIENT SOURCES

INDEX OF AUTHORS

JOURNAL FOR THE STUDY OF THE NEW TESTAMENT

Supplement Series